SPORT AND THE LAW

SPORT AND THE LAW

A Concise Guide

Laura Donnellan

BLACKHALL
Publishing

Published by Blackhall Publishing
Lonsdale House
Avoca Avenue
Blackrock
Co. Dublin
Ireland

e-mail: info@blackhallpublishing.com
www.blackhallpublishing.com

ISBN: 978-1-84218-210-9

A catalogue record for this book is available from the British Library.

Printed and bound in Great Britain by
CPI Antony Rowe, Chippenham, Wiltshire.

Acknowledgements

Thanks to Elizabeth Brennan and Eileen O'Brien at Blackhall Publishing for their support during the writing of this book. I would also like to sincerely thank my colleagues at the School of Law, University of Limerick, and my friends and family, especially Mary Liddane who proofread the initial draft.

for Bubbles

Contents

Table of Cases

IRELAND

NORTHERN IRELAND

SWITZERLAND

Table of Cases

UNITED STATES

DECISIONS OF THE COURT OF ARBITRATION FOR SPORT

EUROPEAN UNION CASE LAW

European Court of Justice

Court of First Instance

Table of Cases

EUROPEAN COURT OF HUMAN RIGHTS

Table of Statutes

UNITED STATES

IRISH CONSTITUTION

EUROPEAN TREATIES

EUROPEAN UNION SECONDARY LEGISLATION: REGULATIONS, DIRECTIVES AND DECISIONS

INTERNATIONAL CONVENTIONS

UNITED STATES CONSTITUTION

List of Abbreviations

AC	Appeal Court
ADR	Alternative Dispute Resolution
AFL	Australian Football League
AFLT	Australian Football League Tribunal
AG	Advocate General
AHD	Ad Hoc Division
AIRE	Association of Irish Riding Establishments
All ER	All England Reports
APCC	Australian Professional Cycling Council
ASC	Australian Sports Commission
BALCO	Bay Area Laboratory Cooperative
BBBC	British Boxing Board of Control
BLE	Bord Lúthchleas na hÉireann
BMA	British Medical Association
BOA	British Olympic Association
CAS	Court of Arbitration for Sport
CCES	Canadian Centre for Ethics in Sport
CERA	Continuous Erythropoietin Receptor Activator
Ch	Chancery
CJ	Chief Justice
CPTE	Crouch, Pause, Touch, Engage
Cr. App Rep	Criminal Appeal Reports
Crim. LR	Criminal Law Reports
DPP	Director of Public Prosecutions
DRA	Disputes Resolution Authority
EBU	European Broadcasting Union
EC	European Community
ECHR	European Convention of Human Rights
ECJ	European Court of Justice
ECR	European Court Reports
ECSC	European Coal and Steel Community Treaty
EEA	European Economic Area

EEC	European Economic Community
EFI	Equestrian Federation of Ireland
EOC	European Olympic Committee
EPO	Erythropoietin
EURATOM	Treaty establishing the European Atomic Energy Community
EWCA	England and Wales Court of Appeal
EWHC	England and Wales High Court
FAI	Football Association of Ireland
FAIFS	Football Association of the Irish Free State
FAW	Football Association of Wales
FEI	Fédération Equestre Internationale
FIBT	Fédération Internationale de Bobsleigh et de Tobogganing
FIFA	Fédération Internationale de Football Association
FIH	International Hockey Federation
FINA	Fédération Internationale de Natation
FSR	Fleet Street Reports
FT	Federal Tribunal
GAC	Games Administration Committee
HC	High Court
HGH	Human Growth Hormone
HL	House of Lords
HSI	Horse Sport Ireland
IAAF	International Association of Athletics Federation
IABA	Irish Amateur Boxing Association
ICAS	International Council for Arbitration in Sport
ICC	International Cricket Conference
IEHC	Irish High Court
IFs	International Sports Federations
ILDRA	Irish Long Distance Riding Association
ILRM	Irish Law Reports Monthly
ILT	Irish Law Times
IMAC	Irish Martial Arts Commission
INEA	Institute for European Affairs
IOC	International Olympic Committee
IR	Irish Reports
IRB	International Rugby Board
IRFU	Irish Rugby Football Union
IRUPA	Irish Rugby Union Players Association
ISC	Irish Sports Council

ITF	International Tennis Federation
IURCA	Irish Universities Riding Club Association
LCCP	Law Commission Consultation Paper
LJ	Lord Justice/Lady Justice
LQR	Law Quarterly Review
LRC	Law Reform Commission
LT	Law Times
MEA	Medical Equestrian Association
MMA	Mixed Martial Arts
MR	Master of Rolls
NADO	National Anti-Doping Organisation
NBA	National Basketball League
NCAA	National Collegiate Athletic Association
NFs	National Federations
NFL	National Football League
NGB	National Governing Body
NHL	National Hockey League
NLJ	New Law Journal
NOC	National Olympic Committees
NSW	New South Wales
NSWRL	New South Wales Rugby League
OCI	Olympic Council of Ireland
OG	Olympic Games
OJ	Official Journal
QB	Queen's Bench
QBD	Queen's Bench Division
QC	Queen's Counsel
R	Regina (The Crown)
RDAI	Riding for the Disabled Association Ireland
RDS	Royal Dublin Society
RSPCA	Royal Society for the Prevention of Cruelty to Animals
RTP	Registered Testing Pool
RVL	Racing Victoria Limited
SJI	Show Jumping Ireland
TCCB	Test and County Cricket Board
TEU	Treaty on European Union
TFEU	Treaty on the Functioning of the European Union
THG	Tetrahydrogestrinone
TLR	Times Law Reports
TUE	Therapeutic Use Exemption
UCI	Union Cycliste Internationale

UEFA	Union des Associations Européennes de Football/ Union of European Football Associations
UFC	Ultimate Fighting Championship
UKHL	United Kingdom House of Lords
UN	United Nations
UNESCO	United Nations Educational, Scientific and Cultural Organisation
USADA	US Anti-Doping Agency
USS	United States Swimming Committee
USTA	United States Tennis Association
VFL	Victorian Football League
WACA	Western Australian Cricket Association
WADA	World Anti-Doping Agency
WBA	World Boxing Association
WHO	World Health Organisation
WLR	Weekly Law Reports
WMA	World Medical Association
WNBA	American Women's National Basketball Association
WRFU	Welsh Rugby Football Union

Introduction

Sport and the Law: A Concise Guide provides an overview of the law relating to sport in Ireland and other common law jurisdictions, namely, England, the United States, Canada and Australia. In recent years we have seen an increase in the involvement of the law in sport. The professionalisation and commercialisation of sport has brought with it a plethora of legal issues. In recent years, sportspersons have seen an increase in earning potential. If an athlete suffers a career-ending injury or is involved in a contract or sponsorship dispute, or a doping allegation, he or she will be more likely to seek redress in the courts. In short, sportspersons are demanding higher standards of justice. As a result of these sporting cases, a cohesive body of law pertaining to sport has developed.

It is important, from the outset, to explain the organisation of sport in Ireland. In Ireland, the regulation of sport falls under the auspices of the Department of Tourism, Culture and Sport.[1] The Department has a number of important functions in relation to sport. Its primary function is the formulation, development and evaluation of sport policy (the implementation of which is, in the main, a matter for the Irish Sports Council (ISC)), and overseeing major sports projects: supervising the National Aquatic Centre at Abbotstown, developing proposals for the provision of a national stadium, and the administration of the Sports Capital and the Local Authority Swimming Pool Programmes.

There is heavy state involvement in the regulation of sport in Ireland. The state's involvement can be characterised as both direct and indirect

---

[1] Previously called the Department of Tourism, Sport and Recreation and also the Department of Arts, Sport and Tourism.

control. The Department of Tourism, Culture and Sport exercises direct governmental regulation, while the ISC, a body created by statute, exercises quasi-governmental regulation. The individual national governing bodies, while recipients of funding from the Department and the ISC, are categorised as autonomous and private associations. Recent litigation has questioned the involvement of the ISC and its interference in the internal affairs of the national governing bodies. The former chief executive of Athletics Ireland was recently dismissed after pressure was placed on the organisation by the ISC. Although the matter was settled out of court, it highlighted the need for the ISC to reassess its role in the promotion and development of sport in Ireland.[2] Allegations of poor governance within the Irish Amateur Boxing Association (IABA) have once again brought the tenuous relationship between the ISC and national governing bodies to the fore.[3]

There are two sport units within the Department of Tourism, Culture and Sport. Sport Unit 1, the Sport Policy and Capital Programmes Division, is responsible for the development of sport and recreational policies. It liaises with the ISC, Horse Racing Ireland (HRI) and Bord na gCon. It administers the Sports Council Programme, a programme funded by the National lottery.[4] It also administers the Local Authority Swimming Pool Programme, using funds from the Exchequer.[5] The unit has an international role as it liaises with the European Union, the Council of Europe and the World Anti-Doping Agency (WADA) on

---

[2] The Irish Sports Council has recently been embroiled in litigation over its involvement in the dismissal of the Chief Executive Officer (CEO) of Athletics Ireland (AAI). Mary Coghlan was appointed as CEO in April 2008 and took up office in May 2008, but was subsequently dismissed. In July 2009, Ms Coghlan initiated legal proceedings in the High Court challenging the validity of her dismissal. Ms Coghlan was alleging misfeasance in public office against the ISC, a distributor of government funds.

[3] The ISC refused to fund the positions of chief executive officer and high performance director within the IABA after it alleged that best practice may not have been followed in the selection process.

[4] Applications for funding are advertised annually. The programme allocates funding to projects that are directly related to the provision of sports facilities and are of a capital nature. This would include the purchase of premises and other assets; improvements to assets; and the purchase of non-personal equipment which will be used for at least five years. Those who may apply for funding include voluntary and community organisations (including sports clubs), national governing bodies, third level institutions (where it can be shown that the proposed facility will contribute to the regional and/or national sporting infrastructure), and, in some circumstances, primary and post-primary schools, and local authorities.

[5] This programme grants funding to local authorities to build new pools or refurbish existing ones. See <http://www.arts-sport-tourism.gov.ie/grants_funding/Swimming_Pool.htm>.

matters pertaining to sports issues and policies. All applications from certified sports bodies seeking approval of sports capital projects are processed by the unit as well as applications from certified bodies claiming tax relief.[6]

Sport Unit 2 is responsible for major sports capital projects, including the redevelopment of Lansdowne Road Stadium[7] and the current development of the National Campus of Sports Facilities at Abbotstown.[8] The unit carries out audits of local sports facilities and presents awards to volunteers in sport. More recently, the unit has been involved in devising a strategy to ensure that Ireland benefits from the proximity of the London 2012 Olympic and Paralympic Games.

As mentioned above, there is also quasi-governmental involvement in sport through a number of agencies. The Department of Tourism, Culture and Sport is assisted by the following agencies: the ISC,[9] Campus and Stadium Ireland Development,[10] Horse Racing Ireland and Bord na gCon.[11] These agencies have all been created by way of statute and have the status of semi-state bodies.

Chapter 1 places in context the social, political and cultural importance of sport in society. Sport, although considered an industry, is

---

[6] See <http://www.arts-sport-tourism.gov.ie/sport/organisation/unit1.html>.

[7] Now called Aviva Stadium. In 2004, the Government agreed to provide funding of €191 million to the joint Irish Rugby Football Union (IRFU)/Football Association of Ireland (FAI) project for the redevelopment of the stadium as a 50,000-capacity all-seating facility. Work began in 2007 following the granting of planning permission, and the revamped stadium opened in 2010.

[8] The development of the campus was approved in 2005. Detailed work began and has recently been completed. The campus has been built on a phase-by-phase basis. Phase 1 provided for the following: a National Field Sports Training Centre (catering for rugby, soccer, Gaelic games and hockey); a National Indoor Training Centre to provide world-class training facilities for over thirty Governing Bodies of Sport; accommodation for sportsmen and sportswomen; sports science and medical facilities; all-weather synthetic pitches for community use; and renovation of existing buildings to cater for needs identified by sports bodies.

[9] Irish Sports Council Act, 1999. The ISC carries out drug testing in all Irish sport, both recreational and competitive. All national governing bodies are bound by the ISC's Anti-Doping rules. In Ireland, the World Anti-Doping (WADA) Code is enforced by the ISC. All national governing bodies in receipt of public funding in Ireland are bound by the WADA rules and the Council of Europe Anti-Doping Convention. As many governments cannot be legally bound by a non-governmental document, the code was implemented by way of international treaty which the United Nations Educational, Scientific and Cultural Organisation (UNESCO) drafted.

[10] National Sports Campus Development Authority Act, 2006.

[11] Horse and Greyhound Racing Industry Act, 2001. This Act established Horse Racing Ireland (HRI), which replaced the Irish Horseracing Authority. Bord na gCon is a semi-state body that was established under the Greyhound Act, 1958.

treated differently from other industries. For instance, men and women are segregated in sporting events. Such segregation would not be tolerated in other sectors. However, sport occupies a special position in society. The intervention of the law in the sporting realm has caused much debate. Some academic commentators see such interference as a positive step; others are of the view that sport is a private matter that should be exempt from the watchful gaze of the law except in the most exceptional of circumstances. It is not just the application of the law of the land to sport that has caused much debate, the actual term for such a branch of law has caused a rift between academic writers. Chapter 1 looks at the difference between the terms 'sport and the law' and 'sports law', as it is perceived by different commentators.

Chapter 2, 'Participator Violence in Sport', examines the role of the criminal law in dealing with participator violence on the field of play. The use of the criminal law in sport in both Ireland and in Britain is quite rare. However, there have been a number of high profile cases involving the Gaelic Athletic Association (GAA), including the case of *DPP v McCartan*.[12] The use of the criminal law in Canada offers an interesting comparative analysis.

Chapter 3 discusses the legality of boxing and other fighting sports. The chapter begins with a historical discussion on the development of bare-knuckle fighting into modern day boxing, as well as referring to mixed martial arts. Boxing provides an anomaly. Sportspersons can consent to harm that is within the rules of the game, or incidental to the playing of the game or the playing culture. However, sportspersons do not consent to harm which is intentional, deliberate or reckless. Boxing, by its very nature, involves the intentional infliction of harm. A detailed discussion is provided on the seminal case of *R. v Brown*, where the House of Lords discussed the continued legality of boxing.[13]

The issue of civil liability in sport is examined in Chapter 4. This chapter looks at the application of the law of tort to sport. The law of tort covers a wide range of issues, including personal injuries, defective

---

[12] Unreported, 1 November 2004, District Court.

[13] [1994] 1 AC 212. *Brown* concerned a group of sadomasochistic homosexual men who engaged in violent activities including genital torture for the purposes of pleasure. All of the men were consenting adults, the acts took place in private and no one suffered permanent injury. This case is important for contact sports, most notably boxing. Organised sports are lawful due to the presence of a referee (in a football match or boxing match), and, more importantly, it is in the public interest to allow lawfully constituted sports to be played. Similarly, it is in the public interest to allow parental chastisement and reasonable surgeries.

products, defamation and nuisance, both public and private. Some of the issues are relevant to sport, particularly the liability of participators, referees, coaches, instructors and governing bodies. With regard to participants, a player is under a duty to take all reasonable care taking account of the circumstances. The standard is objective; it is based on the reasonable person rather than the individual defendant. Liability will not attach in situations where there is an error or lapse of judgment. Something more serious is required for the defendant to be held liable. The threshold for liability is high and thus very difficult to reach.

Drug testing and gender testing in sport are both covered in Chapter 5. The chapter gives a brief account of the history of both gender and drug testing. The rules and procedures of the ISC's doping policy will be examined in detail. The constitutional issues surrounding drugs, namely, privacy, the presumption of innocence and the right to earn a livelihood will also be discussed. In addition, technological doping is briefly alluded to, the LZR Racer swimsuit being a recent example. Gender testing began as a means of preventing men posing as women. However, in more recent times, it has been used to catch women who have genetic abnormalities but who are outwardly female. The position of transsexual athletes is also examined.

As sport has become increasingly commercialised, there is a need to examine a number of commercial issues. Chapter 6, 'Commercial Issues in Sport', examines the application of the law of contract to sport. A brief background to general contract law is given, the main provisions of a professional playing contract are examined and employment issues, such as restraint of trade, are also discussed. The law of agency and the regulation of football agents are briefly discussed. The chapter ends with a cursory glance at media rights in Irish sport with a focus on the impact of European law on media rights in sport.

Chapter 7, 'European Law and Sport', provides a discussion on the initial reluctance of the then European Community to involve itself in sport matters. The European Court of Justice from the 1970s onwards became involved so long as sport was considered to be an economic activity, which then was a matter for the European Community. The case of Bosman introduced major changes for professional sportspersons.[14] The decision in *Bosman* struck down the requirement for a transfer fee for an out-of-contract player. It also held the restrictions on

---

[14] Case C-415/93, *Union Royal Belge des Societies de Football Association ASBL & Others v Jean-Marc Bosman* [1995] ECR I-4921.

non-national players to be a form of discrimination under European law. The case and subsequent developments are discussed.

As many articles of the European Economic Community (EEC) Treaty were renumbered by the treaties of Maastricht, Amsterdam, Nice and Lisbon,[15] reference is made to the article number at the time of the case and its most recent renumbering by Lisbon. In come situations, the article has undergone three number changes. For example, the current Article 101 on restrictive agreements was Article 81 until Lisbon. However, it was Article 85 prior to Amsterdam.

Chapter 8 deals with the types of alternative dispute resolution which are available to sportspersons, including the Court of Arbitration for Sport (CAS) and the Dispute Resolution Authority within the GAA. There are benefits to using the law courts as a means of redress; however, alternative dispute resolution (ADR) is less costly, more expeditious and can offer more specialised arbitrators. This chapter examines the benefits of the courts and ADR.

Chapter 9 traces the involvement of animals in sport from the Middle Ages, looking at the decline of blood sports in the nineteenth century, and current involvement and modern regulation of animals in sport, including horse racing and greyhound racing. The Hunting Act, 2004, enacted in the United Kingdom, is also discussed. There have been recent developments in Ireland, most notably the Wildlife (Amendment) Bill, 2010, the text of which will be briefly examined. The issue of doping in equestrian sports is examined with reference to the recent CAS case of *Hansen v Fédération Equestre Internationale (FEI)*.[16]

---

[15] For a detailed discussion of European law, see J. Fairhurst, *The Law of the European Union* (8th ed.) (Essex: Pearson Education Ltd, 2010), in particular Chapter 1 on the evolution of the EU, Chapter 3 on the institutions (including the Commission, Parliament and Council) and Chapter 5 on the court system.
[16] CAS 2009/A/1768.

The Law and Its Relationship with Sport

INTRODUCTION

Traditionally, sport has been viewed as a private activity that is regulated by private law. Private law governs the legal rights and relationships of individuals, companies and associations. Examples of private law include contract law, tort law and family law.[1] Most sporting bodies are categorised as private and voluntary associations. An association is defined as 'a self-governing body whose members are in an ongoing contractual relationship defined by rules, agreements and customs of the fellowship'.[2] Due to the private structure of sporting bodies, the public law has, in the past, been loath to interfere with the determinations of these organisations. However, in recent times, sports organisations have found it increasingly difficult to evade the watchful eye of the law.

The involvement of the public law can be attributed to the increased commercialisation of sport, which has made the stakes higher for sports bodies and sportspersons. Increased professionalisation and commercialisation of sport has meant sporting bodies and persons have more to lose if their rights have been compromised. Governing bodies have also assumed greater power within their individual sports. They must adhere to their own rules and regulations as failure to do so may result in legal action by one of their athletes. Society as a whole has become more litigious, and sport, as an important social activity, is unable to remain immune from such developments. In recent years sportspersons

---

[1] Public law, on the other hand, governs legal rights and relationships between individuals and the state.

[2] J. Barnes, *Sports and the Law in Canada* (3rd ed., Toronto & Vancouver: Butterworths, 1996), at 68.

have seen an increase in earning potential. If an athlete faces a career-ending injury, a contract or sponsorship dispute, or a doping allegation, he or she will be more likely to seek redress in the courts. In short, sportspersons are demanding higher standards of justice. As a result of these sporting cases, a cohesive body of law relating to sport has developed.

Irish sport is largely amateur and thus much of the discussion in this book will relate to other jurisdictions, namely Britain, Canada, Australia and the United States. However, the developments in these other juris-dictions will be of importance to Ireland in the future. The nature of Irish sport has changed over the years. Rugby, for example, is now a professional sport and professionalism brings with it a plethora of legal issues. As more and more sports become professionalised in Ireland, the issues raised in this book will become increasingly pertinent. In addition, although sport may be classified as a pastime or recreational activity, this does not mean that it is immune from judicial scrutiny. On-field violence is equally illegal in a professional match as it is in a local GAA match.[3] While Ireland has a dearth of case law and material on sport and the law, the comparative analysis of the law in other countries will provide a template from which Irish sporting bodies and the courts can develop a body of sporting jurisprudence.

WHEN SHOULD THE LAW INTERVENE IN SPORT?

Cox *et al.* see sport and law as 'natural enemies'.[4] Sport is 'idealistic and ethereal' and thus 'above the crude machinations of the law'.[5] They are realistic and admit that there are times when the law should get involved in sporting disputes. However, the question is not when the law should intervene but to what extent the law should involve itself in sporting matters.[6] In most cases, decisions should be left to the sports governing bodies. Consequently, sports bodies should not be subjected

---

[3] As will be discussed in Chapter 2, there is reluctance on the part of players and clubs to pursue on-field violence cases through the courts. The adage 'what happens on the field, stays on the field' seems to deter players bringing cases to the courts. Players feel that it is unsportsmanlike to do so and may feel that they are 'letting the team down' by pursuing a case. In contrast, there are many cases where the determinations of gov-erning bodies have been challenged. There have been numerous doping cases where the sportsperson has argued that their right to fair procedures has been breached, or a lengthy suspension has resulted in an unreasonable restraint of trade. This will be dis-cussed in Chapter 5.
[4] N. Cox, A. Schuster and C. Costello, *Sport and the Law* (Dublin: First Law, 2004), at 1.
[5] *Ibid.*
[6] *Ibid.*

'to the dogmatic formalities associated with the law'.[7] Sport is a multi-billion-euro industry and, like other industries, it needs to be regulated by the law. Cox *et al.* raise an interesting argument. They posit that sportspeople are just as prone to irresponsible business decisions and corruption as other businesspersons.[8] Cox *et al.* contend that the law 'should only intervene where it can be certain that it will be effective in doing so'.[9]

Denning MR in the case of *Enderby Town Football Club Ltd v Football Association Ltd* highlighted the reticence of the law to intervene in the determinations of sporting bodies.[10] He remarked that 'justice can often be done in them [that is, domestic tribunals] better by a good layman than a bad lawyer.'[11] In a similar vein, Tadgell J in *Australian Football League v Carlton Football Club Limited*[12] recognised that there are some situations where the courts should not intervene in the decisions of sports governing bodies. However, he continued that governing bodies are not above the law and, if the justice of the case so demands, the courts should be willing to intervene.[13]

Grayson and Gardiner on the Involvement of the Law

It is generally accepted that the law should be involved in sport; however, the extent of its involvement is unclear. There are varying opinions on when the law should intervene and when decisions should be left to the internal disciplinary mechanisms of the sport. The views of two leading academic commentators provide an illuminating discussion.

---

[7] *Ibid.*

[8] *Ibid.*

[9] *Ibid.*, at 3. They give the example of a professional footballer who commits an illegal tackle. A lengthy suspension may be a more appropriate penalty than a court fine. However, the injured party may seek compensation and will need to go to the courts, or the criminal law may need to be involved if the tackle is of a serious nature. In these situations, the law has a role to play.

[10] [1971] 1 Ch 591.

[11] *Ibid.*, at 605. See also the comments of Vice Chancellor Megarry in *McInnes v Onslow-Fane* [1978] 1 WLR 1520, at 1535, where he held the sports governing body to be 'far better fitted to judge than courts'.

[12] [1998] VR 546. This case concerned an application for judicial review by a player who was suspended for nine matches by the AFL Tribunal.

[13] *Ibid.*, at 549–550. Tadgell J held: 'Statutes aside, the courts have been disposed to interfere in a limited way with decisions of private or domestic tribunals in order to protect private rights that have been adjudged to deserve protection, including rights in property. The concept of property has been broadly interpreted for this purpose and, in cases within that category, I believe that there is no decision of a private or domestic tribunal with which the courts will refuse to interfere if interference be considered necessary for the attainment of justice.'

Simon Gardiner and Edward Grayson have very different views on the role of law in sport. Grayson is often referred to as the inventor of sport and the law.[14] He was a barrister who specialised in sports litigation.[15] Grayson viewed the intervention of the law in the regulation of sport as a positive thing. He wrote:

> …the law can and should come to the help of sport; and indeed, how sport with its high profile and image can come to the help of the law. For sport without rules and their control creates chaos. Society without laws and their enforcement means anarchy.[16]

Grayson was inspired by the old Corinthian ideal of fair play, where sportspersons excelled through their own endeavours and where the rules of the sport were respected.[17] He argued that:

> …if sport and its rulers cannot or will not try to preserve that Corinthian tradition, which the citations throughout…and the inspiration for this book demonstrate is an ideal realistically and recognised and capable of attainment to aim for, it is not always achieved, then the courts can and will do it for them, through the law of the land at both criminal and civil levels and certainly if adequate compensation is required.[18]

Grayson refers to sporting history and the sportsmanship that epitomised amateur sport in the mid-1950s.[19] The genesis of sport and the law can be traced back to the early post-war period when the Corinthian ideals of fair play, self-discipline, health and education were espoused by members of the Association of Football Players' and Trainers' Union (now the Professional Footballers' Association).[20] Modern sport is, according to Grayson, beset by violence and ungentlemanly behaviour. Grayson refers to a number of sportspersons, including Gary Lineker, David Gower and Lawrence Dallaglio, as examples of post-war sportspersons who embody the Corinthian ideal. Simon Gardiner is not persuaded by Grayson's arguments. Gardiner sees the Corinthian ideal

---

[14] Grayson published the first edition of his book *Sport and the Law* in 1988 and a second edition in 1994.

[15] Edward Grayson passed away on 23 September 2008 at the age of 83. See <http://www.telegraph.co.uk/news/obituaries/3111068/Edward-Grayson.html> (last accessed on 4 January 2010).

[16] E. Grayson, *Sport and the Law* (2nd ed., London: Butterworths, 1994), at vii.

[17] E. Grayson, 'Sport and the Law: A Return to Corinthian Values' (1998) 6(1) *Sport and the Law Journal*, 5–12; E. Grayson, *Sport and the Law* (3rd ed., London, Edinburgh, Dublin: Butterworths, 2000).

[18] Grayson, *Sport and the Law* (2nd ed.), at xxxvi.

[19] Grayson, *Sport and the Law* (3rd ed.), at 65.

[20] *Ibid.*

as being intertwined with class. The sportspersons who emerged in the 1900s and personified the Corinthian ideal were all from upper-class backgrounds and received their education in public schools.[21] Their background and subsequent entry into the professions, including law, education and medicine, instilled in them a respect for the laws and spirit of sport.[22] The writer and academic C.B. Fry, best known for his career as a cricketer, in reference to the cricketer R.E. ('Tip') Foster, remarked that 'his feet had, as it were, the Oxford accent.'[23]

Grayson's utopian view of sport is at variance with historical accounts of sport. Violence and competitiveness are not only synonymous with today's sports. Gardiner notes that, in the past, sports were rife with violence, secularism, partisanship and competitiveness.[24] Gardiner questions whether the Corinthian ideal ever existed in the manner Grayson suggests.[25] The Corinthian values of fair play and the love of participation are still relevant in modern sports, but these values are largely confined to amateur and recreational sports.[26] Fair play and the joy of participation in competitive sport, while noble virtues, are not the instigating factors for involvement in modern competitive and elite sports.[27] The professionalisation and commercialisation of sport has resulted in the nature of sport becoming increasingly complicated and beset by legal rules and regulations. In short, Grayson believes that the intervention of the law is necessary, given the increased commercialisation of sport.

Gardiner admits that over the years the Corinthian spirit has been absent.[28] Sport has been regulated by the state for centuries, from

---

[21] S. Gardiner *et al.*, *Sports Law* (2nd ed., London: Cavendish, 2001), at 36. D. Porter, 'Amateur Football in England, 1948–1963: The Pegasus Phenomenon' (2000) 14(2) *Contemporary British History* 1–30, notes at 1–2 that 'It is not easy to discern exactly what contemporary references to the Corinthian spirit implied beyond playing the game for its own sake in a manner which reflected creditably on gentlemen who had enjoyed the benefits of a good school and one or other of the ancient universities.'

[22] Gardiner *et al.*, *Sports Law*, at 36.

[23] *Life Worth Living: Some Phases of an Englishman* (London: Ian Allen, 1957), at 27. See also Porter, 'Amateur Football in England, 1948-1963: The Pegasus Phenomenon' and D. Porter and A. Smith, *Amateurs and Professionals in Post-War British Sport* (London: Frank Cass, 2000).

[24] Gardiner *et al.*, *Sports Law*, at 35. See also E. Dunning 'Social Bonding and Violence in Sport' in *Quest for Excitement: Sport and Leisure in the Civilising Process* (eds. N. Elias and E. Dunning) (Oxford: Blackwell, 1986), 224–244.

[25] Gardiner *et al.*, *Sports Law*, at 37.

[26] *Ibid.*, at 36.

[27] *Ibid.*

[28] *Ibid.*, at 37.

gaming laws to the Book of Sport.[29] State involvement varied from pre-
serving men for the King's army, to preventing drinking and gambling
at Sunday sports to preventing the lower classes from hunting on royal
land. The intervention of the state in sporting matters is not a recent
development. However, in more recent times the law is becoming more
involved in the regulation of all aspects of sport;[30] testament to this is the
growing academic commentary,[31] specific legislation,[32] cases, and law
firms specialising in sport and the law. Gardiner sees that the law has a
role to play but should only intervene in the most exceptional circumstances. Gardiner contends that sport should be largely self-regulated.
There are situations when the law should be involved, for example, in
a situation where an athlete had been unfairly treated by his or her governing body. In this situation, recourse to the law should be as a last
resort. All the internal disciplinary mechanisms of the sport should first
be exhausted before an individual or governing body seeks the intervention of the law.[33] There are situations where the governing body is
best equipped to deal with a problem. For example, a footballer who
commits a foul can be banned for a number of matches instead of being
fined by a court. A fine of €3,000 imposed by a court will not have the
same deterrence for a player as a lengthy suspension.

Sport as a Vertical Branch of Law

Cox *et al.* highlight the flaws in the arguments raised by Grayson and
Gardiner. The debate centres on whether the law of self-regulation will
improve a sport (Gardiner) or whether some form of external control
would be more beneficial (Grayson).[34] Cox *et al.* note that there are also
public policy considerations. While the interests of sport are important, it is also in the public interest that violence on the field is
dissuaded, that an injured athlete has an interest in seeking redress
if the injury sustained ends their career, and that anti-competitive
practices are prohibited.[35]

---

[29] This will be discussed in more detail in Chapter 9.
[30] Laws regulating football agents, media rights, personal injuries, liability of stadium
owners, liability of equipment manufacturers, liability of referees, assault cases, etc.
[31] Numerous books and specific journals, for example, the *Journal of Sport and the Law,
Sports Law Administration and Practice*, the *Marquette Sports Law Review*, to name but a
few.
[32] For example, the Irish Sports Council Act, 1999.
[33] The internal disciplinary procedures do not require the involvement of the courts,
solicitors or barristers. It is less costly and more expeditious.
[34] Cox, Schuster and Costello, *Sport and the Law*, at 3.
[35] This will be discussed in more detail in Chapter 7.

Michael Beloff adds an interesting dimension to the debate. Beloff makes the point that some areas of life are regulated by the law, while others are not.[36] For example, air travel and sea travel are regulated by aviation and shipping law respectively. However, gardening, flower arranging and cooking are all human activities not governed by any legal principles.[37] Beloff argues that something more than the existence of law is needed to justify the term 'sports law'. In supporting his argument, Beloff notes that other areas of human activity are regulated by law.[38] He gives the examples of the law of trusts and tort law. Both the law of trusts and tort law contain legal rules that encapsulate rights and obligations 'which apply irrespective of the subject matter of the particular case in which they are relevant'.[39] The law of trusts and tort can be termed 'horizontal law' (rule-led law), whereas categories of law that are defined by reference to human activity can be termed 'vertical law'. In using Beloff's distinction, we can place the relationship between sport and law as a human-led activity under the category of vertical law. Activities under this category are not distinct areas of law but borrow their content from rule-led branches of law such as tort, contract, criminal and trusts.[40] If a sportsperson breaches a term of a contract, the applicable law here is contract law, as there is no specific sports law that would apply here.

WHY DOES SPORT HAVE ITS OWN SYSTEM?

Sport is different to other industries or businesses. Sport has existed since antiquity and its importance has survived. Sport is important leisure activity, and, as Beloff notes, sport 'is a primary and atavistic form of self-expression'.[41] Bill Shankly, a former Liverpool Football Club manager, famously stated that football is not just a matter of life and death, it's much more important than that.[42]

Sport is also international in nature. The commercialisation of sport has resulted in international competition. There is a huge international public interest in sport. A form of international law relating to sport has

---

[36] *Sports Law* (Oxford, Portland, OR: Hart Publishing, 1999), at 1, para 1.2.
[37] *Ibid.*, at 1–2, para 1.2.
[38] *Ibid.*
[39] *Ibid.*
[40] *Ibid.*, at 2, para 1.3.
[41] *Ibid.*, at para 1.4. Beloff gives the example of Georgia, who on the dissolution of the USSR almost immediately applied for membership of FIFA.
[42] Shankly made these comments on a Granada TV chat show in 1981.

emerged. One only has to look at Nafziger's book of this name.[43] The relationship between sport and the law is also non-governmental, which again distinguishes it from other forms of law.

Sport enjoys certain privileges that would not be permitted in other industries. Men and women are segregated in sport, and take part in separate races and events. If such segregation was practised in an ordinary workplace, it would be considered sex discrimination. A manager who fires an employee on the spot and fails to follow the disciplinary procedures as required by law could be challenged in the courts for unfair dismissal. However, in the sporting realm, a team manager who sends home a national team player from a sporting event, as was the case of Roy Keane at the World Cup in 2002, would be considered to be entitled to do so. However, the player has the right to be given a number of warnings before being sent home.[44]

These peculiarities differentiate sport from other sectors and thus justify its special treatment. However, such peculiarities do not seem to embody the professionalisation of sport. Cox *et al.* issue a word of caution: 'as long as the consequences of professionalisation are *not* fully appreciated, the law will find sport to be a fertile ground for *its* business.'[45]

In order to understand the importance of sport, a cursory glance at its historical evolution is necessary.

Historical Evolution of Sport

The word 'sport' is a shortened version of the word 'disport', meaning a diversion, merriment or to amuse oneself. For early man, sport was not a mere diversion but a necessity. Sport provided an outlet for primitive man to release aggression and tension through play, which 'served as an innocuous outlet for otherwise harmful urges'.[46] Sport gave man a sense of achievement and served to further his innate desire to compete with and dominate others, and created muscular strength and skill, while in colder climes it helped with blood circulation.[47] Sport was a

---

[43] *International Sports Law* (2nd ed., Ardsley, NY: Transnational Publishers, 2004). See also J. Nafziger 'International Sports Law as a Process for Resolving Disputes' (1996) 45 *International and Comparative Law Quarterly* 130–149; J. Nafziger, 'Dispute Resolution in the Arena of International Sports Competition' (2002) 50 *American Journal of Comparative Law* 161–179.

[44] Cox, Schuster and Costello, *Sport and the Law*, at 5. The relationship between a national team player and the manager is different to the contractual relationship that exists between a player and his club.

[45] *Ibid* (italics in original).

[46] R. Brasch, *How Did Sports Begin?* (London: Longman, 1972), at 1.

[47] *Ibid.*, at 2.

medium through which man could establish victory over his foes.[48] Perhaps most importantly, sport provided man with the necessary training to defend his family and property and to escape danger.[49] Even ball sports, including football and baseball, were created as a means of battle between tribes.[50] Sport aroused a sense of mysticism as early man regarded it as a gift from the gods.[51] Children used play as a form of training in order to learn the hunting and gathering skills needed to ensure survival. Over time, sport changed from being seen as having a function that reflected the realities of life, to having one of reflecting pleasure and distraction.

Early Modern Period and Organised Sport

The early modern period saw the emergence of organised sport. Sport was given a very wide definition to include activities as diverse as stone throwing, pantomime and ballet. Joseph Strutt, in his seminal work *Sports and Pastimes of the People of England*, observed that sport, like other activities, was closely related to class.[52] A gentleman would not compete with a person below his rank.[53] Hunting, hawking and horse racing were rural exercises practised by persons of rank.[54] Townspeople and city dwellers engaged in quintain (an ancient military exercise), plays, dramas, pantomimes, juggling, dancing, gymnastics, ballet and fire eating. Animals amused crowds by performing tricks, while other animals were trained for baiting. Bull- and bear-baiting became synonymous with the English royal family. Those living in or adjacent to towns and cities played bowls and enjoyed bull running, badger-baiting, cockfighting, throwing at cocks, duck hunting, squirrel hunting and rabbit hunting. Sports were often associated with a particular festival, for instance, cockfighting was a popular activity on Shrove Tuesday. Domestic sports included bell ringing, chess, cards, backgammon and draughts. Children's pastimes often involved animals, including playing with insects and cockfighting.

---

[48] *Ibid.*, at 1.
[49] *Ibid.*
[50] *Ibid.*, at 2.
[51] *Ibid.*
[52] *Sports and Pastimes of the People of England* (London: Thomas Tegg & Son, 1838). This book was originally published in 1801 and reprinted in 1810. The sports are listed in pages IX to XVI.
[53] J. Williams, 'Sport and the Elite in Early Modern England' (2008) 28(3) *Sport in History* 389–413, at 392.
[54] Also included: archery, slinging of stones, throwing of weights and stones, handball, tennis, hurling, football, cricket, sailing, rowing and skating.

Sport became a symbol of wealth and power among the elite members of society. Relationships developed at tournaments and hunting created a sense of 'good neighbourliness' which, if used properly, could propel a gentleman into a place of power.[55] Sport had the ability to create friendly relations between nations as sporting events, including jousting and hunting, provided visiting dignitaries with a recreational activity or a spectator sport. For the monarch, sport was a tool to keep courtiers occupied during times of peace.[56]

Process of Civilisation

What emerges from the sixteenth century onwards is a process of civilisation. Standards of social behaviour, conduct and sentiment began to change drastically. As Norbert Elias observes: '[t]he ruling of conduct and sentiment became stricter, more differentiated and all embracing, but also even, more temperate, banishing excesses of self-castigation as well as of self-indulgence.'[57] The state had become more involved in the regulation of the behaviour of its citizens, and with that came stricter control of the warrior classes and the nobles.[58] Sport also experienced a change in conduct and sentiment. The modern regulation of football in England can be traced back to the nineteenth century when the Football Association was formed in 1863. The rules of football have undergone little change since 1863.[59] In earlier centuries violence was often associated with games but a new sensitivity towards violence was to emerge in the nineteenth century. A similar development occurred in boxing.[60]

---

[55] Williams, 'Sport and the Elite in Early Modern England', at 389.

[56] *Ibid.*, at 390.

[57] N. Elias (1986), 'Introduction' in Elias and Dunning (eds.), *Quest for Excitement: Sport and Leisure in the Civilising Process*, at 21.

[58] *Ibid.*

[59] P. Murphy, J. Williams and E. Dunning, *Football on Trial: Spectator Violence and Development in the Football World* (London and New York: Routledge, 1990), at 3. The modern game of football seems to have emerged during the 1840s in public schools and by the 1850s and 1860s the game became increasingly popular among upper- and middle-class adults (Murphy *et al.*, at 5). Football became more civilised, rules were introduced and players were forced to exercise self-restraint and physical control. Two forms of football emerged: football and rugby. Rugby was largely confined to the countries of the former British Empire. Initially, the modern game of football was played by the more affluent members of society who would solve on-field disputes through discussion and who would voluntarily follow the rules. However, as football 'spread to wider social circles' (at 6), more formulised rules were needed. Referees, linesmen and free kicks were introduced.

[60] This will be discussed in Chapter 3.

Prizefighting and bare-knuckle fighting were not devoid of rules but lacked a uniform set of principles.[61] In 1743 the Broughton Rules were introduced and, in 1865, the Queensberry Rules were introduced by the eighth Marquis of Queensberry. The introduction of rules and regulations into English boxing attracted the attention of other countries, most notably France, who adopted the English rules as a blueprint.[62] This global export of English sporting rules, or 'sportization' was not just confined to boxing but also included horse racing, tennis and athletics.[63]

Governing Bodies in the Nineteenth Century

In the mid-nineteenth century, modern organised rules for sport emerged. The industrial revolution and subsequent automation gave people more time to engage in leisurely pursuits.[64] Sporting associations were established and organised rules of sport were created. The primary function of these newly created governing bodies was to draw up and enforce rules in the particular sport.[65] The governing body would organise national competitions and select national teams to play against teams from other countries.[66]

The functions of modern governing bodies are more onerous. Nowadays, sporting bodies range from local teams to international level. The national body, which is responsible for regulating sport at local and national level, is also affiliated with the European body or the relevent supra-national organisation, which in turn is affiliated with the international body. In the mid-nineteenth century, governing bodies had little interaction with governmental policy.[67]

As will be discussed at the end of this chapter, governments are not directly involved in sport but have assigned the regulation of sport to sports councils. In Ireland, the Irish Sports Council Act, 1999 established the Irish Sports Council. Sports councils provide funding, grants, advice

---

[61] A formal roped-off section was rarely used; often the ground would be marked with chalk. There was no such thing as rounds and there was no limit on the duration of the fight. See J. Anderson, *The Legality of Boxing: A Punch Drunk Love?* (Abingdon: Birbeck Law Press, 2007), at 15.

[62] Elias, 'Introduction', at 21.

[63] *Ibid.*, at 21–22.

[64] D. Thorpe and A. Buti *et al.*, *Sports Law* (South Melbourne: Oxford University Press, 2009), at 3.

[65] B. Houlihan and A. White, *The Politics of Sports Development: Development of Sport or Development through Sport?* (London: Routledge, 2002), at 164.

[66] *Ibid.*

[67] *Ibid.*

and draft policies on various issues, including drugs in sport, participation and non-discrimination, and child protection.

Revival of the Olympics

As mentioned, one of the first governing bodies to be established was the Football Association in 1863. This was followed by associations being established for swimming (1869), rugby (the Rugby Football Union (1871)), cycling (1878), rowing (1879), skating (1879), athletics (1880), boxing (1881), hockey (1886), tennis (1886) and skiing (1903).[68]

Before the close of the century, a significant revival of the ancient Olympics took place in Athens in 1896.[69] Baron Pierre de Coubertin, a French aristocrat, had voiced his concerns about the lack of physical education in French schools and attributed this to French military defeats.[70] He contended that French schools were too academic and intellectual and that there was not enough physical training and sports. De Coubertin travelled to the United States and Britain to observe the administration of athletes. As his attempts to overhaul the French education system never materialised, he instead turned his focus to a larger-scale plan. The French Government commissioned de Coubertin to hold athletic congresses and in 1892, at a jubilee of the French Union of Athletic Sports Societies, de Coubertin spoke of his intention to revive the Olympic Games.[71] At this time, the idea was very much in its

---

[68] J. Horne, A. Tomlinson and G. Whannel, *Understanding Sport: An Introduction to the Sociological and Cultural Analysis of Sport* (London: Spon Press, 1999), at 261. The writers note that at the end of the nineteenth century sport began to attract regular fee-paying spectators and this was in effect the starting point of the commercialisation of sport.

[69] The ancient Olympics had ended in 393 AD as Emperor Theodosius I banned the Games due to their alleged affiliation with pagan rituals. Theodosius wished to eradicate from Greek society any non-Christian activities and festivals.

[70] France had suffered defeat in the Franco-Prussian War in 1871. De Coubertin remarked: 'How well one understands that France should go and play dominoes instead of exercising its tired muscles. Sated with victory, France gradually fell asleep while its black, total, horrible defeat had awakened energies which laboured grimly at the undertaking that you know: the German Empire. It was thus that military athletics was born in Berlin,' taken from a lecture given at the Sorbonne in November 1892, entitled 'Physical Exercises in the Modern World' and cited by I. Weiler, 'The Predecessors of the Olympic Movement, and Pierre de Coubertin' (2004) 12(3) *European Review* 427–443, at 435–436.

[71] De Coubertin is often referred to as the father or inventor of the modern Olympics. However, some commentators disagree. Before the War of Independence (1821–1829), the Greeks, drawing their inspiration from the Romantic poets, endeavoured to revive the Olympics. However, their attempts never came to fruition. Thirteen Olympic Games are said to have taken place before the revival in 1896, the first being the

infancy; however, in 1894 de Coubertin convened a meeting, which was attended by 79 delegates from 12 countries. At this meeting, the International Olympic Committee (IOC) was formed. It was agreed that the Games would be held every four years, beginning in 1896 in Athens. The Games opened on 6 April and ended on 15 April.[72] The Olympic Games remained amateur until 1984. At the Los Angeles Games in 1984 the rules relating to the admittance of professional athletes were changed to reflect economic realities.[73] Boxing remains the only amateur sport at the Olympic Games for safety reasons. Amateur boxers wear protective headgear, while professional boxers do not.

Sport enjoys a privileged position within society. It enjoys peculiarities that would not be tolerated in other areas of life. While commentators may disagree on the extent to which the law should intervene in the determinations of sports governing bodies, the fact remains that the law has become increasingly involved. The law has a role to play in sport. While the extent to which it may be involved is unclear, the benefits of the intervention of the law cannot be underestimated. Sports governing bodies have a vested interest in the outcome of a case. Sports governing bodies are often judge and jury in a dispute.[74] Redress to the law can offer a sportsperson a 'copper bottomed guarantee of ultimate justice for individual sportsmen embroiled in stormy long running (invariably disciplinary) disputes with their governing bodies'.[75]

Cotswold Games in 1612; see Weiler, 'The Predecessors of the Olympic Movement, and Pierre de Coubertin', at 428 and further examples at 428–429. Weiler questions de Coubertin's knowledge of Ancient Greece (at 435) and argues that de Coubertin's 'chief contribution should primarily be seen in the fact that he emphasised certain pedagogical and philosophical views, created the ideology of Olympism, the internationalism of the Olympics (of course, in the background of the international sports movement) and helped to organise the so-called Olympic movement'.

[72] Fourteen countries took part with the largest group of competitors coming from Greece, Germany, France and Great Britain. A total of 241 athletes competed in 43 events. It was a male-only Games. See <http://www.olympic.org> (last accessed 7 January 2010). Women did not compete until 1900. De Coubertin did not wish for women to compete as he stated: '…the true Olympic hero, in my view, is the individual adult male.' He was not against women participating in sport *per se*, 'provided that they do not make a public spectacle of themselves. In the Olympic Games, as in the contests of former times, their primary role should be to crown the victors.' (Weiler, 'The Predecessors of the Olympic Movement, and Pierre de Coubertin', at 435).

[73] Many of the Eastern Bloc states were funding full-time amateur athletes. The Western athletes were self-financing amateurs. From the 1970s onwards, there were requests to change the criteria as Western athletes argued that they were at a disadvantage.

[74] Most notably in doping cases. This will discussed in Chapter 5.

[75] P. Morris and G. Little, 'Challenging Sports Bodies' Determinations' (1998) 17 *Civil Justice Quarterly* 128–148, at 129.

'SPORTS LAW' OR 'SPORT AND THE LAW'?

For some time, a debate has centred on whether or not the branch of the law dealing with sport is called 'sport and the law' or 'sports law'. Various academic writers have proffered their views on the matter. Some books are titled *Sports Law*,[76] while others have used the title *Sport and the Law*.[77] While such differences in titles may seem unimportant at first glance, there is a marked difference between the terms 'sports law' and 'sport and the law'. Sports law implies that there is a unique body of law that applies specifically to sport. Sport and the law suggests an inter-disciplinary relationship between law and sport. A situation may arise in a sporting context that requires reference to contract law, the law of torts, employment law, the criminal law or European law. In this situation, a recognised branch of law is being applied to a particular industry, that industry being sport. Some academic commentators have argued that 'sports law' is a 'misleading term' and 'in reality, sports law is nothing more or less than law as applied to the sports industry.'[78]

Beloff emphasises the need to define 'sports law'.[79] He contends that 'one must delineate its scope, however blurred its edges and however indistinct its outline.'[80] Beloff succinctly defines sports law as:

> ...a loose but increasingly cohesive body of rules governing the practice of sport and the resolution of disputes in law. That body of rules straddles the boundaries between many well-known branches of our law, but has at its centre an unusual form of international constitutional principle prescribing the limited autonomy of non-governmental decision-making bodies in sport.[81]

Beloff argues that sport should not treated any differently to any other field of human activity and that legal rules and regulations should be applied without exception.[82]

---

[76] Gardiner *et al.*, *Sports Law* (3rd ed., London: Cavendish, 2006); Beloff *et al.*, *Sports Law* (Oxford: Hart, 1999); M. Fewell, *Sports Law: A Practical Guide* (Sydney: LBC Information Services, 1995); R. Parrish, *Sports Law and Policy in the European Union* (Manchester: Manchester University Press, 2003).

[77] Cox, Schuster and Costello, *Sport and the Law*; J. Barnes, *Sports and the Law in Canada* (3rd ed., Toronto: Butterworths, 1996); E. Grayson, *Sport and the Law* (3rd ed., 2000). See also S. Greenfield and G. Osborn (eds.) *Law and Sport in Contemporary Society* (London: Frank Cass, 2000).

[78] M.J. Cozzillio and M.S. Levinstein, *Sports Law: Cases and Materials* (Durham, NC: Carolina Academic Press, 1997), at 5. See also T. Davis, 'What Is Sports Law?' (2001) 11 *Marquette Sports Law Review* 211–244.

[79] Beloff *et al.*, *Sports Law*, at 3, para 1.5.

[80] *Ibid.*

[81] *Ibid.*, at 6, para 1.12.

[82] *Ibid.*, at 4, para 1.8.

Morris and Little, in contrast, see sport as having its own 'micro legal systems' due to its special characteristics, which validates the restraint of the legislature and judiciary from devising legal doctrines and procedures which may be employed to examine the determinations of sport governing bodies, thus interfering with their inherent functions.[83]

The 'sport and the law' versus 'sports law' debate can be divided into three arguments.[84] The first position holds that there is no separate identifiable body of law that relates exclusively to sport and the possibility that such a corpus of law will emerge in the future is extremely remote.[85] The second position contends that there is no separate identifiable body of law currently relating to sport. However, as the public law has begun to intervene and this has resulted in cases being brought before the courts, it is predicted that in the near future a substantive corpus of law pertaining to sport will emerge.[86] The third position asserts that there is a body of law that can be referred to as sports law.[87]

The first approach reflects the traditional view that there is no specific branch of law that applies exclusively to sport.[88] Traditionalists argue that the term 'sports law' is misleading as sport as an activity and form of entertainment is governed by the overarching legal system.[89] It is superfluous to contend that there is a body of law that can be designated as sports law. Sports law is seen as the application of basic legal rules to a particular industry, the industry at issue being sport.

The second approach encapsulates a more moderate view. Academic commentators, including Professor Kenneth Shropshire, see sports law as developing into a field of law in the future.[90] Shropshire refers to state and federal legislation in the United States that has impacted on sport, from the regulation of sports' agents to anti-discrimination under Title IX, Education Amendments Act, 1972.[91] Shropshire considers the term 'sport and the law' as the appropriate term. He posits that there is a 'growing sports-only corpus of law'.[92] The moderates see sports law as

---

[83] Morris and Little, 'Challenging Sports Bodies' Determinations', at 129.
[84] Davis, 'What Is Sports Law?'
[85] *Ibid.*, at 211.
[86] *Ibid.*
[87] *Ibid.*
[88] *Ibid.*, at 212.
[89] *Ibid.*
[90] *Ibid.* K. Shropshire, 'Introduction: Sports Law?' (1998) 35 *American Business Law Journal* 181–184, at 182.
[91] Title 20 USC Sections 1681-1688. This Act banned sex discrimination in schools. The prohibition applies to education and athletics.
[92] Shropshire, 'Introduction: Sports Law?', at 182.

an emerging field of law which will develop into its own substantive branch of law in the future. Weisart and Lowell support the view that sports law is a field of study. They point to the anomalies that exist, in some situations a specific provision may apply to sport and nowhere else.[93] For example, baseball in the United States is exempt from anti-trust legislation.[94] Sport permits peculiarities, including the segregation of men and women in races, which would ordinarily constitute sex discrimination, and consequently these peculiarities require the unique application of legal principles.[95] In the words of Davis:

...thus, while not expressly adopting the position that recognizes the existence of a course of study called sports law, Weistart and Lowell strongly suggest that two phenomena, the unique application of legal doctrine to the sports context and the factual uniqueness of sports problems that require the need for specialized analysis, support the notion that a body of law called sports law might exist.[96]

The third approach sees sports law as a separate field of law.[97] Proponents of sport as a separate field of law, including Gardiner, argue that sport is being marginalised and is not being treated like other forms of business.[98] Sport is viewed more as entertainment and this perception has resulted in it being considered less serious than other forms of business. There is a great reluctance among the traditionalists to recognise sport as being the subject matter of legal relationships.[99] Given its

[93] J.C. Weistart and C.H. Lowell, *The Law of Sports* (Indianapolis, IN: Bobbs-Merrill Co, 1979), at xviii.
[94] Under the Sherman Act, 1890 and the Clayton Act, 1914, any business that operates across state borders and participates in interstate commerce is subject to anti-trust legislation. In 1922, an exemption was given to baseball. The Supreme Court held that baseball was exempt from the Sherman and Clayton Acts in the case of *Federal Baseball Club of Baltimore, Inc. v National Baseball Clubs* 259 US 200 (1922). The Supreme Court ruled even though there was scheduling of games across state lines, those games were intrastate events, as the travel from one state to another was 'not the essential thing'. See J.W. Neville, 'Baseball and the Antitrust Laws' (1947) 16 *Fordham Law Review* 208–230.
[95] Cozzillio and Levinstein, *Sports Law: Cases and Materials*, at 214. Weistart and Lowell, *The Law of Sports*, at xviii–xix.
[96] Davis, 'What Is Sports Law?', at 214.
[97] Similar arguments have been made in respect of computer law. See Davis, 'What is Sports Law?', at 216. Davis provides a list of factors that demonstrate that sports law has reached a level of common acceptance, see 217-218. See also Davis at 219-238 where he discusses the substantive areas of law that are applicable to sports, namely, contract law, employment law, antitrust law, tort law and constitutional law.
[98] Davis, 'What Is Sports Law?', at 215.
[99] *Ibid*. Similarly, marriage is a social relationship yet it is governed by legal rules.

peculiarities, its uniqueness, the growing body of cases and commentary, proponents of the third category hold sports law has become a separate body of law. Gardiner notes that 'there is no official recognition procedure', but rather 'it is a process of legal practitioners and academics recognising the growing application of the law to a new area of social life'.[100]

What Is A Sport?

There is no legal definition of a sport. There are many reasons why a sports body or individual would want a particular activity to be defined as a sport. A sporting body may receive tax relief or state funding. Certain contact sports, including boxing and rugby, may result in injury that would ordinarily be defined as an assault but if it's received in the context of a sport, it is treated as an exception to the common law rules on consensual assault. Section 2 of the Irish Sports Council Act, 1999 defines recreational sport as 'all forms of physical activity, which through casual or organised participation, aim at expressing or improving physical fitness and mental well-being and at forming social relationships'. Section 2 defines competitive sport as 'all forms of physical activity which, through organised participation, aim at expressing or improving physical fitness and at obtaining improved results in competition at all levels'.

There are limits to what can be defined as a sport, as the case of *R. v Brown* demonstrates.[101] This case concerned a group of sadomasochistic homosexual men who engaged in violent activities, including genital torture, for the purposes of pleasure. All the men were consenting adults, the acts took place in private and no one suffered permanent injury. Video cameras recorded the activities. However, these recordings were not for public viewing but for the group of men involved. The men were charged with assault occasioning actual bodily harm under section 47 of the Offences Against the Person Act, 1861. The men argued that there could be no offence if the parties involved consented. The trial court rejected this contention and the case was appealed by five of the men to the Court of Appeal. The case was sent to the House of Lords which upheld the illegality of the acts. The House of Lords held that the practice of sadomasochistic activities for the satisfaction of sexual desires did not constitute 'good reason'. Thus, their criminal

---

[100] Gardiner *et al.*, *Sports Law*, at 73.
[101] [1993] 2 All ER 75. This case will be discussed in more detail in Chapter 3.

conviction was upheld even though the men had consented to the harm suffered. This case is important for contact sports, most notably boxing. Boxing, which can cause actual bodily harm, is legal because it is regulated by rules. It is socially acceptable in contrast to the sadomasochistic activities of the men in *Brown*. Lord Jauncey referred to organised sports and held that organised sports can be distinguished from the activities in *Brown*. Organised sports are lawful due to the presence of a referee (in a football match or boxing match), and, more importantly, there is a public interest in allowing lawfully constituted sports to be played.[102]

There are definitional problems when it comes to applying the word sport to some activities and not to others. Cycling down the road would not be considered a sport, yet cycling in the Tour de France is a sport. To Kris Lines, head of the Sports Law Programme at Staffordshire University, 'the key is whether the overall activity would be a sport (however defined) if played in a competitive environment, not whether the activity could be a sport in some environments and not others. Basketball clearly is a sport, even if I am just shooting the ball at home.'[103]

However, while playing baseball at home is a sport, it needs further refinement in order for it to be considered a sport in legal terms.[104] Brown suggests that for a sport to be classified as such it needs to be regulated by law and be deemed socially acceptable. The United Kingdom Law Commission consultation paper on consent in the criminal law provides some guidance on what constitutes a legal definition of sport.[105] The Commission, in reference to field violence (para 13.11), proposes that sports participants should not be held criminally liable for injury caused if the injury in question is inflicted in the 'course of playing or practising a recognised sport in accordance with its rules'. Thus, liability should only attach if the injury inflicted is done so outside the rules of the sport. The Commission recognises (para 13.1) the need to define what constitutes a lawful sport. The rules and regulations, and what would be acceptable, differ between sports. In boxing, for example, it is within the rules to hit an opponent from the waist up, yet in a non-contact sport such as tennis, any form of physical contact would

---

[102] Similarly, Lord Jauncey added that there is a public interest in allowing for reasonable surgeries and parental chastisement.

[103] 'Defining a Sport: An Illustration', 28 September 2009 (available online: <http://sports-law.blogspot.com/2009/09/defining-sport-illustration.html>, last accessed 8 January 2010).

[104] See G. McFee, *Sport, Rules and Values: Philosophical Investigations into the Nature of Sport* (London: Routledge, 2004), 15-32.

[105] LCCP 139 *Criminal Law: Consent in the Criminal Law* (1995) (London: HMSO).

be outside the rules of the sport. In order to provide a legal definition of sport, the rules and regulations of a particular sport need to be verified in order for it to be recognised as a lawfully constituted sport.[106] The Law Commission refers to criteria devised by the then British Sports Council.[107] The Council identifies the following criteria used by it in determining whether an activity is recognised as a sport:[108]

- Physical skill
- Physical effort
- Accessibility
- Rules and organisation
- Essential purpose
- Physical challenge
- Risk
- Uniqueness
- Strategies and tactics
- Level of participation
- Martial arts
- Other considerations

This final point is of particular relevance to the activities practised in *R. v Brown*.[109] The guidelines ask if there any political, moral or other ethical considerations which might prohibit the Sports Council from recognising the activity? Cox *et al.* note that such a clause clearly prohibits the activities described in *Brown* from being recognised as a lawfully recognised sport.[110]

The above guidelines provide some assistance in the quest to find a clear and precise legal definition of what constitutes a sport. Reference may also be made to sports that are recognised by the International Olympic Committee (IOC). However, some anomalies may denigrate the effectiveness of using the IOC as a guide. Men's ski jumping is recognised, yet women's ski jumping is not. It would seem that the IOC

---

[106] As will be discussed in Chapter 3, this is an important consideration for emerging forms of martial arts.

[107] 'Recognition of Activities and Governing Bodies', Sports Council Paper SC (93) 68, para 4.3 (updated in 1998). The Sports Council is now known as UK Sport. It was established by Royal Charter in 1996 and began operating on 1 January 1997. It is sponsored by the Department of Culture, Media and Sport.

[108] See Gardiner *et al.*, *Sports Law*, at 21, for a more detailed description of the criteria.

[109] [1993] 2 All ER 75.

[110] Cox, Schuster and Costello, *Sport and the Law*, at 8-9.

is more concerned with organising a popular and successful competition.[111] However, neither golf nor rugby were recognised as Olympic sports, both arguably very popular participant and spectator sports. In October 2009, the IOC decided to allow both sports to be included in the 2016 Olympics.[112]

IRISH SPORTS COUNCIL ACT, 1999

In Ireland, sport falls under the auspices of the Department of Tourism, Culture and Sport. The Department and the Minister are aided by the Irish Sports Council (ISC), which was established under the Irish Sports Council Act, 1999. The main of aim of the ISC is to encourage participation in sport from people of all ages and abilities, from recreational to high performance level. The ISC recognises the importance of sport and its contribution to enhancing the quality of Irish life.[113]

The ISC is a statutory authority comprising of eight major divisions:

• Anti-doping
• Corporate services
• Finance
• High performance
• Local sports partnerships
• National governing bodies
• National Trails Office
• Irish Institute of Sport

The 1999 Act bestowed upon the ISC the task of combating drugs in Irish sport.[114] The ISC has a three-pronged approach to doping: testing, education and research. Under Article 6(1)(d) of the Act, the Council is empowered 'to take such action as it considers appropriate, including testing, to combat doping in sport'. Article 18(3) of the Act provided for the creation of a:

> Committee to be known as the Anti-Doping Committee of the Irish Sports Council, to (a) assist and advise the Council in relation to the performance of its functions under section 6(1)(d), and (b) exercise such powers and carry out such duties relating to that function as the Council may from time to time delegate to the Committee.

---

[111] Lines, 'Defining a Sport: An Illustration'.
[112] Golf was last an Olympic sport at the 1904 Games in St Louis. Karate and squash had also applied but were not given recognition.
[113] See the website of the Irish Sports Council: <http://www.irishsportscouncil.ie>.
[114] This will be discussed in more detail in Chapter 5.

The ISC sets out its objectives for a three-year period in its strategic documents. The first document, *A New Era for Sport (2000–2002)*, was replaced by *Sport for Life* in 2003. In 2006, the ISC launched *Building Sport for Life*, followed by the current document for the period of 2009–2011, *Building Sport for Life: The Next Phase*.

HOW IS SPORT GOVERNED?

In a domestic setting, sports are governed by their national governing body or federation. For example, football (soccer) in Ireland is regulated by the Football Association of Ireland (FAI).[115] The regional body for football in Europe is UEFA (Union des Associations Européennes de Football).[116] FIFA (Fédération Internationale de Football Association) is the international governing body for football.[117] The FAI is affiliated with UEFA and FIFA. This means that the FAI is bound by the rules and regulations of both organisations. National governing bodies must keep up to date with any changes in the rules or regulations of their affiliates. At international level, sporting bodies are governed by international sports federations (IFs) and the IOC.

The status of domestic sports bodies differs among sports organisations in Ireland. Some are created by way of legislation. These are called statutory bodies. The Irish Greyhound Board, or Bord na gCon, is one such statutory body, established by the Greyhound Industry Act, 1958.[118] Other governing bodies are established as private limited companies and are regulated by the Companies Acts 1963–2009. Some sports bodies have charitable status, which gives them certain exemptions when it comes to income tax and corporation tax.[119]

---

[115] The FAI was originally known as the Football Association of the Irish Free State (FAIFS), which was established in 1921. Until 1950, a player could play for the FAIFS and for the Northern Ireland association, the Irish Football Association (IFA). In 1946, the IFA rejoined FIFA as Northern Ireland. Subsequently, the FAIFS became known as the FAI. Until 1985, Derry FC played in Northern Ireland but joined the League of Ireland. For more details see <http://www.fai.ie> and <http://www.loi.ie/>.

[116] Established in 1954 in Basle, Switzerland. UEFA comprises 53 national football associations. It is recognised by FIFA as one of the six continental federations. The FAI joined in 1954.

[117] Established in 1904, governed by Swiss law and based in Zurich. It has 208 member associations. The FAI joined in 1923.

[118] The board has wide powers ranging from issuing licences to use certain tracks to issuing permits to officials, bookmakers and trainers. It controls 9 of the 17 licensed tracks in the Republic of Ireland. See <http://www.igb.ie/top/About-Us/>.

[119] The Charities Act, 2009 has excluded some sports bodies. Section 2 of the Bill excluded 'bodies established for and existing for the sole purpose of promoting athletic

At the apex is the Olympic movement. The Olympic movement encompasses three constituent parts: the IOC, the IFs[120] and National Olympic Committees (NOCs).[121] The Olympics is a worldwide movement which governs 33 sports.[122] Sportspersons who participate in a sport governed by an IF that is not recognised by the IOC are not permitted to compete in the Olympics. The IOC may seem remote to those taking part in particular sports at national level. However, the matrix of affiliations make it necessary for the sport to comply with IOC rules at all levels. Taking the example of the FAI above, a player in the League of Ireland, although not part of the Olympics, is bound by the rules of the FAI, the FAI in turn is bound by the rules of the IF, FIFA. Thus the rules of the IOC have the ability to pervade through many levels of sport.[123]

Each country has a NOC.[124] In Ireland, the Olympic Council of Ireland (OCI) promotes the Olympics in accordance with the Olympic Charter. The OCI has been in existence since 1922 and its main objectives are:

- To provide Team Ireland with the most effective athlete-centred, performance-driven operational planning and management at each Olympiad
- To maximise commercial value of the Olympic brand and provide long-term financial security for the OCI
- To develop and protect the Olympic movement in Ireland
- To provide strategic leadership and representation of Olympic sport within government, the EOC[125] and the IOC[126]

---

or amateur games or sports'. In order to qualify for tax exemptions, the sports body must show the Revenue Commissioner that all income has been or will be used for the sole purpose of promoting that amateur game or sport. The body must be a not-for-profit, member-controlled and-owned organisation. See <http://www.revenue.ie/en/tax/it/leaflets/gs1.pdf>.

[120] International federations require athletes to adhere to their rules and regulations, ranging from on-field conduct (e.g. violence) to off-field conduct (e.g. bringing the sport into disrepute), doping and player eligibility.

[121] Rule 1.2 of the Olympic Charter. Rule 28 of the Charter provides that the role of the NOCs is to 'develop and protect the Olympic Movement in their respective countries, in accordance with the Olympic Charter'.

[122] Not all sports are recognised by the Olympics.

[123] Thorpe and Buti *et al.*, *Sports Law*, at 14, state: 'One can therefore see how the rules established by the IOC find their expression at all levels of sport, even in events that are not officially part of the Olympic Games.'

[124] There are currently 205 NOCs.

[125] European Olympic Committee, see <http://www.eurolympic.org/> (last accessed 27 July 2010).

[126] Taken from <http://www.olympicsport.ie/Content.aspx?pageid=59> (last accessed 27 July 2010).

The IOC is based in Lausanne, Switzerland and operates under Swiss law. The IOC falls under the jurisdiction of the international legal system. It operates within a framework similar to that of the United Nations (UN). Thorpe notes that the IOC 'plays a key role in determining the international legal norms which govern sport'.[127] The IOC has fostered close relations with a number of UN agencies, including the United Nations Educational, Scientific and Cultural Organisation (UNESCO). The IOC and UNESCO forged links in 1984 but in 2004 a new cooperation agreement was signed to reinforce the commitment of both organisations. The IOC and UNESCO work together to promote common interests in the areas of physical education and sport.[128] Given the importance of sport in promoting well-being and health, the IOC also works closely with the World Health Organisation.

The legal status of the IOC is somewhat vague. It is generally accepted as a non-governmental organisation (NGO).[129] It is recognised as a legal entity, but, as Thorpe notes, it is not 'incorporated in the usual sense of the word'.[130] The Olympic Charter is the constitutional document of the Olympic movement. It is a codification of all the principles of Olympism,[131] and the rules and bye-laws adopted by the IOC. Rule 1.1 of the Charter recognises the IOC as the supreme authority of the Olympic movement. The IOC establishes rules governing eligibility to participate in the Olympic Summer and Winter Games, and has some input into the rules governing each Olympic sport, as all Olympic sports must be in compliance with the rules and spirit of the Olympics. Rule 27.1.1 provides that it is the mission and role of the IFs within the Olympic movement to 'establish and enforce, in accordance with

---

[127] Thorpe and Buti et al., Sports Law, at 12.
[128] In 2005, UNESCO adopted the International Convention against Doping in Sport. It came into force on 1 February 2007. The Convention presents formalised global anti-doping rules and regulations with the aim of eradicating prohibited substances from sport. The Convention also endeavours to enforce the World Anti-Doping Code in international law by placing obligations on nations to ensure compliance with the Code. See <http://portal.unesco.org/shs/en/ev.php-URL_ID=9682&URL_DO=DO_TOPIC&URL_SECTION=201.htm> (last accessed 27 July 2010).
[129] Rule 15.1 of the Olympic Charter provides that 'the IOC is an international non-governmental non-profit organisation, of unlimited duration, in the form of an association with the status of a legal person, recognised by the Swiss Federal Council in accordance with an agreement entered into on 1 November 2000.' The most recent version of the Charter is from 2007, available online at
<http://multimedia.olympic.org/pdf/en_report_122.pdf> (last accessed 27 July 2010).
[130] Thorpe and Buti et al., Sports Law, at 12.
[131] Olympism is a philosophy of life that exalts and combines a balanced approach to body, mind and will.

the Olympic spirit, the rules concerning the practice of their respective sports and to ensure their application'. International Federations are responsible for developing their sports throughout the world (Rule 27.1.2) and must establish eligibility criteria for participation in the Olympics in conformity with the Olympic Charter. These criteria must be submitted to the IOC for approval (Rule 27.1.5).

Each IF comprises all the national federations (NFs) of the relevant sport (Rule 29.1.2). This rule is augmented by bye-law 1.2, which provides that at least five national federations must be affiliated with each IF governing sports included in the programme of the Olympic Games.

A more recent development in the organisational structure of sport is the creation of the Court of Arbitration for Sport (CAS).[132] The CAS, based in Lausanne in Switzerland, provides athletes and governing bodies with an alternative to the law courts. The CAS is an arbitration body created by the IOC in 1983.

For those embroiled in a sporting dispute recourse may also be made to national arbitrators.[133]

CONCLUSION

In the past, sporting bodies were able to immunise themselves from judicial intervention. However, in recent years, sport has become a big business due to its increased commercialisation and professionalism. As athletes have more to lose if their rights are unduly comprised, redress from the law has assumed a greater importance. Governing bodies must keep within the powers conferred upon them as failure to do so may invoke the wrath of the law.

At present, there is no specific branch of law that pertains exclusively to sport. Admittedly, sport enjoys peculiarities not found or tolerated in other industries. However, to say that there is a branch of law called sports law is premature. The proper, and broader, term to encompass the relationship would seem to be sport and the law. Sport and the law recognises the cultural, political and social importance of sport but also recognises that the law has a role to play. Perhaps in the near future a body of law called sports law will emerge and be accepted in the same way as other branches of law.

The matter of the appropriate terminology aside, the law should intervene in the sporting realm, albeit in exceptional circumstances.

---

[132] See Chapter 8.
[133] See L. Donnellan, 'Player Eligibility and Club Sanctions: The Position in Ireland' (2007) 14(2) *Sports Law Administration and Practice* 12–16.

Recourse to the law should be seen as a last resort and should only be used when all the internal mechanisms of the sport have been exhausted. The following chapters will demonstrate the law's involvement in sporting disputes, from violence in sport (criminal and civil), to the constitutional issues arising from drug testing and the involvement of the European Union. The legal relationship between sport and the law is both complex and sometimes unclear. Beginning with a discussion on violence in sport, Chapter 2 will examine the role of the criminal law in dealing with participator violence on the field of play.

CHAPTER 2

Participator Violence in Sport

INTRODUCTION

Violence in sport can attract either the criminal law or civil law, or indeed both. If a sportsperson is injured by reason of an intentional or reckless challenge, the individual may seek redress through the criminal law by instituting an assault case against the perpetrator, and may also seek damages for the injury sustained. The focus in this chapter is on contact sports and the intervention of the criminal law in cases involving participator violence.

Dearth of Prosecutions

The use of the criminal law in sport in both Ireland and Britain is quite rare.[1] In the United States there is a marked reluctance to bring criminal cases as the encroachment of the criminal law can be seen as curbing the vigour of certain sports due to participants fearing prosecution.[2] Most sportspersons are reluctant to bring charges against an opponent as to do so may be considered unsportsmanlike or may be deemed to be letting the team down. Sports cases present evidentiary problems as it is difficult to prove *mens rea* (mental element) or criminal intent on the

---

[1] This chapter focuses on criminal liability in relation to on-field violence. The criminal law can apply in other ways, including match fixing, illegal gambling pertaining to a match and the use of illegal drugs (cocaine, heroin, etc.) by sportspersons.

[2] J. Yates and W. Gillespie, 'The Problem of Sports Violence and the Criminal Prosecution Problem' (2002–2003) 12 *Cornell Journal of Law & Public Policy* 145–168, at 168. The authors (at 146) note that, while prosecutions and civil litigation are low, nevertheless '...society is willing to hold sports participants accountable for their actions.' Some critics refer to violence in sport and its societal effects, including the influence on children and spectators, see 150–151.

part of the defendant.[3] Also, the issue of consent is an important factor. When an individual joins a sports club he or she agrees to be bound by the rules of that club. Typically, disputes are submitted to the internal disciplinary mechanisms of the sport. When an individual plays a contact sport, it is reasonably foreseeable that he or she will sustain an injury, as contact sports by their very nature involve contact between the players. Individuals consent to the inherent risks that are associated with the sport. However, there are limits to what an individual can consent to.[4]

Most infractions are dealt with by the internal disciplinary mechanisms of the sport or league. The case law suggests that only incidents of excessive violence will be subject to the criminal law. For more trivial infringements of the rules, self-regulation by the sporting bodies will continue to be the more popular and effective method of dealing with violence in sport.

LAWFUL AND UNLAWFUL SPORTS

As seen in the previous chapter, an activity classified as a sport enjoys certain privileges. A recognised sport may be given fiscal benefits in the form of funding and tax exemptions. Certain activities that would be rendered illegal in a situation outside the sporting sphere are deemed acceptable within the realm of a recognised sport.

If a sport is recognised as lawful, this does not mean that the law will never intervene. If a sportsperson deliberately and recklessly disregards the rules of the sport and intentionally goes beyond the limits of that sport, the criminal law may be invoked. Even in a contact sport like boxing, there are limits. For example, a boxer may not hit below the belt or hold, trip, kick or butt his opponent with the foot or knee. Nor can a boxer hit with the open side of the glove or the inside of the glove.[5]

---

[3] As many incidents arise in the heat of the moment in a fast-paced contact sport, it may be an arduous task for the plaintiff to prove that the opponent deliberately or recklessly intended to injure him or her.

[4] P. McCutcheon, 'Sports Violence and Consent and the Criminal Law' (1994) 45(3) *Northern Ireland Legal Quarterly* 267–284, at 267 notes: '...there is a point beyond which the consent of the participation in sport is considered immaterial and the conduct is treated as unlawful.'

[5] A boxer may not bite the ear of an opponent as the incident involving Mike Tyson and Evander Holyfield in 1997 demonstrated. At a World Boxing Association (WBA) title fight at the MGM Hotel in Las Vegas, Tyson bit a chunk out of Holyfield's ear. Tyson had his boxing licence revoked for one year by the Nevada State Athletic Commission and was fined $3 million plus costs. He was not sentenced to prison.

Similarly, in rugby, there are many instances in which violent conduct is permitted. While a tackle may not be within the rules of the sport, some have become part of what is known as the playing culture. This has caused a blurring of the distinction between breaches of the rules of the game and those which are breaches but are deemed to be acceptable. As Cox *et al.* note, '…in simple terms then, the rules of most contact sports seem to permit and encourage uncivilised behaviour, and remarkably the law of the land allows them to do so, provided only that the sport in question is recognised as lawfully constituted.'[6]

Many sports attract followers due to their violent nature,[7] as the discussion on ice hockey at the end of this chapter will examine. Indeed, in some sports, violence is encouraged and considered to be an acceptable part of the playing culture. Jean Fuggett, a former American footballer who played for the Dallas Cowboys, once remarked: 'The game is legalized violence…. I can go into a game and just literally try to break somebody's neck…. It happens all the time.'[8]

Some sports are illegal irrespective of consent,[9] the use of rules or the presence of a referee. The following sports are illegal in Ireland and in most countries: prizefighting,[10] gladiatorial fights to death, cockfighting, cock-throwing[11] and bear-baiting.[12] These blood sports were banned due to the rioting and drinking that often accompanied them. Similarly, prizefighting was declared illegal in the seminal case of *R. v Coney.*[13] Prizefighting was declared unlawful as it was considered to serve no useful purpose and had a tendency to incite riots and breaches of the peace.

---

[6] N. Cox, A. Schuster and C. Costello, *Sport and the Law* (Dublin: First Law, 2004), at 165.
[7] W. Hechter, 'The Criminal Law and Violence in Sports' (1976–1977) 19 *Criminal Law Quarterly* 425–453, at 432.
[8] Hechter, 'The Criminal Law and Violence in Sports', at 437. Hechter, at 431, notes that in the 1974–1975 hockey season in the United States, there were over 44,000 treatments recorded in hospital emergency rooms. Most of the injuries related to minors engaging in amateur hockey games.
[9] *R. v Donovan* [1934] 2 KB 498.
[10] *R. v Coney* (1882) 8 QBD 534.
[11] Also known as cock-threshing, shying at cocks, cock-running, cock-squailing and in Devon it was referred to as cock-kibbit. See T. Collins, 'Cockthrowing' in the *Encyclopaedia of Traditional British Rural Sports* (eds. T. Collins, J. Martin and W. Vamplew) (Oxford: Routledge Sports Reference Series, 2005), at 75. The bird was tied to a stake with strings. Passersby, standing 20 yards away, would pay to throw stones or broomsticks at the cock. The cock would endeavour to avoid the thrown object. The owner of the bird would often charge two pence for three throws.
[12] Bear-baiting was the preferred pastime of the British royal family. See Chapter 9 on animals in sport.
[13] (1882) 8 QBD 534.

Until October 2009, it was an offence in New South Wales in Australia for women to take part in boxing contests by virtue of sections 8(1) and 15 of the Boxing and Wrestling Control Act, 1986 (NSW). In October 2009, the ban was lifted and now women may engage in boxing and kickboxing under the Combat Sports Act, 2008. This now means that women boxers can take part in national competitions and also be eligible to compete in the Olympic Games.

As will be discussed in the next chapter on boxing, emerging martial arts such as cage rage are in a precarious legal position. In Ireland, there are legal mixed martial arts (MMA) clubs. These martial arts are not illegal *per se*; they derive their legal status from boxing, which is defined in negative terms: boxing is legal because it is *not* prizefighting. In some American states amateur MMA is illegal whereas professional MMA is permitted.

A sport may be legal in itself but it may involve the commission of a separate crime, for example, prizefighting is illegal as it leads to breaches of the peace.

SPORT AND THE CRIMINAL LAW

Range of Offences

In the area of criminal liability in sport, cases can range from assault to manslaughter. It is highly improbable that a case involving murder would ever occur on the field of play.[14] Prosecutions for criminal sporting assaults are rare; however, a small number have been recorded in ice hockey in Canada. In the United Kingdom a few cases involving rugby have resulted in the intervention of the criminal law.[15] In criminal cases, the standard of proof required is 'beyond reasonable doubt'. If in doubt,

---

[14] D. Thorpe and A. Buti *et al.*, *Sports Law* (South Melbourne: Oxford University Press, 2009), at 76, notes that a murder charge, in theory under Australian law, could be brought in a situation where the opponent intentionally inflicts grievous bodily harm and as a result the victim dies. For example, if a player deliberately strikes an opponent with the intention of fracturing his jaw, but the victim dies as a result of the blow. D. Healey, *Sport and the Law* (4th ed., Sydney: University of New South Wales Press, 2009), at 194, notes that a murder charge would only ensue if a sportsperson pulled a knife on an opponent and stabbed him or her to death. For a charge of murder to succeed, proof of premeditation on the part of the defendant is required.

[15] In the United States between 1933 and 1976, there were 1,198 deaths in organised football. In 1905, President Theodore Roosevelt threatened to ban football unless it became less violent, see Yates and Gillespie, 'The Problem of Sports Violence and The Criminal Prosecution Problem', at 148, and also Hechter, 'The Criminal Law and Violence in Sports', at 436. Roosevelt was present at a football game where the entire Pennsylvania team tried to win by beating a Swarthmore player into a 'bloody pulp'. Yates and Gillespie (at 149) also note that basketball, although generally considered a

the judge or jury must acquit. As sports cases raise evidentiary problems (given the fact, for example, that the incident in question can arise in the 'heat of the moment'), the court may find the accused guilty of reckless or intentional disregard for the safety of an opponent.

DEFENCES

When a sportsperson is faced with a criminal charge, a number of defences are available to them, depending on the circumstances.

Consent

The defence of consent is often used in sports cases. There is a public interest or benefit derived from the playing of contact sports.[16] Sportspersons consent to the reasonably foreseeable hazards of the sport, and consent to harm that is within the rules of the game or incidental to the playing of the game. However, athletes do not consent to harm that is intentional, deliberate or reckless. The state has an interest in the well-being of its citizens. It is important to note that consent is implied rather than explicitly granted. The extent or the degree of the consent depends on objective criteria that surrounds 'the incident rather than on a determination of the subjective willingness of the victim'.[17] The courts will take into account whether the incident occurred during official play or during time-out or at end of play. In the case of *State v Floyd*,[18] the violent act occurred during a time-out in a game of basketball. The court held that there was 'no nexus between the defendant's acts and playing the game of basketball'.[19] The court reiterated the point that the violent act was not a reasonably foreseeable incident. It created an unreasonable risk of serious injury or breach of the peace.[20]

Hechter sums up the defence of consent in sporting cases. He asserts that:

---

non-contact sport, has experienced violence. In 1977, a peacemaker tried to intervene in a fight and sustained a broken jaw, broken nose, skull fracture, facial lacerations, brain concussion and spinal injury. Hechter (at 440–442) gives a number of examples from baseball.

[16] See *State v Gudugli*, 2004-Ohio-2871; 811 NE 2d 567 (Ohio Ct App. 2004). The court discussed the social utility of sport.

[17] Yates and Gillespie, 'The Problem of Sports Violence and the Criminal Prosecution Problem', at 161.

[18] (Iowa App. 1990), 466 NW 2d 919, at 922.

[19] *Ibid.*

[20] *Ibid.*, at 923. The defendant tried to argue self-defence but this was rejected by the court.

...the test is, in situations involving bodily injury: if an assault results in bodily injury consent is not a defence, unless the assault serves a socially useful purpose. As sports have a social utility, some leniency is generally allowed. But the focus is not on the sport in general, but on the incident or assault in particular.[21]

Generally, it is accepted that sportspersons consent to risks that are permitted by the rules of the game. The rules of the sport serve a dual purpose. They provide for the protection of the player and provide that the game is played uniformly, thus ensuring a better game. However, the court in *R. v Green* disagreed with this hypothesis. The court held that contact in violation of the rules may also be consented to, for example, there are situations where the conduct is a common occurrence (outside the rules of the game, but within the playing culture) and does not create a high risk of injury.

In *State v Shelley*,[22] the appeal court held that the assault arising from the incident was not a reasonably foreseeable hazard as 'there is nothing in the game of basketball, or even rugby or hockey, that would permit consent as a defence to such conduct'.[23]

Self-Defence

For self-defence to be raised, the defendant's force must be proved to be proportionate to the perceived or actual infliction of harm. A player could not invoke this defence if there was an element of vindictiveness. Self-defence is only available to players who reacted honestly and in good faith.[24] Self-defence was successfully raised in the case of *R. v Maki*.[25] The court in *Maki* acknowledged that the incident between the two hockey players, Maki and Green, took place in the heat of the game and thus it was difficult to identify the initial aggressor.[26]

---

[21] Hechter, 'The Criminal Law and Violence in Sports', at 450. Hechter adds that public acceptance of violence is not a justification for its continuance.
[22] (Wash. App. 1997), 929 P. 2d 489, at 493.
[23] *Ibid*. For a critical analysis of the appellate court's reasoning see J. Standen, 'The Manly Sports: The Problematic Use of Criminal Law to Regulate Sports Violence' (2009) 99(3) *Journal of Criminal Law and Criminology* 619–642, at 631–633. Standen calls for the need for flexibility in the application of the criminal law. He argues that, in hockey, blows to the head and other parts of the opponent's body with a gloved hand are not uncommon, yet can result in severe injuries.
[24] Hechter, 'The Criminal Law and Violence in Sports', at 451.
[25] [1970] 3 OR 780, 14 DLR (3d) 164 (Prov. Ct).
[26] In 'The Criminal Law and Violence in Sports', at 451, Hechter notes that mutual fighting nullifies self-defence. *R. v Green* arose from the same incident.

Involuntary Reflex

For an injury to be the result of an involuntary reflex, the requisite *mens rea* must have been absent in the defendant. In *R. v Green*,[27] Green's stick chop to Maki's shoulder was not an assault but rather an 'instinctive' reaction to a prior blow from Maki.[28] Sports agent Bob Woolf disagrees with the defence. He argues that the 'heat of the game has always been a kind of moral defence in sports to excuse bad manners and irrational acts'.[29]

Provocation

In *Agar v Canning*[30] the defence of provocation was raised but not accepted by the court. However, it was used as a mitigating factor in the award of damages.[31]

Diminished Capacity

This defence has never been invoked by a sportsperson.[32] Standen remarks that it is surprising that no athlete has endeavoured to rely on this defence given the volume of sociological research that supports the view that sportspersons' 'conditioned behaviour tends to produce violent conduct off of the playing field'.[33]

When Will the Criminal Law Intervene?

In most instances of on-field violence, violent play is usually dealt with by the referee. In other situations, the club or league may discipline the player in the form of a suspension or fine.[34] Criminal prosecutions in

---

[27] (1970) 16 DLR (3d) 137 (Prov. Ct).

[28] See also *R. v Wolfe* (1974) 20 CCC (2d) 333, 10 CRNS 268, [1970] 3 OR 780, 14 DLR.

[29] B. Woolf, *Behind Closed Doors* (New York: Atheneum, 1976), at 141.

[30] (1965) 54 WWR 302 (Man. QB), affd 55 WWR 384 (CA).

[31] Hechter, 'The Criminal Law and Violence in Sports', at 453, states that unless there are specific statutes that provide for the defence of provocation, the defence will not be allowed in a prosecution for assault, battery or aggravated assault. This is based on the old common law belief that individuals should not take the law into their own hands. It may be considered a mitigating factor.

[32] Standen, 'The Manly Sports: The Problematic Use of Criminal Law to Regulate Sports Violence', at 619–620.

[33] *Ibid*.

[34] For example, see the case of Rory O'Connell, the Westmeath player who was banned for 12 weeks for allegedly stamping on an opponent. O'Connell held that he made a scramble for the ball and he made an attempt to free his foot which had become entangled. Consequently he argued that there was no intent to injure Kelleghan, the Offaly

sporting assaults are rare due to the issue of consent and also due to the fact that injuries can occur in the 'heat of the moment'. A player consents to injuries which are 'reasonably foreseeable hazards' of the particular sport.[35] In this situation, criminal liability will not attach to the perpetrator even if the victim suffers a serious injury.[36] In fast-paced and robust contact sports, it is very difficult to ascribe intent to the conduct of a player.[37] That is not to say that the criminal law will never intervene. Recent cases have shown that the criminal law will intervene if a player intentionally or recklessly injures an opponent and the violent act is beyond that which is ordinarily incidental to the playing of the game.[38]

Anderson notes that the criminal law will intervene in certain situations as 'no particular segment of society, even one adjudged to have a high social value such as sport, should be permitted to commit crime with impunity.'[39] In light of recent cases involving Gaelic Athletic

---

player. See L. Donnellan, 'The GAA Disciplinary Procedures and Player Reinstatement' (2004) 11(6) *Sports Law Administration and Practice* 14–16.

[35] *State v Shelley*, 929, P. 2d 489, 491 (Wash. Ct App. 1997).

[36] See *McAdams v Windham* 208 Ala. 492, 94 So. 742 (1922). This case involved a legal bare-fisted boxing match. The defendant's blow to the heart of the victim resulted in his death. The civil suit was dismissed. The court noted (at 743) that, although an individual in a violent sport assumes inherent risks, that assumption does not extend to 'wrongful and intentional infliction of injury'. In citing the case of *Drum v Miller* 135 NC 204, 47 SE 421 (1904), Gardner J approved the following: 'Where an act is itself lawful, liability depends not on the particular consequences or results that may flow from it, but whether a prudent man, in the exercise of ordinary care, would have foreseen the injury or damage that would naturally or probably have resulted from the act.'

[37] Hechter, 'The Criminal Law and Violence in Sport', at 442, gives the example of a baseball catcher who used finger gestures to give authorisation to the pitcher to strike the person batting.

[38] D.V. White, 'Sports Violence as Criminal Assault: Development of the Doctrine by Canadian Courts' (1986) 6 *Duke Law Journal* 1030–1054, notes (at 1039) that this standard has drawbacks. She gives the example of *R. v Henderson* [1976] 5 WWR 119 (BC Co. Ct 1976), at 123, where the judge held that 'fighting is part of the game of hockey.' White (at 1040) states that 'defining "incidental" broadly enough to include gratuitous fighting makes a mockery of the entire test.' This case involved an innocent bystander. Examples of conduct that is not incidental are often extreme, and thus the guidelines given by the court are not always helpful; see White, at 1039–1041. For a discussion on *Henderson* and the contrasting case of *R. v Gray* [1981] 6 WWR 654 (Sask. Prov. Ct 1981), see White, at 1043–44.

[39] J. Anderson, 'Law and a New Order', *Sunday Tribune*, 16 November 2008 (available online: <http://www.tribune.ie/sport/article/2008/nov/16/law-and-a-new-order/>, last accessed 14 January 2010). Similarly, Hechter, 'The Criminal Law and Violence in Sport', at 425, states: 'criminal liability for an athlete's actions should not stop as a player leaves the realm of ordinary citizen and enters the realm of athletic competition.'

Association (GAA) players (as discussed below), the criminal law may, in the future, feature more frequently in Irish sport.

The law is more likely to intervene if the sport's governing body is not seen to be taking action against violence on the field. In one Australian case, the police in Victoria brought charges against a football player who engaged in violent conduct on the field. The police felt that the Victorian Football League (VFL), which had not taken immediate action, was not handling the matter appropriately. After police intervention, the player was suspended for four weeks.[40]

Similarly, in the United Kingdom, Lee Bowyer pleaded guilty to an offence under section 5 of the Public Order Act, 1985 after a brawl erupted between him and his teammate Kieron Dyer when Dyer failed to pass him the ball during a soccer game.[41] The fact that the brawl took place between two players from the same team would have made it very difficult to argue that the incident was part of the game.[42] The comments of the Northumbria Police Deputy Chief Constable David Warcup are noteworthy. He explained that the reason behind his decision to prosecute was based on public policy as a number of complaints were received from the public. Deputy Chief Warcup stated: '...policing at football matches is to ensure the effective safety of the public, and any incidents of violence, whether they be on the pitch or in the stands, can affect the safety of people attending the event. Therefore, it's not only the spectators who have a responsibility to behave themselves, but also the players on the pitch.'[43]

The Intervention of the Criminal Law

In the late 1800s, a number of sporting cases were brought before the courts. The following three cases demonstrate the judicial recognition of the application of criminal law to sport.

In *R. v Bradshaw*,[44] the accused jumped in the air and struck an opponent in the stomach with his knee during a football match. The injury

---

[40] Healey, *Sport and the Law*, at 197. The incident occurred in 1985. Leigh Matthews hit an opponent in the jaw. He pleaded guilty to assault causing harm and received a $1,000 fine, which was later dropped to a 12-month good behaviour bond.

[41] The incident took place in front of 52,000 fans in St James's Park during a match against Aston Villa in April 2005.

[42] Healey, *Sport and the Law*, at 198.

[43] As quoted by T. Wilkinson, 'Bowyer Fined £600 for On-Pitch Brawl', *Independent*, 5 July 2006 (available online: <http://www.independent.co.uk/news/uk/crime/bowyer-fined-pound600-for-onpitch-brawl-406735.html>, last accessed 23 January 2010). For other recent examples, see Cox, Schuster and Costello, *Sport and the Law*, at 179–180.

[44] (1878) 14 Cox CC 83.

caused the death of the victim. Bramwell L.J., in his direction to the jury, outlined the criminal law's involvement in sport. The judge directed the jury to find the accused guilty of manslaughter if they were satisfied that the accused intentionally or recklessly caused serious harm to the deceased.[45] The accused was acquitted after testimony from the referee showed that there had been no unfair play. Twenty years later, in *R. v Moore*,[46] the accused was found guilty of manslaughter after a violent tackle in a football match resulted in the death of the victim. Similar to Bramwell L.J., Hawkins J. directed the following to the jury, 'no one has the right to use force which is likely to injure another and if the prisoner used such force and death resulted, he was guilty of manslaughter.'[47] As mentioned, in the case of *R. v Coney*,[48] the court held that prizefighting was an unlawful sport as it amounted to a breach of the peace. The court not only found the fighters and the organisers guilty, but also held a number of spectators guilty of aiding and abetting.[49]

In the late 1970s a number of sports cases came before the courts. Although, as the three cases above demonstrate, the courts were willing to intervene in cases involving violence, it was not until some one hundred years later that a number of cases resulted in prosecutions. The reluctance of the courts to prosecute can be attributed to the traditional belief that the sports governing bodies were best equipped to deal with matters of this nature. However, the level of violence began to escalate in the 1970s, and the courts could not longer remain aloof from such developments.

In the case of *R. v Billinghurst*,[50] the defendant punched an opponent, resulting in a broken jaw, during an amateur rugby match in south Wales. The court, in handing down a nine-month sentence (which was suspended for two years given the previous good nature of the accused), held that rugby was a physical game which involved the use of force and, as such, players were deemed to consent to force that was reasonably foreseeable. However, it was not a licence for thuggery and participants were not deemed to have consented to the intentional or reckless infliction of harm. Similarly, in *R. v Bishop*,[51]

---

[45] See Bramwell's seminal direction at (1878) 14 Cox CC 83, at 85.
[46] (1898) 14 TLR 229.
[47] *Ibid.*, at 230.
[48] (1882) 8 QBD 534.
[49] This case will be discussed in more detail in Chapter 3.
[50] [1978] Crim LR 553.
[51] (1986) *The Times*, 12 October 1986. See also *R. v Hardy, The Guardian*, 27 July 1994; *R. v Shervall* (1989) 11 Cr. App. R. 284; *R. v Davies* 12 Cr. App. Rep. (s) 308 {1991} Criminal LR 7.

the Welsh international rugby player David Bishop punched an opponent who lay on the ground during an off-the-ball incident in a club rugby match in Wales. Bishop was initially given a one-month sentence but this was changed by the Court of Appeal to a twelve-month suspended sentence.[52]

Playing Culture – Recent Developments

The courts traditionally confined consent to incidents that fell within the rules of the game. The courts in both *R. v Bradshaw*[53] and *R. v Billinghurst*[54] implied that consent could be interpreted in a broader manner. In *Bradshaw*, the court referred to the 'rules and practices of the game', while in *Billinghurst*, the court referred to players consenting to force that could be 'reasonably expected to happen during a game'. In the case of *R. v Blissett*[55] the doctrine of playing culture received tacit recognition. However, the English courts, unlike their Canadian counterparts (as discussed below), remained reluctant to expressly recognise that consent could include the playing culture of the sport. Playing culture has been defined to include codes of conduct, tactics and commonly occurring incidents of foul play.[56]

The case of *R. v Barnes* is an important development as for the first time an English court, the Court of Appeal, considered a wider definition of consent to include the playing culture.[57] It stated that consent could be a defence in the case of a legitimate sport if the use of force by the defendant was of the kind that could be expected during the game. The Court of Appeal relied heavily on Canadian jurisprudence;[58] it held that the following factors should be considered by the jury:

- The level of the game (was it amateur or professional)
- The nature of the act

---

[52] See McCutcheon, 'Sports Violence and Consent and the Criminal Law', at 270. See also J. Anderson, 'International Sports Law Perspective: Citius, Altius, Fortius? A Study of Criminal Violence in Sport' (2000–2001) 11 *Marquette Sports Law Review* 87–106, at 98–99.
[53] *R. v Bradshaw* (1878) 14 Cox CC 83.
[54] *R. v Billinghurst* [1978] Crim LR 553.
[55] *Independent*, 4 December 1992.
[56] A. Pendlebury, 'Perceptions of Playing Culture in Sport: The Problem of Diverse Opinion in the Light of *Barnes*', (2006) 4(2) *Entertainment and Sports Law Journal*, October 2006 (available online: <http://go.warwick.ac.uk/eslj/issues/volume4/number2/pendlebury>, last accessed 6 July 2010).
[57] *R. v Barnes* [2004] EWCA Crim 3246.
[58] Pendlebury, 'Perceptions of Playing Culture in Sport', at para 12, argues that the court took the 'vague approach of stating that only conduct that was sufficiently grave to be labelled as criminal should result in conviction'.

- The degree of force used
- The extent of the risk of injury
- The state of mind of the defendant[59]

While the case presented the Court of Appeal with an opportunity to expressly adopt the concept of playing culture, its analysis is somewhat flawed. Pendlebury notes that the Court of Appeal did not properly apply the criteria to the case, if it had then Barnes' conviction would have been upheld.[60] Evidence from the match officials showed that the tackle was a two-foot lunge and the force used was not of a degree that the victim would have consented to.[61] The decision is disappointing in this respect and until a future case provides a clearer definition of playing culture or the governing bodies are entrusted to develop more precise guidelines, 'sportspersons will still struggle to compete within the boundaries of the law'.[62]

IRISH LAW AND ASSAULT

In Ireland, the Non-Fatal Offences Against the Person Act, 1997 governs assault. Section 2 of the Act defines assault as the actual carrying out or threat of reckless or intentional direct or indirect force or as causing impact to the body of another without the consent of that person. Section 3 concerns 'assault causing harm' with consent being absent. Section 4 relates to assault 'causing serious harm'. Serious harm is defined as 'injury which creates a substantial risk of death or which causes serious disfigurement or substantial loss or impairment of the mobility of the body as a whole or of the function of any particular bodily member or organ'.[63] This section is silent as to the absence of consent. However, it is extremely doubtful that the defence of consent could be invoked under section 4 as the offender, if found guilty of the offence, could face life imprisonment. Section 22(1) provides the following: 'the provisions of this Act have effect subject to any enactment or rule of law providing a defence, or providing lawful authority, justification or excuse for an act or omission.' Section 22 retains the basic

---

[59] *R. v Barnes* [2004] EWCA Crim 3246, Lord Woolf CJ, at para 15.
[60] Pendlebury, 'Perceptions of Playing Culture in Sport', at para 14.
[61] *Ibid.*
[62] *Ibid.*, at para 40, concedes that the governing bodies may be the more appropriate body to devise rules in relation to the playing culture as 'they act responsibly and they certainly have the expertise to set an appropriate boundary for sportspersons'.
[63] Section 1 of the Non-Fatal Offences Against the Person Act, 1997.

common law rule that consent cannot be an absolute defence to all forms of assault.[64]

The Law Reform Commission Report on Non-Fatal Offences and Its Application to Sport

The 1997 Act was largely based on the recommendations of a Law Reform Commission (LRC) Report from 1994.[65] The report examined the position of contact sport in Chapter 9. It acknowledged that contact sports, by their very nature, entail violent conduct. Quoting from the Canadian Law Reform Commission's working paper,[66] the LRC proposed that the criminal law should be used as a 'policeman' of last resort or as an 'enforcer'.[67] The LRC recommended that no general exemption should be given to contact sports where the victim does not expressly or impliedly consent to the infliction of injury.[68] In referring to the Canadian Working Paper on assault, the LRC recommended the need for a more long-term strategy.[69] In order to dissuade on-field violence in the long term, a series of administrative and educational measures are needed which would involve local governments, sporting bodies, coaches and parents.[70]

The LRC summarised the situations in which a person is said to have consented in a contact sport. A person is said to have consented:

1. To any contact within the rules of the game

---

[64] F. McAuley and P. McCutcheon, *Criminal Liability* (Dublin: Round Hall Sweet & Maxwell, 2000), at 533.

[65] (LRC 45–1994).

[66] No. 38, *Assault*, at 35.

[67] (LRC 45–1994), at 271, para 9.148.

[68] *Ibid.*, at para 9.149. The LRC noted that, while the occasional prosecution will have some deterrent in the short term, it will not solve the wider problem of violence in sport.

[69] *Ibid.*, at para 9.150.

[70] The LRC also suggested that those who aid or abet in the commission of on-field violence could be subject to the criminal law, at 272, para 9.151. This would include coaches or managers who encourage players to injure a key player from an opposing team. See *Pinkerton v United States* 328 US 640 (1946). See also J.H. Kerr, *Motivation and Emotion in Sport: Reversal Theory* (Hove: Psychology Press, 1997), at 115–116. Kerr states: 'In general, aggression is seen as an unprovoked hostility or attacks on another person which are not sanctioned by society. However, in the sports context, the aggression is provoked in the sense that two opposing teams have willingly agreed to compete against each other. Aggression in team contact sports is intrinsic and sanctioned, provided that plays remain permissible within the boundaries of certain rules, which act as a kind of contract in the pursuit of aggression (and violence) between consenting adults.'

2. To any contact of an accidental nature arising incidentally in the course of it

3. To incidental pain and to the risk of hurt or injury from such contact[71]

For example, a footballer impliedly consents to be tackled, to being kicked accidentally and to the risk of being injured, but does not consent to being punched or kicked.[72] As most sports do not authorise intentional or reckless tackles or injury, there should be no exemption given to contact sports.[73] If a player does not have the requisite intent or recklessness and the contact is within the rules of the sport, it is irrelevant that the force used was likely to cause injury.[74]

The LRC acknowledged that it is very difficult if not impossible to ascertain whether a contact is intentional or reckless. The courts, when faced with a sporting case, often refer to the standards of the particular sport in deciding whether or not the conduct is acceptable.[75] Such an approach is understandable given that 'sports produce valuable social benefits through the practice and example of fair play within an agreed set of rules.'[76] This approach has attracted criticism as it is contended that 'the participants' right to bodily integrity is no longer adequately protected by the standards of professional sports in which the stakes are high and violence is a not uncommon occurrence.'[77] The Canadian Law Reform Commission suggested that the criminal law should apply irrespective of the rules (with the exemption of boxing) of the sport and thus treat on-field and off-field violence uniformly.[78] In the United States, Congress put forward the Sports Violence Act, 1980 in order to reduce the levels of violence in professional sport.[79]

---

[71] (LRC 45–1994), at 273, para 9.152.

[72] *Ibid.*, at para 9.153.

[73] *Ibid.*

[74] *Ibid.*

[75] *Ibid.*, at para 9.154.

[76] *Ibid.*

[77] *Ibid.*, at para 9.155.

[78] *Working Paper on Assault* (1984). The Commission subsequently dispensed with the suggestion and instead favoured an exemption of a general nature.

[79] (LRC 45–1994), at para 9.156; HR 7903, 96th Cong. (1980). Although referred to as an Act, it did not get past the bill stage. This Bill was never passed into law. The Bill was introduced by former professional baseball player and United States Representative Ronald Mottl. It created a new federal criminal offence of 'excessive violence during professional sporting events'. The Bill failed as it was felt that on-field violence could be better dealt with at a local prosecutorial level – Yates and Gillespie, 'The Problem of Sports Violence', at 155. It was introduced again in 1981 but again failed. See White, 'Sports Violence as Criminal Assault', at 1031–1033. The Bill provided for a punishment of a year in prison and a $5,000 fine. White (at 1032) adds

In reference to the amateur nature of most Irish sport, the LRC noted that the rules of most sports place reasonable limits on the degree of violence to which one may consent. Consequently, the LRC concluded that no specific penalties should be devised for sporting violence.[80] It was also concluded that boxing should not be signalled out for exemption. Any proposed changes to the rules of the sport are a matter for the relevant regulatory sports body in accordance with public debate and medical evidence.[81]

In the absence of any statutory intervention, the LRC concluded that the criminal law would continue to apply in situations where the rules of the sport are breached. It did, however, note its limitations.[82] In some martial arts, a serious injury may result from a kick which is within the rules of the sport. Failure to prosecute and attempts to prosecute would both attract public debate. It would seem unjust to hold the opponent criminally liable for conduct that is part of the rules of the sport. The victim would have also consented to the risk. Public opinion may call for sports that can cause serious injury, including professional boxing, to be declared unlawful. The LRC recommended that a specific provision be made for consent to injuries inflicted in the course of, and in accordance with, the rules of a lawful sporting activity. It summed up its position as follows:

> Every person is protected from criminal responsibility for causing harm or serious harm to another where such harm is inflicted during the course of, and in accordance with the rules of any bona fide sporting activity.[83]

The 1997 Act did not incorporate the findings of the LRC report in relation to sport. However, section 22 implies that the sporting exemption is retained.[84]

VIOLENCE IN IRISH SPORT – THE GAA

Given the amateur nature of Irish sport, there are very few cases where a sportsperson has been prosecuted. The fact that a sport is amateur

---

that it was felt that few prosecutions would be brought under the Bill. However, a federal bill on sports violence would have a 'strong symbolic effect'.

[80] (LRC 45–1994), at 274, para 9.157.

[81] *Ibid.* The World Medical Association (WMA) had called for a worldwide ban on boxing.

[82] *Ibid.*, at 274–275, para 9.158.

[83] *Ibid.*, at para 9.159.

[84] For a detailed discussion on the position in Britain, see the Law Commission Consultation Paper No. 134, *Consent and Offences Against the Person* (1994) and Consultation Paper No. 139, *Consent in the Criminal Law* (1995).

does not mean that the criminal law will not intervene. The Irish courts have traditionally taken a 'soft' approach to on-field violence in sport.[85] There is a marked reluctance on the part of the players, sports bodies and indeed the public to invoke the criminal law in on-field disputes. The Irish courts have a tendency to be lenient on sportspersons in situations where they have paid compensation to the victim in advance of the trial or a donation has been made to a charity. In the case of the *DPP v McCartan*,[86] James McCartan, a Down footballer, was found guilty of assault (under section 3 of the Non-Fatal Offences Against the Person Act, 1997) after breaking the jaw of an opponent, Kenneth Larkin, during a match between Down and Westmeath. Judge William Early decided to postpone sentencing and stated that his final determination would be influenced by any offer of compensation to the victim.[87] On 22 November, Judge Early decided against a prison sentence as McCartan had made a generous donation to a charity.[88] McCartan was ordered to pay €1,243 in legal costs.[89]

The judge recognised that Larkin's marking of McCartan would have caused much irritation. However, he held: 'to strike someone without legal justification is a crime, whether it takes place in the street, in the family home, or the football pitch or elsewhere'.[90] There is nothing new in this sentiment. Similar comments have been made in other sports cases. What is interesting from the case is the attitude of GAA's Games Administration Committee (GAC). The GAC had convened an inquiry into the matter but decided to drop it.[91] The matter had gone before the GAC and subsequently to an Appeals Management Committee and, after a 17-month inquiry, it was dropped on procedural grounds.[92] The GAC attracted much criticism as this case involved a very serious injury and it seemed to be making light of serious incidents of on-field violence. Perhaps the criticism was somewhat harsh given that the GAA

---

[85] J. Reilly, 'Courts Soft on Violent Tackles on Sports Field', *Sunday Independent*, 1 April 2007.

[86] Unreported, 1 November 2004, District Court.

[87] The case was first heard on 1 November 2004 at Dublin District Court.

[88] McCartan made a €10,000 donation to the Lions Club in Portlaoise at the behest of Larkin, who was stationed there as a Garda. See 'GAA Man in Assault Donates €10,000', *Irish Times*, 11 January 2005, at 4.

[89] 'McCartan to Pay €10,000 to Charity of Victim's Choice', *Irish Times*, 6 November 2004.

[90] F. McNally, 'McCartan Found Guilty of Assaulting Westmeath Player', *Irish Times*, 2 November 2004, at 1.

[91] Down had appealed the decision of the GAC to the Management Committee.

[92] J. Anderson, 'Policing the Sports Field: The Role of the Criminal Law' (2006) 2 *International Sports Law Review* 25–31, at 26.

has made a concerted effort of late to deal with ill-discipline in sport.[93] The GAA showed a great reluctance to involve the authorities and was reported to have criticised the Gardaí as they attempted to question McCartan after he left a hearing at Croke Park.[94]

Implications of the McCartan Case

The comments of Anderson in his article 'Ignorance of the Law Is No Defence' are noteworthy. He argues that the repercussions of the McCartan case have more to do with a review of football's playing and safety rules (in particular, the tackle rule and introduction of a sin-bin[95]) and less to do with increased legal exposure.[96] Anderson notes that the GAA does not want to have its rules dictated by lawyers, but if a change in the tackle rules could alleviate some of the legal risks, than perhaps this is the best option for the GAA. In referring to the incident that arose between Larkin and McCartan, Anderson proffers that the 'incident may have been related to frustrations with the tackle-rule.'[97] Although defined in the rule book, the tackle rule has caused problems for referees and players alike who have difficulties with its application and interpretation. If a defender feels that the only way he can hinder a forward is by pulling, dragging or obstructing that player, then it is no surprise that forwards will often be frustrated and retaliate. Anderson is quick to add that this is no excuse for 'unacceptable violent reaction'; however, it may explain why some players, like in the McCartan case, resort to excessively violent acts in order to free themselves from their opponent.

The GAA introduced an experimental sin-bin in 2005; however, it was abandoned within one month.[98] The case of Rory O'Connell highlights the problems within GAA disciplinary procedures.

---

[93] J. Anderson, 'Ignorance of the Law Is No Defence', *Irish Times*, 18 December 2004, at 3. Anderson adds, '...its mooted independent appeals tribunal is to be welcomed, and if given precise terms of reference and adequate resources will enhance the GAA.' Anderson, 'Policing the Sports Field', states at 26: '...in sum, the GAC/AMC's handling of the investigation is a classic example, from a sports administration point of view, of how not to deal with such incidents.' Anderson adds that Westmeath may have been frustrated with the delay in proceedings and decided to go to the courts to seek redress.

[94] McNally, 'McCartan Found Guilty of Assaulting Westmeath Player'.

[95] If a player has committed a foul, instead of sending him off, the referee can send the player to an off-field area (sin-bin) for a specified time.

[96] Anderson, 'Ignorance of the Law Is No Defence', at 3.

[97] *Ibid.*

[98] 'GAA Sin-bin Lasts Barely One Month', *BBC Sport Northern Ireland*, 24 January 2005 (available online: <http://news.bbc.co.uk/sport2/hi/northern_ireland/gaelic_games/4203723.stm>, last accessed 28 January 2010).

The Rory O'Connell Case

The Rory O'Connell case is an example of a player using the court system as a way of avoiding suspension.[99] It is also a situation where the use of a sin-bin may have been the more appropriate punishment.[100] The case is important in a number of respects. It brought to the fore once again the use of the public law in matters which are quintessentially private. Mr Justice O'Leary of the High Court granted an interlocutory injunction[101] to Mr O'Connell, which enabled O'Connell to resume playing for his county, even though he had been suspended following an alleged stamping incident involving an opponent, Paschal Kelleghan. O'Connell contended that he was 'completely innocent' of any wrongdoing.

Rory O'Connell was banned for 12 weeks following an alleged stamping incident involving Offaly's Paschal Kelleghan in a Leinster Championship game.[102] O'Connell argued that he had not stamped on his opponent and the linesman had misinterpreted an innocent tackle for the ball.[103] The player was found to have committed an offence under Rule 138 of the GAA Rules and was handed down a 12-week suspension by the GAC. Paschal Kelleghan had sent the GAC a letter stating that he was not sure who had stamped on him.[104] This letter followed contact between O'Connell and Kelleghan where Kelleghan stated that he did not know who had stamped on him. However, this

---

[99] This is similar to the situation in the United States where it is called an 'ambush' injunction. See Anderson, 'Ignorance of the Law Is No Defence', at 3. *O'Connell v GAA* (2004) Record 2004 105 34 P (High Court).

[100] Anderson, 'Ignorance of the Law Is No Defence'.

[101] An injunction is an order of the court directing a party to an action to do (mandatory injunction) or to refrain from doing something (prohibitory injunction). An interlocutory injunction is temporary and is given pending the full hearing. The court must be satisfied that there is a fair and bona fide question to be tried and the balance of convenience favours the granting of the injunction. The granting of an interlocutory injunction in favour of the party does not mean that the party will be successful. In many sports cases, the applicant obtains the injunction and the case never proceeds to a full hearing.

[102] Arguably, a 12-week suspension was somewhat draconian in the latter part of the football season. In March 2004, a Cavan player received a four-week ban for allegedly punching an opponent, occasioning a broken jaw. There seems to be a lack of uniformity in the issuance of bans.

[103] One of the linesmen stated that O'Connell had manoeuvred his foot back and in doing so made contact with Kelleghan.

[104] In referring to the letter, the GAC contended that the letter had arrived without an address and had not come through the Offaly County Board and consequently the letter could have been written by anyone. Mr Justice O'Leary, in response to this contention, stated that the GAA Rules did not require that a letter should come through a particular official channel.

letter was held by the GAC to be inadmissible as evidence at the GAC meeting. O'Connell appealed against his suspension and at this hearing he discovered that the letter had not been taken into account by the GAC.

O'Connell referred the matter to the High Court, arguing that he had been denied the right to fair procedures. In the High Court, Mr Justice O'Leary held that the letter should have been admissible as evidence and failure to allow this evidence to be used at the hearing was a denial of O'Connell's right to fair procedures.[105] An interlocutory injunction was granted which allowed O'Connell to be reinstated on the Westmeath team. The Westmeath manager Páidí Ó Sé welcomed the decision and placed O'Connell on the substitutes' bench for the Leinster football final against Laois.[106] The County Board Chairman Seamus Whelan hailed the decision as a vindication for O'Connell, who had maintained his innocence throughout the proceedings.

The GAA is not in favour of players seeking redress in the courts.[107] However, denying an individual access to the courts would further compound the problems of the GAA, an organisation already accused of denying players the right to fair procedures and due course of law.

Not surprisingly, the granting of the injunction attracted much criticism from the GAA. The GAA viewed the decision as an encroachment upon the determination of the GAC. The decision has serious implications for the future of the GAC disciplinary system. Every player is entitled to the right to fair procedures. Sporting organisations must conduct their disciplinary procedures in accordance with accepted practices and failure to do so should entitle the players to redress in a court of law. Lord Woolf MR in *Modahl v British Athletic Federation*[108] made a similar point and argued:

> …generally a court will not interfere with the findings of fact by an independent tribunal, because an independent tribunal is somebody who has the experience of matter. But it does have a right to interfere where a

---

[105] *O'Connell v GAA* (2004) Record 2004 105 34 P (High Court).

[106] O'Connell played in both the final and replay. Westmeath won their first ever senior provincial football title with O'Connell being praised for his contribution in both matches.

[107] After the O'Connell case, Seán Kelly, the then president of the GAA, came out strongly against players who look for redress in the courts. He held that the GAA should challenge all High Court injunctions taken by players and clubs. Kelly alluded to the Waterford hurler John Mullane, who decided not to pursue a case in the High Court following his one-match suspension, holding the player up as an example to other players.

[108] An unreported interlocutory judgment of the Court of Appeal, dated 28 July 1997.

point of law is involved, or where there is alleged to be a breach of natural justice.[109]

Tomás Keane: Prison Sentence Imposed

In October 2008, Tomás Keane, a hurler from Fethard GAA club, was found guilty of assault at Clonmel Circuit Court. Brian Ryan, the victim, was bitten on both ears and required reconstructive surgery. Keane was sentenced to twelve months in Limerick Prison, with nine suspended. Keane was also ordered to pay €12,000 in compensation to Ryan.

This was the first time, in recent years, that a GAA player was imprisoned for on-field violence.[110] There have been other instances where players have been given suspended sentences and one player was ordered to enter a peace bond for five years, which means he was prohibited from playing Gaelic football for five years.[111]

Not surprisingly, the decision was not welcomed by the GAA. The player had been suspended for 96 games and compensation had been paid to the victim under the GAA's player injury scheme. A spokesman for Fethard GAA was quoted as saying, '...the GAA would not have survived a century-and-a-half if people went running to the courts.'[112]

Reform in the GAA

The increase in on-field violence has not gone unnoticed by the GAA. At its 2009 Congress a disciplinary reform package was presented; however, it was defeated by eight votes.[113] The disciplinary task force spent hours examining the impact of certain types of fouls, including body checking, frontal charging and high-neck tackles. It was decided that penalties would be awarded to deter players from engaging in the above mentioned fouls.[114] Although the reforms were shelved after

---

[109] *Ibid.*, at 32.
[110] In the early days of the GAA, a number of players were imprisoned for on-field violence and the occasional unlawful killing. See Anderson, 'Law and a New Order'.
[111] Anderson, 'Law and a New Order'. The case was heard by Judge Neilan at Tullamore District Court. The defendant kicked his opponent in the head during a club game. The victim spent 13 days in hospital and made a full recovery. The defendant was given a suspended 11-month sentence and paid €15,000 in compensation.
[112] Anderson, 'Law and a New Order'.
[113] A two-thirds majority was needed. See E. Sweeney, 'GAA Can't Avoid the Ugly Truth', *Irish Times*, 31 January 2010. Sweeney refers to the on-field brawl that erupted on 24 January 2010 at an inter-county match in Portlaoise.
[114] Sweeney, 'GAA Can't Avoid the Ugly Truth' and I. O'Riordan, 'Cooney Insists that GAA Have Not Gone Soft on Discipline', *Sunday Independent*, 31 January 2010.

the vote, it is hoped that they will be introduced in the near future, although no definite date has been mooted.[115]

It had been suggested that the GAA could adopt the model of the disciplinary tribunal, as used by Australian Rules Football (AFL), albeit with some modifications as the Australian Football League Tribunal is used in a professional game.[116] The GAA has proposed the introduction of the Australian mark, a popular element of Australian Rules Football.[117] The rule states that 'a free-kick shall be awarded to a player who catches the ball from a kick-out between the two 45-metre lines. This free-kick must be taken by the player who catches the ball'.[118] An exception to this is that 'the kick may be taken by another member of the player's team if the player who catches the ball is injured prior to the free-kick being taken.'

Other suggestions for reform have included the professionalisation of the GAA, as the evidence suggests that professional rugby players are less likely to inflict serious injuries on each other. Anderson outlines the financial and contractual implications for a professional player who inflicts serious harm on another.[119] A player may be fined, be docked wages, lose out on bonuses, or, if the player is found guilty of gross misconduct, he may have his contract terminated. The professional player's career could end abruptly if he were to commit a dangerous foul.

Amateur players may also bring actions. While criminal cases might be rare, an amateur player who is injured and cannot work for a period of time may be more likely to bring a civil action in order to claim compensation. While a sport may have an insurance scheme for injured players, this may not adequately cover their medical or living expenses.[120]

The GAA may be forced to radically re-examine its disciplinary procedures if players begin to sue other players.[121] Clubs, coaches, county boards and even selectors could be held vicariously liable for injuries inflicted by one of their players on an opponent.[122] Often an injured player will sue the player and the club (under the deep pocket theory).

---

[115] S. Moran, 'Confidently Facing the Challenges Ahead', *Irish Times*, 30 January 2010.
[116] Anderson, 'Policing the Sports Field: The Role of the Criminal Law', at 26.
[117] 'GAA Clarify "Mark" Experimental Rule', *Breaking News.ie*, 12 January 2010 (available online: <http://www.breakingnews.ie/world/gaa-clarify-mark-experimental-rule-441675.html>, last accessed 5 July 2010).
[118] *Ibid.*
[119] As quoted by D. Whelan, 'Sport Here Must Take Arbitration Route', *Irish Times*, 6 November 2004.
[120] Anderson, as quoted by Whelan, 'Sport Here Must Take Arbitration Route'.
[121] *Ibid.*
[122] *Ibid.*

While the GAA has recently encountered the intervention of the criminal law, Canada has long used the criminal law to regulate on-field
violence. The following discussion on Canada will provide an interesting comparative analysis.

CANADA: ICE HOCKEY AS A CASE EXAMPLE

Ice hockey, or hockey as it is more commonly referred to, is one of
Canada's most popular sports. Ice hockey is a combination of field
hockey and skating and its rules are based on the rules of soccer.[123]

Hockey has a reputation as one of the most violent contact sports.
Often players are encouraged to fight and knock out an opponent.[124]
Violence in hockey has become an expected part of the game.[125] However, there are limits. Although there are risks inherent in the sport, a
player does not consent to unprovoked attacks resulting in serious
injury. Attacks of this nature are subject to the intervention of the criminal law. The more common assaults that produce serious injury tend to
be dealt with by the game officials.[126]

As mentioned, in the United States there has been a marked reluctance to prosecute incidents of excessive violence. Prosecutions in the
area of sporting assaults are very rare. Often prosecutors are reluctant
to take an action against a popular sportsperson. Canada, in contrast,
has shown a great willingness to use the criminal law. However, the
Canadian approach has posed a number of problems. Many of the cases
have come before trial courts where evidence has been given orally.[127]
Consequently, there is a lack of detailed written judgments. The Canadian courts cite precedent sparingly and there is an overreliance on the
seminal cases of *R. v Green*[128] and *R. v Maki*.[129] In short, these sporting

---

[123] R. Brasch, *How Did Sports Begin?* (London: Longman, 1972), at 136.

[124] See Yates and Gillespie, 'The Problem of Sports Violence and the Criminal Prosecution Problem', at 150. See also B. Woolf, *Behind Closed Doors*. Bob Woolf
chronicled his life as a sports agent. A Boston-based lawyer, Woolf spoke of the
pressure put on players to be able to fight. Players who were considered unable to
fight were often asked to enrol in boxing classes. Woolf recalls one hockey couch
sizing up a young amateur player in the way a boxing coach would a potential boxer
(at 146).

[125] Hechter, 'The Criminal Law and Violence in Sports', at 430–431 states: 'No hockey
player enters onto National Hockey League ice without the knowledge that he may
soon be hit.'

[126] Hechter, 'The Criminal Law and Violence in Sports', at 431.

[127] White, 'Sports Violence as Criminal Assault', at 1037.

[128] (1970) 16 DLR (3d) 137 (Prov. Ct).

[129] (1970) 14 DLR (3d) 164 (Prov. Ct).

cases often tend to lack precision and terminology.[130] However, more recent cases, including *R. v Cey*[131] and *R. v Ciccarelli*,[132] have established invaluable judicial analysis that can be adopted by other jurisdictions, including Ireland.

Origins of the Intervention of the Criminal Law in Ice Hockey

There are two views which prevail in regard to the use of the criminal justice system in sport. One view holds that the law should not get involved and that sport should be given special treatment. Players consent to any injuries that are sustained in a fast-paced contact sport. The other view holds that sport should be subject to the rigours of the law and should not be immune to criminal prosecution. Sportspeople are seen as important role models and their actions on the field of play can influence young children and adults alike. Sportspersons should face criminal prosecution for egregious acts of violence like any other individual would if he or she committed an assault.

In the case of *Agar v Canning*,[133] the Canadian Supreme Court sided with the latter view and found the defendant liable. During the course of a game of hockey, the plaintiff attempted to delay the defendant by hooking him with his stick. The defendant was carrying the puck at the time. The plaintiff hit the defendant on the back of the neck. The defendant retaliated and hit the plaintiff in the face, resulting in the loss of one of his eyes. The plaintiff brought a civil action for damages against the defendant and succeeded, even though he had initially provoked the defendant. Bastin J remarked that the 'conduct of a player in the heat of battle is instinctive and unpremeditated and should not be judged by standards suited to polite social intercourse'.[134]

The judge continued to hold that there are limits to a player's immunity from liability. Each case must be decided on its facts. However, 'injuries inflicted in circumstances which show a definite resolve to cause serious injury to another, even when there is provocation and in the heat of the game, should not fall within the scope of implied consent.'[135]

The defence of consent was not allowed in *Agar* and the subsequent civil case of *Martin v Daigle*.[136] These two cases suggest that the courts

---

[130] White, 'Sports Violence as Criminal Assault', at 1037.
[131] (1989) 48 CCC (3d) 480.
[132] (1989) 54 CCC (3d) 121.
[133] (1965), 54 WWR 302 (Man. QB), affd 55 WWR 384 (CA).
[134] (1965), 54 WWR 302 (Man. QB), at 304.
[135] *Ibid.*
[136] (1969) 6 DLR (3d) 634, 1 NBR (2d) 755 (SC App. Div.).

are more likely to accept the defence of consent in criminal cases than in civil suits.[137] The comments of Hawkins J in *R. v Coney* support this view.[138] Hawkins J held: 'It may be that consent in all cases be given so as to operate as a bar to civil action; upon the ground that no man can claim damages for an act to which he himself was an assaulting party.'[139] As long as the participants gave full, informed and free consent, then an action for trespass to the person could not be brought by the plaintiff.[140]

The Reaction of the Canadian Government and the Canadian Criminal Code

The escalation of violence in hockey prompted the commission of an investigation. In 1974, a brawl erupted at the Hamilton–Bramalea Hockey Association game. The brawl on the ice led to a brawl among the spectators. In response, the Canadian Government commissioned a study on violence in hockey.[141] The study was led by an Ontario attorney, William R. McMurtry. The report found that violence was being used as 'tactical instrument' by professional players and that this in turn contributed to a use of violence among amateur players.[142] The report recognised the importance of sport in society and concluded:

> Sport, and particularly hockey, need not be a symptom of a sick society. Hockey can be an effective instrument to improve the social conditions...rather than a divisive force by calculated animosities.[143]

In 1975, Ontario Attorney General Roy McMurtry used the report as a basis to prosecute players for acts of violence on the rink. McMurtry ordered police and prosecutors to begin rigorous enforcement of law against 'clear breaches of the Criminal Code' in the rink.[144]

---

[137] Hechter, 'The Criminal Law and Violence in Sports', at 445.

[138] (1882) 8 QBD 534.

[139] *Ibid.*, at 553.

[140] S. Gardiner *et al.*, *Sports Law* (3rd ed., London: Cavendish, 2006), at 642, suggests that a participant may be able to consent to more injury being inflicted upon him in a civil case than under the criminal law.

[141] *Investigation and Inquiry into Violence in Amateur Hockey* (Toronto: Ministry of Community and Social Services, 1974).

[142] Canadian Government, *Investigation and Inquiry into Violence in Amateur Hockey*, at 15. See Hechter, 'The Criminal Law and Violence in Sports', at 427.

[143] Canadian Government, *Investigation and Inquiry into Violence in Amateur Hockey*, at 41–42.

[144] Hechter, 'The Criminal Law and Violence in Sports', at 428.

At the time of the report, assault was defined in section 244 of the Criminal Code. Over the years, the Criminal Code has been amended. Currently, assault is defined under section 265. Under section 265(1) a person commits an assault when (a) without the consent of another person, he applies force intentionally to that other person, directly or indirectly; (b) he attempts or threatens, by an act or a gesture, to apply force to another person, if he has, or causes that other person to believe on reasonable grounds that he has, present ability to effect his purpose; or (c) while openly wearing or carrying a weapon or an imitation thereof, he accosts or impedes another person or begs.[145] If the sports person is found to have committed an assault under section 265, he or she is usually charged under Section 267(1)(a) or (b). Section 267 refers to persons who, in committing an assault, either (a) carry, use or threaten to use a weapon or an imitation thereof or (b) cause bodily harm to the complainant.

Assault causing bodily harm is usually used in sports violence prosecutions as opposed to common assault.[146]

Most hockey cases come within the ambit of section 267(1)(b), and not section 267(1)(a).[147] Bodily harm, similar to the Non-Fatal Offences Against the Person Act, 1997, is defined as any hurt or injury that interferes with a person's health, comfort or psychological well-being. The harm must be something that is more than brief, fleeting or minor in nature. Although hockey involves the use of a stick and would thus seem to fit within the definition of section 267(1)(a), section 267(1)(b) is deemed more appropriate in these cases as they involve sports stars and assault with a weapon attracts far more negative press.[148] However, in *R. v McSorley*[149] the accused was charged under section 267(a). This change in approach shows that the 'criminal justice system is beginning

---

[145] RS, c. C-34, s. 244; 1974-75-76, c. 93, s. 21; 1980-81-82-83, c. 125, s. 19.

[146] Section 267(1)(b).

[147] A. Husa and S. Thiele, 'In the Name of the Game: Hockey Violence and the Criminal Justice System' (2001–2002) 45 *Criminal Law Quarterly* 509–529, at 513. Section 267(1)(b) is used even though sticks are used to cause injury.

[148] *Ibid.*

[149] 2000 BCPC 116 (BC Prov. Ct). McSorley was convicted of assaulting the Vancouver Canucks' Donald Brashear in 2000. He was placed on probation for 18 months after he slashed Brashear in the head with a stick. Brashear was knocked unconscious on the rink. McSorley maintained that he meant to hit the shoulder and not Brashear's head. The court rejected this contention and the judge held that a NHL player would never miss (para 108). This suggests that the court would not have accepted defence of consent even if McSorley had intended to hit Brashear's shoulder.

to take a more interventionist role in hockey violence'.[150] McSorley was convicted and given a 18-month conditional discharge. He never played in the National Hockey League again.

The Seminal Cases of *R. v Green* and *R. v Maki*

One of the most notorious Canadian cases occurred in 1969 in an exhibition hockey match between the Boston Bruins and the St Louis Blues. Ted Green, of the Boston Bruins, swung and hit Wayne Maki of the St Louis Blues on the head. Maki then turned and speared Green in the abdomen with his hockey stick. Green retaliated by swinging the stick at Maki's shoulder. Maki ended the fray by hitting Green on the head with his stick, which fractured Green's skull and required the insertion of a steel plate in his head. The incident took place over a ten-second period. The two players were tried in two separate actions.

In *R. v Maki*[151] the accused was charged with assault causing harm. The court acknowledged that players assume certain risks and hazards when they step on the rink, however, 'no sports league...should thereby render the players in that league immune from criminal prosecution. And no athlete should be presumed to accept malicious, unprovoked, or overly violent attacks.'[152] Maki successfully pleaded self-defence and was acquitted of all charges. The court held that the Crown had failed to prove beyond reasonable doubt that the accused did not feel that he was under reasonable apprehension of bodily harm or that he had used excessive force in the circumstances.[153] The court cautioned that criminal charges could be allowed 'in the future where the circumstances warrant and the relevant authorities deem it advisable to do so.'[154]

In *R. v Green*[155] the accused was also acquitted. However, the trial judge construed the facts of the case differently than the court in *Maki*. The court concluded that 'no hockey player enters onto the ice of the National Hockey League without consenting to and without knowledge of the possibility that he is going to be hit in one of many ways once he is on that ice.'[156] Green was acquitted on the grounds of self-defence.

---

[150] Husa and Thiele, 'In the Name of the Game', at 513. The writers continue: 'No longer will a high-priced athlete be treated differently from the ordinary Canadian.'
[151] [1970] 3 OR 780, 14 DLR (3d) 164 (Prov. Ct).
[152] *Ibid.*, at 4.
[153] Up to the point of Maki's blow, Green had been the aggressor.
[154] [1970] 3 OR 780, 14 DLR (3d) 164 (Prov. Ct).
[155] (1970) 16 DLR (3d) 137 (Prov. Ct).
[156] *Ibid.*, at 594.

New Approach – *Cey* and *Ciccarelli*

In *R. v Cey*[157] the accused body checked[158] an opponent into the boards surrounding the ice rink, resulting in the infliction of facial injuries and concussion on the opponent. The trial court acquitted Cey on the grounds that he had not intended to injure his opponent more than what was customary for the game. He argued that the opponent had consented to incidents of this nature. The Saskatchewan Court of Appeal overturned the acquittal and a re-trial was ordered. The Court of Appeal agreed that the consent given in sport was an exception to the general rule that consent to force, which is likely to result in bodily harm, was not normally a defence. However, the court qualified this by asking whether the force used (i.e. body checking in close proximity to the boards) by the accused was 'so violent and inherently dangerous as to have been excluded from the implied consent'.[159] The court held that egregious acts of violence which went beyond that which was incidental to the game would negate consent. The court also noted that the state of mind of the accused was not the only consideration. It identified a number of objective criteria in order to determine the scope of the participant's implied consent, including the setting of the game, whether the game was part of a league and the nature of such a league, the age of the players, conditions under which the game was played, the extent of the force used, the degree of risk and the probability of serious harm occurring.[160]

The case was welcomed as it created a set of principles which the court can take into account in comparison to the vague tests that earlier cases suggested.[161] Any acts of violence that go beyond what is customary to the playing of the game will be deemed to exceed the implied consent. The court clearly found that conduct which carried a high risk of injury would be rendered unlawful regardless of consent or the frequency with which it occurs in the sport.[162] The level of force permitted would depend on the circumstances of the game.

---

[157] (1989) 48 CCC (3d) 480 (Sask. CA).

[158] A body check occurs 'when a hockey player bumps or slams into an opponent with either his hip or shoulder (the only legal moves) to block his progress or throw him off-balance; it is only allowed against an opponent in control of the puck or against the last player to control it'. This definition is taken from the Ice Hockey Glossary (available online: <http://www.firstbasesports.com/hockey_glossary.html#backcheck>, last accessed 6 July 2010).

[159] *Ibid.*, at 491–492.

[160] *Ibid.*, at 490–491.

[161] McCutcheon, 'Sports Violence and Consent and the Criminal Law', at 276.

[162] *Ibid.*

Anderson succinctly summarises the *R. v Cey* case as follows:

...the court attempted to clarify the vagueness of the earlier approach by providing that in future the consent of sports participants should be recognised by reference to a number of specific factors such as the nature and standard of the game played, the nature of the act from the point of view of the degree of force and harm inflicted and the state of mind of the accused.[163]

The *Cey* criteria were adopted in the cases of *R. v Ciccarelli*,[164] *R. v Leclerc*[165] and *R. v Jobidon*.[166] In *Ciccarelli*, the accused became the very first professional athlete from the NHL to serve a jail sentence.[167] The player was jailed for one day and fined CA$1,000. He appealed his conviction but was unsuccessful. The NHL suspended him for ten days, costing the player CA$25,000 in salary.

In *Leclerc*, the court took the view that participants gave implied consent to those assaults that were inherent and reasonably incidental to the normal playing of the game in the particular context of the game.

In *Jobidon*, the Supreme Court of Canada applied *Cey* to a case involving a brawl between two men. The victim died and the accused argued that he could not be found guilty as the victim had consented. The court disallowed the defence of consent as the case involved a fist fight and fist fights are deemed to be socially useless activities and have a tendency to escalate into larger brawls and cause breaches of the peace. Barnes makes an important observation. He notes that, 'criminal liability will sometimes turn on the social or economic value that the judge places on a particular recreation or entertainment.'[168]

Bertuzzi–Moore Incident

More recently, Todd Bertuzzi of the Vancouver Canucks faced criminal charges after he assaulted Steve Moore of the Colorado Avalanche in 2004.[169]

---

[163] J. Anderson, 'Mens Sana In Corpore Sano? Violence in Sport and the Criminal Law' (1998) 6 *Irish Student Law Review*, at 64–78.

[164] [1990] 54 CCC 3d 121 (Ont. Dist. Ct 1989).

[165] (1991) 4 OR (3d) 788, 67 CCC (3d) 563 (CA).

[166] (1991) 66 CCC (3d) 454.

[167] Yates and Gillespie, 'The Problem of Sports Violence and the Criminal Prosecution Problem', at 154.

[168] J. Barnes, *Sports and the Law in Canada* (3rd ed., Butterworths: Toronto & Vancouver, 1996), at 261.

[169] J.H. Kerr, 'Examining the Bertuzzi–Moore NHL Ice Hockey Incident: Crossing the Line between Sanctioned and Unsanctioned Violence in Sport' (2006) 11 *Aggression and Violent Behaviour* 313–322, at 313.

As a result of the incident, Bertuzzi was sent off and suspended for a month. He was made apply for reinstatement for the 2004–2005 season. Bertuzzi was also required to forfeit CA$501,926.23 to the NHL players' emergency fund.[170] The incident attracted widespread media attention. The Prime Minister of Canada informed Canadian hockey of its need to clean up. Bertuzzi made a public apology to Moore at a press conference two days after the game. He insisted that he did not intend to harm Moore.

Violence in ice hockey is often accepted as being part of the game. The Bertuzzi case attracted much attention as this case involved premeditation due to previous incidents between the teams. In the Bertuzzi–Moore incident, the injuries were extensive and the assault was premeditated, unsanctioned and vindictive.[171] Charges were brought against Bertuzzi by the criminal justice branch of the Attorney General's office. Bertuzzi pleaded guilty to common assault. He was fined CA$500 (in addition to the sum for the emergency fund), ordered to complete 80 hours of community service and was given a year's probation.[172]

While the criminal aspects of the case were resolved in December 2004, there is ongoing civil litigation between the parties. Moore initiated a civil case against Bertuzzi. Moore never recovered from the injuries and has never played hockey since the incident. He is seeking $35 million in damages. Moore's parents have also initiated a civil action against Bertuzzi. They are seeking $1.5 million in damages for nervous shock after witnessing the incident on television. Bertuzzi issued civil proceedings against the Canucks' head coach Marc Crawford in 2008. Bertuzzi alleges that he was contractually obliged to follow the directions of Crawford. He alleges that Crawford was also responsible for the incident. Crawford has insisted that Bertuzzi acted in complete disobedience of the direction given to him from the bench.

Is the Criminal Law an Effective Tool?

The cases above demonstrate that incidents of intentional or deliberate infliction of injury are not permitted and will expose the perpetrator to criminal liability. Sportspersons consent to injuries that are normally incidental to the playing of the game. For more minor infractions of

---

[170] *Ibid.*, at 316.

[171] *Ibid.*

[172] *Ibid.* He was also given a conditional discharge: if he abided by the terms set by the court, he would not have a criminal record.

rules, the governing body of the particular sport is best suited to deal with the matter.

However, some commentators are critical of the use of the governing body to deal with on-field violence or indiscipline.[173] The comments of Flakne and Caplan are noteworthy.[174] Flakne and Caplan equate the use of the governing body determining the appropriate sanction with:

> ...granting the board of directors of General Motors jurisdiction over the determination of guilt or innocence and the appropriate punishment for one of their employees who, while on the job killed his foreman. It would seem that if violence in sports is to be curtailed, the only effective remedy lies with the state, where the capability of meting out effect deterrent sanctions exists.

CONCLUSION

The internal disciplinary mechanisms should be able to deal with most incidents. Only acts of egregious violence should attract criminal prosecution. In general, a person may not consent to infliction of actual bodily harm or serious harm (see sections 3 and 4 of the Non-Fatal Offences Against the Person Act, 1997). However, contact sport is given an exemption. There is a public interest or benefit derived from the playing of contact sports. Sportspersons consent to harm that is within the rules of the game or incidental to the playing of the game, or within the playing culture. However, sportspersons do not consent to harm that is intentional, deliberate or reckless. This, however, presents an anomaly as, for instance, boxing, by its very nature, involves the intentional infliction of harm. As the Lords in *R. v Brown* held, contact sports including boxing are permitted because they constitute 'good reason'.[175] The next chapter turns to the issue of the legality of boxing.

---

[173] Similar arguments have been raised in doping cases. This will be dealt with in more detail in Chapter 5.
[174] G.W. Flakne and A.H. Caplan, 'Sports Violence and the Prosecution' (1977) 13 *Trial* 33–35, at 33–34.
[175] [1994] 1 AC 212.

CHAPTER 3

The Legality of Boxing and Other Fighting Sports

INTRODUCTION

The previous chapter noted that sportspersons can consent to harm that is within the rules of the game, incidental to the playing of the game or within the playing culture. However, sportspersons do not consent to harm which is intentional, deliberate or reckless. The sport of boxing presents an anomaly. The primary objective of boxing is to inflict harm on your opponent.[1] While no court has ever countenanced a case regarding the legality of boxing, in *R. v Brown*[2] Lords Templeman (at 232),[3] Slynn of Hadley (at 278)[4] and Mustill (at 263)[5] did question the legal acceptance of boxing.

The comments of McInerney J from the civil case of *Pallante v Stadiums Pty (No. 1)* are also noteworthy.[6] The judge contrasted boxing with assault. Assault differs from the sport of boxing as in an assault there is no consent and the infliction of harm is done in a hostile or angry

---

[1] S. Gardiner *et al.*, *Sports Law* (3rd ed., London: Cavendish, 2006), at 621.
[2] [1994] 1 AC 212.
[3] 'Rightly or wrongly the courts accepted that boxing is a lawful activity.'
[4] 'It seems to me that the notion of consent fits ill into the situation where there is a fight. It is also very strange that a fight in private between two youths where one may, at most, get a bloody nose should be unlawful, whereas a boxing match where one heavyweight fighter seeks to knock out his opponent and possibly do him very serious damage should be lawful.'
[5] 'Thus, although consent is present in both cases the risks of serious violence and public disorder make prize-fighting something which "the law says shall not be done", whereas the lesser risk of injury, the absence of the public disorder, the improvement of the health and skills of the participants, and the consequent benefit to the public at large combine to place sparring into a different category, which the law says "may be done".'
[6] [1976] VR 331.

manner. The comments of McInerney J have been criticised. An assault need not take place in a hostile or angry manner. Some assaults are permissible where the parties consent to intentional harm and the harm does not exceed the limits in law. Such a narrow construction did not take into account that sporting contests often invoke hostility and anger, particularly contact sports.[7] McInerney J, aware of the inconsistency in his argument, qualified his comments and stated that consent would only be negated in situations where the mind of the accused boxer was predominated by either hostility or anger.

Boxing is a legal and recognised sport.[8] As a recognised sport, the law provides it with significant protection. If a fight took place in the street, it would be considered illegal as it would be a breach of the peace and charges under the Non-Fatal Offences Against the Person Act, 1997 may ensue.[9] In the fight that takes place on the street, the combatants could be adults with capacity to consent, yet their actions are deemed illegal. However, an organised boxing match is legal because boxing is a recognised sport.[10] The national governing body for boxing in Ireland is the Irish Amateur Boxing Association (IABA). All local boxing clubs are affiliated to the IABA. What distinguishes the example of the two consenting adults settling their differences by fighting in the street from boxing is the fact that a recognised boxing match has rules which must be followed. There is a referee, there are safety measures in place, and the pugilists wear padded gloves and safety helmets.[11]

Rules are devised for sports to ensure fairness and uniformity, but they also are devised in a way to ensure that the likelihood of participants being injured is minimised. However, the legality of boxing has long been debated. Over the years there have been calls to declare it illegal. Boxing remains a sport due to its popularity and there is a public interest in it continuing as a lawful sport.

---

[7] D. Thorpe and A. Buti *et al.*, *Sports Law* (South Melbourne: Oxford University Press, 2009), at 101.

[8] It is a recognised Olympic sport along with other fighting sports – fencing, judo, taekwondo and wrestling.

[9] For an Irish perspective see, B. Foley, 'Boxing, the Common Law and the Non-Fatal Offences Against the Person Act 1997' (2002) 12(3) *Irish Criminal Law Journal* 15–20, at 15.

[10] In the case of *Commonwealth v Collberg*, 119 Mass, 350 (1876) two boxers consented to a fight. However, the court held that boxing served no useful purpose and tended to cause breaches of the peace. The court (at 353) held that boxing matches were 'unlawful even when entered into by agreement and without anger or mutual ill will'. Consent of the parties was irrelevant.

[11] The IABA Rule Book is available online: <http://www.iaba.ie/Rule_Book/rule_book.html>.

HISTORY OF BOXING

Prizefighting and bare-knuckle fighting were not devoid of rules but lacked a uniform set of principles.[12] Prizefighting, as the name suggests, involved financial reward for the fighter who had physically overcome his opponent. In 1743 the Broughton Rules were introduced, which became the sport's first uniform set of rules.[13] The Broughton Rules, while welcomed at first, proved to be inadequate.[14] In 1865 the Queensberry Rules were introduced by the eighth Marquis of Queensberry.[15] Under these rules there would be no wresting or hugging permitted; rounds would be three minutes in length, with one minute's time between rounds; the ring would be twenty-four feet in diameter; gloves of the best quality would be worn and if a glove burst or came off it would be replaced to the referee's satisfaction.[16]

Gunn and Ormerod refer to the legal recognition of boxing as being by 'default rather than design'.[17] In the nineteenth century, prizefighting became increasingly associated with breaches of the peace.[18] A number of cases came before the courts, which presented the courts with an opportunity to outlaw the sport. While prizefighting was banned, a tamer version of the sport, namely boxing, gained judicial acceptance.

The Courts and Prizefighting

As prizefighters began to wear gloves, the distinction between boxing (sparring) and prizefighting became quite blurred. The courts

---

[12] A formal roped-off section was rarely used, often the ground would be marked with chalk, there was no such thing as rounds and there was no limit on the duration of the fight. See J. Anderson, *The Legality of Boxing: A Punch Drunk Love?* (Abingdon: Birkbeck Law Press, 2007), at 15.

[13] Anderson, *The Legality of Boxing*, at 14. For a historical discussion of boxing, see R. Brasch, *How Did Sports Begin?* (London: Longman, 1972), at 39–43.

[14] Anderson, *The Legality of Boxing*, at 25.

[15] In 'Pugilistic Prosecutions: Prizefighting and the Courts in Nineteenth Century Britain' (2001) 21(2) *The Sports Historian* 37–57, at 45, J. Anderson notes that changes introduced by the Queensbury Rules were superficial and may even have intensified the physicality of the sport.

[16] Anderson, *The Legality of Boxing*, at 28.

[17] M. Gunn and D. Ormerod, 'Despite the Law: Prize-Fighting and Professional Boxing' in *Law and Sport in Contemporary Society* (eds. S. Greenfield and G. Osborn) (London: Frank Cass, 2000), at 23.

[18] Anderson, 'Pugilistic Prosecutions', at 44, sums up the position of the courts up until the 1840s in relation to prizefighting: 'the law on prizefighting can be said to be clear; they were illegal primarily on the grounds that they were riotous, unlawful assemblies…as the nineteenth century progressed, increased policing…resulted in the emphasis in prizefighting prosecutions switching away from unlawful assembly and riot towards assault.'

distinguished between sparring matches and prizefighting on the basis of the likelihood of one of the fighters suffering serious injury.[19] The courts, finding it difficult to distinguish the two, decided to leave the issue to the jury.[20]

In the leading case of *R. v Coney*,[21] the court established that prize-fighting was illegal as it caused a breach of peace. The court did not hold boxing or sparring legal, but declared prizefighting illegal. While the case considered a charge of aiding and abetting at a prizefight, it 'provides an ideal starting point in contemporary legal attitudes to violence in sport'.[22] The defendants argued that their attendance at the fight was merely passive in nature as they were not involved in the management or organisation of the fight. In the trial court, the chairman left it to the jury to decide whether this was a prizefight and therefore illegal and an assault. He also directed that all persons who attend a prizefight to watch the combatants strike each other, and who are present when they do so, are also guilty of assault. The chairman added the words of Justice Littledale in *R. v Murphy* to his direction: '…if they were not casually passing by, but stayed at the place, they encouraged it by their presence, although they did not say or do anything.'[23] The jury, in following the direction of the chairman, found the defendants Gilliam, Tully and Coney guilty of assault. Burke and Mitchell, as the two fighters, were found to be guilty of an assault. Similarly, Parker and Symonds, the organisers of the fight, were also found guilty. The case was appealed to the Criminal Court of Appeal as the trial judge sought confirmation regarding his direction to the jury in relation to Coney, Gilliam and Tully. In an 8–3 majority, the convictions of the three men were quashed. The majority held that mere voluntary presence at such an event could not be equated with aiding and abetting a criminal

---

[19] Gunn and Ormerod, 'Despite the Law: Prize-Fighting and Professional Boxing', at 24.
[20] See *R. v Orton* (1878) 39 LT 293. Here the court held (at 294) that if a fight were a mere exhibition of skill in sparring it was not unlawful. However, if the combatants had met intending to fight until one gave into exhaustion or injury he had received, it was a breach of the peace and thus unlawful irrespective of whether the fighters wore gloves. In *R. v Young* (1866) 10 Cox CC 371, a boxer faced charges for the manslaughter of an opponent during an indoor sparring match. Bramwell J (at 373) instructed the jury as follows: 'If a death ensued from a fight, independently of it taking place for money, it would be manslaughter, because a fight was a dangerous thing and likely to kill; but the medical witness here stated that this sparring was not dangerous, and not a thing likely to kill.'
[21] (1882) 8 QBD 534.
[22] J. Anderson, 'International Sports Law Perspective: Citius, Altius, Fortius? A Study of Criminal Violence in Sport' (2000) 11 *Marquette Sports Law Review* 87–106, at 87.
[23] 172 Eng. Rep. 1164, 1165 (1833).

activity. The issue of passive and active presence was not an issue for the Court of Appeal. What is most interesting from this case is the court's attitude to prizefighting.[24] The court unanimously held prize-fighting to be illegal as it caused a breach of the peace. Cave J held:

> The true view is, I think, that a blow struck in anger, or which is likely or is intended to do corporal hurt, is an assault, but that a blow struck in sport, and not likely, nor intended to cause bodily harm, is not an assault, and that an assault being a breach of the peace and unlawful, the consent of the person struck is immaterial.[25]

The judgments of Cave J and Hawkins J are instructive in regard to the issue of consent.[26] Hawkins J reaffirmed the 'general proposition...that there can be no assault unless the act charged as such be done without the consent of the person alleged to be assaulted, for want of consent is an essential element in every assault, and that which is done by consent is no assault at all'.[27] Cave J continued to hold that a blow struck in anger or which is intended to do corporal harm constitutes an assault.[28] However, a blow struck in sport which is not likely or intended to cause bodily harm is not an assault.[29] Assaults that result in a breach of the peace are unlawful, irrespective of the consent of the parties.[30] In applying this to sport, Cave J held prizefighting to be illegal as it amounted to a breach of the peace, but playing with single-sticks (wooden sticks used in martial arts) or wrestling did not amount to an assault; 'nor does boxing with gloves in the ordinary way'.[31] Matthew J, in a similar vein, referred to the 'trained fists of pugilists' as 'dangerous weapons, which they are not at liberty to use against each other'.[32]

The Court of Appeal declared prizefighting illegal as it encouraged a breach of the peace and gambling. The dangerous nature of the sport seemed to be a secondary consideration.[33] Judges Stephen and

---

[24] Anderson, 'International Sports Law Perspective', at 89.

[25] (1882) 8 QBD 534, at 539.

[26] Judges Stephens, Lopes, North and Huddleston all agreed with Cave J that the trial judge had erred in relying on Littledale in *R. v Murphy* 172 Eng. Rep. 1164, 1165 (1833). Similar to Cave J, the judges distinguished between active presence and mere casual attendance. Except for Cave J and Hawkins J, the other judges did not discuss the issue of consent at length. See Anderson, 'International Sports Law Perspective', at 91.

[27] (1882) 8 QBD 534, at 539.

[28] *R. v Coney* (1882) 8 QBD 534, at 539.

[29] *Ibid.*

[30] *Ibid.*

[31] *Ibid.*

[32] *Ibid.*, at 547.

[33] Gardiner *et al.*, *Sports Law*, at 622, criticises the reasoning of the court. If they had

Matthew were the only judges who seemed concerned about the degree of harm inflicted on a combatant during a fight. Stephen J held prizefighting to be not only injurious to the public but also to the fighters themselves.[34] A fighter's health may be endangered by blows and because prizefights are disorderly exhibitions, they are 'mischievous on many obvious grounds'.[35]

In short, the Court of Appeal held prizefighting to be unlawful due to its tendency to draw riotous crowds. The court made a distinction between prizefighting and sparring. Prizefighting satisfied the *mens rea* requirement of assault, whereas sparring involved a test of skill with an absence of intent to cause harm.[36] Anderson comments that:

...on this dubious thread of policy does the legality of boxing hang. The legality of this sport is defined in entirely negative terms, i.e., it is not prize fighting which is illegal because it disturbs the peace and may incite rioting and social disorder.[37]

Parpworth also questions the Court of Appeal's rationale in distinguishing between two very similar activities on the basis of intent.[38] Parpworth asserts that 'both prize fighter and boxers seek the same end; to hurt the opponent more than he is hurt himself.'[39] The court upheld sparring, wrestling and fighting with single-sticks, yet held prizefighting to be an unlawful activity. The distinction is even more difficult to understand when one considers modern-day professional boxing. Professional boxers are paid to fight and fighters often knock each other out. The aim of the fight is to score more points than your opponent, and one way to ensure your opponent does not score any points is to knock him out.[40] Gardiner argues that modern boxing may place 'an unnecessary premium on the knock-out punch at the expense of more skilful fighting'.[41] Sparring was held to be legal as there was an absence of intent to inflict injury and there was less of a

adopted a paternalistic approach, they should have declared prizefighting illegal on the grounds of the safety and health of the fighters. Instead, the court held prizefighting to be illegal due to its 'potential for crowd disorder'.
[34] *R. v Coney* (1882) 8 QBD 534, at 549.
[35] *Ibid.*
[36] Gardiner *et al.*, *Sports Law*, at 622.
[37] Anderson, 'International Sports Law Perspective', at 93.
[38] N. Parpworth, 'Boxing and Prizefighting: The Indistinguishable Distinguished?' (1994) 2 *Sport & the Law Journal* 5–8, at 8.
[39] *Ibid.*
[40] Gardiner *et al.*, *Sports Law*, at 622.
[41] *Ibid.*

likelihood of causing harm.[42] However, 'modern day boxing appears strikingly similar to the prize fights that the House was intent on banning.'[43]

The case *People v Fitzsimmons* shows the American approach.[44] A sparring match resulted in the death of an opponent. The fight was held in public and the defendant argued that it was lawful. The New York Supreme Court found in favour of the defendant, holding that the rules and practices of the fight were reasonable and thus criminal liability could not attach. Had Fitzsimons been heard by an English court, and the sparring had been defined as a prizefight, the rules and practices of the fight would have been deemed to be unreasonable and thus criminal liability would attach.[45]

SHOULD BOXING BE BANNED?

Arguments in Favour of Boxing

Those in favour of the continued legality of boxing note that boxing provides an outlet for young people in disadvantaged areas. It demands skill, strength and courage on behalf of the participants. Boxing instils discipline; it offers a chance for self-advancement for young men from poorer backgrounds. If boxing was banned it could drive the sport underground and it would develop into an unregulated sport similar to prizefighting. In applying liberal principles, boxing should remain legal on the grounds of civil liberties.[47]

R. v Brown

The case of *R. v Brown* provides a contemporary discussion on the legality of boxing.[48] As briefly mentioned in Chapter 1, *Brown* involved a group of sadomasochist homosexual men who engaged

---

[42] *Ibid.* M. James, *Sports Law* (London: Palgrave MacMillan, 2010), at 129, distinguishes sparring on the grounds that sparring tests the skill, strength and dexterity of the combatants.

[43] Gardiner *et al.*, *Sports Law*, at 622.

[44] 34 NYS 1102 (1895).

[45] James, *Sports Law*, at 133 views the American approach as the better approach. James views it as a 'much simpler approach to the determination of legality of an activity and would have allowed English law to have developed incrementally in a more structured manner than it has when confronted by some of the less traditionally British fighting sports that are currently popular'.

[46] Gunn and Ormerod, 'Despite the Law: Prize-Fighting and Professional Boxing', at 32–34.

[47] *Ibid.*, at 21–22 and Anderson, *The Legality of Boxing*, at 135–170.

[48] [1994] 1 AC 212.

in violent activities, including genital torture, for the purposes of pleasure. All the men were consenting adults, the acts took place in private, and no one suffered permanent injury. Video cameras recorded the activities. However, these recordings were not for public viewing but for the group of men involved. The court, in adopting a paternalistic approach, held that the activities of the men were unlawful, irrespective of consent. The court referred to contact sports as being lawful as there is a public interest in the continued practice of contact sports, including boxing. Contact sports are deemed to be socially acceptable whereas the acts of the men in *Brown* were perceived as being deviant and contrary to public policy. The House of Lords held that it was in the interests of the men involved and also for society to prevent a 'cult of violence'.[49] None of the men involved ever required hospital treatment nor did any of the men suffer permanent injuries. According to McArdle, 'these players were true professionals'.[50] The activities took place in private chambers, code words were used when the pain inflicted had gone beyond an acceptable level and all the equipment was sterilised. Lord Jauncey noted that the activities of the men were unlike a situation in sport where there is a 'referee present, such as there would be in [a] boxing or a football match'.[51] The absence of a referee meant that the sadomasochistic activities were unregulated.[52]

In his dissenting judgment, Lord Mustill showed a more liberal approach. He reasoned that the Offences Against the Person Act, 1861 was not appropriate in a case involving the private sexual acts of consenting adults. Lord Mustill argued that the case should be about the 'criminal law of private sexual relations, if about anything at all'.[53] The 1861 Act was devised to deal with behaviour which 'involves brutality, aggression and violence, of a kind far removed from the appellants' behaviour which, however worthy of censure, involved no animosity, no aggression, no personal rancour on the part of the person inflicting the hurt towards the recipient and no protest by the recipient'.[54]

---

[49] [1994] 1 AC 212, at 237.
[50] Meaning that the men in *Brown* were skilled in sadomasochism so that they very rarely were injured and were thus comparable to a skilled athlete or professional. D. McArdle, *From Boot Money to Bosman* (London: Cavendish, 2000), at 146.
[51] [1994] 1 AC 212, at 238.
[52] McArdle, *From Boot Money to Bosman*, at 147.
[53] [1994] 1 AC 212, at 256.
[54] *Brown*, at 256, 258.

Lord Mustill recognised that the case presented a new challenge for the courts. His discussion of boxing, prizefighting and sparring, and contact sports, is of importance.[55] In reference to boxing, Lord Mustill stated: '…it is in my judgment best to regard this as another special situation which for the time being stands outside the ordinary law of violence because society chooses to tolerate it.'[56]

Cox *et al.* make a compelling argument in relation to *R. v Brown*.[57] Boxing takes place in public, unlike the activities of the men in *Brown*. A boxer may be considered a social role model. Arguably, the intentional infliction of harm that takes place in a boxing match has greater potential to cause social problems than have the private sexual acts of the men in *Brown*.[58]

Those who favour the abolition of boxing highlight the health dangers associated with boxing.[59] As the head is the primary target, safety precautions are of little benefit.[60] The British Medical Association (BMA) has long called for boxing to be banned. While there may be fewer fatalities in comparison to other sports, boxers can suffer more long-term brain injury. It may take years for the injuries to manifest. It was suggested that doctors could withdraw their support and refuse to attend bouts.[61] If there was no medical cover, it would mean that the sport would become illegal. However, given that doctors are under a legal duty to provide medical cover at bouts, this suggestion was not feasible and could expose doctors to civil liability.

In the United Kingdom, a bill to abolish boxing for profit was defeated by two votes in the House of Lords. In 1994 the Law Commission published a consultation paper.[62] The Law Commission did not review the legality of professional boxing. However, the Commission concluded that boxing would remain legal so long as public policy

---

[55] *Brown*, at 266–267. Lord Mustill also looked at surgery, parental chastisement, dangerous pastimes and rough horse play.

[56] *Brown*, at 265.

[57] N. Cox, A. Schuster and C. Costello, *Sport and the Law* (Dublin: First Law, 2004), at 171.

[58] *Ibid.*

[59] See Anderson, *The Legality of Boxing*, at 117–133. See also H. Brayne, L. Sargeant and C. Brayne, 'Could Boxing Be Banned? A Legal and Epidemiological Perspective' (1998) 316(7147) *British Medical Journal* 1813–1815.

[60] Professional boxers do not wear helmets.

[61] 'Medical Notes: Boxing', *BBC News World Edition*, 24 September 1999 (available online: <http://news.bbc.co.uk/2/hi/health/medical_notes/363957.stm>, last accessed 10 February 2010).

[62] Law Commission, Consultation Paper No. 134, *Consent and Offences Against the Person* (London, 1994).

supported its continued legality. In 1995 the Commission stated 'that the continuing legality of boxing, amateur or professional, is a matter for Parliament to decide'.[63]

CONTINUED LEGAL RECOGNITION OF FIGHTING SPORTS

While *R. v Brown* provides the more recent discussion on the continued legal recognition of fighting sports, there are two other important authorities. In *R. v Donovan*, the defendant caned a 17-year-old girl for purposes of sexual gratification.[64] The girl was left with red marks on her body. Although the girl had consented, Swift J held that to be immaterial. Swift J argued that consent would only be considered in situations where the blows struck were neither likely nor intended to do bodily harm. The judge, in referring to the exemption given to sport, held: '…another exception to the general rule is to be found in cases of rough and undisciplined sport or play, where there is no anger and no intention to cause bodily harm'.[65]

Similarly, in the *Attorney General's Reference (No. 6 of 1980)*,[66] Lord Lane CJ held:

> It is not in the public interest that people should try to cause, or should cause, each other bodily harm for no good reason…. This means that most fights will be unlawful regardless of consent. Nothing we have said is intended to cast doubt upon the accepted legality of properly conducted games and sports, lawful chastisement or correction, reasonable surgical interference, dangerous exhibitions, etc. These apparent exceptions can be justified as involving the exercise of a legal right, in the case of chastisement or correction, or as needed in the public interest, in the other cases.[67]

The Legality of Mixed Martial Arts

Mixed martial arts (MMA) encompasses hybrid sports in that it combines traditional martial arts sports with non-traditional ones. MMA is an ancient sport; however, its modern inception dates back to 1993 when the Ultimate Fighting Championship was founded. MMA has few

---

[63] Law Commission Consultation Paper No. 139, *Consent in the Criminal Law* (London, 1995), at para 12.38. Professional boxing has been banned in Sweden, Norway and Iceland.

[64] [1934] 2 KB 498.

[65] [1934] 2 KB 498, at 508.

[66] [1981] QB 715.

[67] *Ibid.*, at 719.

rules and permits wrestling holds, punching, marital arts throws and kicking.[68] MMA has posed a number of difficulties as it appears to have little regulation and a lack of universally accepted standardised rules.[69] The New Jersey State Athlete Control Board's Mixed Martial Arts Unified Rules of Conduct have been adopted by many of the high profile contests.[70] There is no international federation or governing body that regulates MMA. It is largely self-regulated.

In Ireland, the traditional martial arts (including aikido, kickboxing, tae kwon do, karate, sumo, kung fu, jiu jitsu, tai chi, muaythai, ninjitsu and bujitsu) are governed by the Irish Martial Arts Commission (IMAC). IMAC, as a recognised national governing body, falls under the auspices of the Irish Sports Council (ISC). MMA is not recognised under the sports and governing bodies listed by the ISC. MMA is organised by MMA Ireland, which has its headquarters in Dublin. MMA is considered a properly constituted sport so long as the rules and regulations are adhered to, there are appropriate safety procedures, the rules are enforced by independent referees, and it is appropriately administered.[71] If these criteria are followed, then MMA will be 'at least as safe as boxing as it places so much less emphasis on blows to the head that so concern the BMA'.[72]

CONCLUSION

Boxing remains legal because society continues to tolerate it. There are many advantages connected with the sport: it is popular, it instils discipline, it promotes fitness and it offers young people in disadvantaged areas an outlet. The arguments against boxing have centred on the health implications and dangers for the boxers, the promotion of a cult of violence, the accompaniment of gambling and riotous crowds. While boxing for profit has been banned in some countries, both professional and amateur boxing are legal in Ireland. There has been little debate on its continued legality in Ireland. The Law Reform Commission (LRC) in its *Report on Non-Fatal Offences against the Person* concluded that boxing should not be singled out for exemption.[73] The LRC was of the opinion

[68] James, *Sports Law*, at 145.
[69] *Ibid.*
[70] *Ibid.*, at 146.
[71] *Ibid.*
[72] *Ibid.*
[73] See LRC 45–1994, at 275, para 9.160. Prizefights were referred to in the LRC report. The LRC noted that prizefighting remained illegal under the common law.

that any proposed changes to the rules of the sport would be a matter for the relevant regulatory sports body in accordance with public debate and medical evidence.[74] In contrast, in the United Kingdom boxing has been discussed in a number of cases and Law Commission papers. Parliament in the United Kingdom attempted to ban boxing for profit but the Bill was defeated.

MMA is legal due to its association with boxing and other lawfully recognised fighting sports. It is not accepted as a mainstream sport. The legal status of MMA is somewhat undefined and precious. Boxing is legal because it is not prizefighting. Prizefighting was declared illegal as it caused a breach of peace. The legality of boxing is defined in negative terms. At the moment, the state has not concerned itself with MMA and the sport continues to garner support from members of the public.

---

[74] LRC 45–1994, at 274, para 9.157.

CHAPTER 4

Civil Liability in Sport

INTRODUCTION

In simple terms, a tort is a civil wrong. Tort involves acts or omissions on the part of the defendant which causes physical, economic or psychological injury to the plaintiff. An individual will bring a case in tort in order to obtain damages. Tort covers a wide range of issues, including:

- Personal injuries
- Defective products
- Defamation[1]
- Passing off (where the customer is misled as to the origin of goods or services of another)
- Nervous shock (psychological damage or post-traumatic stress disorder)[2]

---

[1] Defamation involves the protection of an individual's right to his or her reputation against false allegations. Defamation, prior to the Defamation Act, 2009, encompassed two constituent torts: slander and libel. Slander was defined as defamation by way of an oral comment or gesture, for example, a comment made on radio. Libel was a more permanent form of defamation, for example, an allegation in a newspaper. The 2009 Act, Part 2, sections 6(1)(a) and (b) collectively refer to slander and libel as the tort of defamation. For a discussion of the law relating to defamation, see E. Quill, *Torts in Ireland* (2nd ed., Dublin: Gill & Macmillan, 2004), at 315–351. See *Tolley v J.S. Fry & Sons* [1931] AC 333; [1931] All ER Rep 131. See also the Australian case of *Ettingshausen v Australian Consolidated Press* (1991) 23 NSWSC 443, where a footballer was pictured without his consent in the shower after a match. He successfully sued Australian Consolidated Press on the grounds that the publication of the picture suggested that he was the type of person who would consent to a picture of this nature being published.

[2] The parents of ice hockey player Steve Moore are claiming CA$1.5 million in damages

- Private and public nuisance
- Vicarious liability, where the employer is held liable for the torts of an employee committed during the course of his or her employment

Tort liability may arise in a number of sporting situations. Civil liability may arise from participation in sport. A sportsperson may be injured by an opponent and thus unable to play for a few weeks or months, or the injury may be career-ending.[3] Such individuals will seek damages in the form of compensation for the loss of earnings, medical expenses or pain and suffering caused by the injury.[4] A player may also suffer harm due to the negligence of a coach, a referee, a league manager, an association official or medical personnel. A spectator may bring proceedings against the operator of a facility, the occupiers or owners of the ground, the security, or the policing and stewarding. A sportsperson may be injured due to defective equipment and consequently bring an action against the manufacturer of the equipment.[5] A governing body may be sued for changes in the rules or administration of the sport. If the sporting body does not have an adequate insurance scheme, the injured player is more likely to go through the courts to secure damages.

THE RULES OF THE SPORT AND THE NATURE OF THE SPORT

The rules of the sport are of great importance in tort cases. The rules of sports vary and what is permitted in one sport may not be permitted in another. In the case of *Sibley v Milutinovic*, the plaintiff and defendant were playing in a training soccer match.[6] During the course of the

---

after the shock of seeing their son being assaulted by Todd Bertuzzi. See '3 Years Later Moore Can't Forgive Bertuzzi' (available online: <http://nbcsports.msnbc.com/id/17520012/>, last accessed 15 March 2010). See Chapter 2 for details of the incident.
[3] Most sports entail some inherent risk. In many situations the injured party is injured and no one is to blame.
[4] See Quill, *Torts in Ireland*, at 527–533.
[5] *McCormick v Lowe & Campbell Athletic Goods Co.* 144 SW 2d 866 (Mo. Ct App. 1940). In this case a high school pole vaulter was seriously injured after the vaulting pole broke while in use. The Appeal Court held that the defendant manufacturer owed a duty of care to exercise ordinary care to test the product and to determine whether or not it was fit for the purpose intended. As the plaintiff was using the pole in the ordinary and usual manner, failure to inspect the pole rendered the defendant liable. For a discussion on injuries sustained from football helmets, see R.L. Yasser, *Torts and Sports Legal Liability in Professional and Amateur Athletics* (Westport, CT; London: Quorum Books, 1985), at 78–82.
[6] (1990) Australian Torts Reports 81–013.

match, Sibley made a number of low sliding tackles on the defendant from behind. After one such tackle, the defendant punched Sibley in the jaw with a closed fist. Sibley brought an action to sue Milutinovic, while Milutinovic counter-sued, alleging that Sibley had kicked him in his right ankle.

Miles CJ noted that, while soccer was mainly a non-contact sport, some contact was inevitable.[7] However, the intentional application of force was outside the rules of the game whenever the degree of force used was likely to result in injury. The actions of Milutinovic were clearly outside the rules of the game, and thus outside the scope of Sibley's consent. As it was a training match, Miles CJ noted that the extent to which players were entitled to adopt tactics that could result in injury to opposing players had to be distinguished from conduct that was justifiable in an actual competitive match.[8] The judge was influenced by evidence presented that the actions of Sibley in a competitive match would have resulted in him being sent off. Miles CJ held that he was 'not satisfied that the action of the plaintiff was within the ambit of the rules which the players on that evening expected to be observed'.[9] The judge dismissed Sibley's action and held in favour of Milutinovic. This case is important for two reasons. First, it demonstrates the importance of the rules of the sport and, second, it shows the potential complications that can arise in a situation where there is no referee or other match officials.[10]

There is one Irish case that illustrates the weight the court will give to the nature of the sport involved: *McComiskey v McDermott*.[11] McComiskey was acting as a navigator for the defendant in a car rally. On the dashboard there was a sign which stated that passengers travelled at their own risk. The car crashed and McComiskey issued civil proceedings against McDermott. The court was faced with two important factors, namely, what was the effect of the sign and was the defendant guilty of a breach of duty? With regard to the first question, the Supreme Court held that the plaintiff had not waived his right to sue the defendant for negligence. The sign was deemed to ineffective unless the plaintiff expressly assented to its terms. On the second question the Supreme Court held that the defendant was not in breach of his duty

---

[7] *Ibid.*, at 67.888.
[8] *Ibid.*
[9] *Ibid.*
[10] D. Thorpe and A. Buti *et al.*, *Sports Law* (South Melborne: Oxford University Press, 2009), at 107.
[11] [1974] IR 75.

owed to the plaintiff. The duty of care depends on the circumstances, which in this case was a car rally. The defendant was required to drive as a reasonably careful, competitive rally driver would be expected to drive in the prevailing circumstances.

THE TORT OF NUISANCE AND SPORT

With regard to the tort of nuisance, an occupier of land may initiate civil proceedings if their enjoyment of the land is disturbed. There are two types of nuisance: public and private. Public nuisance concerns interference with the rights of the general public, rather than a particular individual. Civil proceedings may only be brought by the attorney general, as the representative of the public interest. An individual may bring an action if he or she suffers special or peculiar damage above that suffered by the general public. For an incident to be considered a nuisance, it must be ongoing and not a one-off event.[12]

A private nuisance arises where the defendant uses his or her land in a manner which interferes with the enjoyment of another's land or damages another's land. A plaintiff may seek an injunction or damages, or both. Private nuisance cases require the law to strike a balance between the competing interests of the plaintiff and the defendant.[13] The law must reconcile the right of the defendant to use their land or property as they so wish and the right of the plaintiff to the peaceful enjoyment of their land. A private nuisance covers physical injuries and activities which cause discomfort to the plaintiff, for example, noise, dust, fumes, smells, vibrations, objects leaving the defendant's land, projectiles and overhanging trees. The plaintiff must show that this is an ongoing state of affairs rather than a one-off incident. The test employed in private nuisance cases is that of reasonableness. In assessing whether the defendant is acting reasonably, a number of factors must be considered, including the nature of the activity and the nature of the locality.[14] What may be considered acceptable in a rural area may not be deemed acceptable in an urban area.[15]

---

[12] See *Bolton v Stone* [1949] 1 All ER 237 and the Court of Appeal's decision in [1951] AC 850, [1951] 1 All ER 1078.

[13] See *Miller v Jackson* [1977] 3 WLR 20.

[14] See *O'Kane v Campbell* [1985] IR 115. In this case a shop was open 24 hours a day and was located near a residential area. The plaintiff complained that the loud noises emanating from the shop were disturbing his sleep.

[15] See *Dewar v City and Suburban Racecourse* [1899] 1 IR 345 where an injunction was granted to prohibit the operation of a racecourse on Sundays.

CRIMINAL LAW AND CIVIL LAW CONTRASTED

In a criminal case, the Director of Public Prosecutions (DPP) brings the action in the name of the state. The victim is a mere witness for the prosecution. In a tort case, the injured party usually brings the action against the wrongdoer. The primary remedy under tort is damages. The primary function of the criminal law is to punish those who commit a crime. In a criminal case, if damages are awarded, they are normally paid to the state and not to the injured party. In a criminal case, the prosecution must prove beyond reasonable doubt that the defendant is guilty. If the jury are in doubt, they must acquit the accused. In civil cases, the burden is on the balance of probabilities, which, in contrast to beyond reasonable doubt, is a lower threshold given that the defendant's liberty is not at stake, as it would be in a criminal case.

Similar to the criminal case, a tort case may be brought on the grounds of assault and battery.[16] However, given the evidentiary requirements in assault and battery in tort, i.e. proving the deliberate infliction of harm, the majority of sports cases are based on negligence. Negligence refers to behaviour that falls below a certain standard.

NEGLIGENCE

The seminal case of *Donoghue v Stevenson* is a suitable starting point for a discussion on negligence.[17] The plaintiff, Donoghue, drank from a bottle of ginger beer that contained a decomposed snail. Ms Donoghue later complained of stomach pains and was diagnosed by her doctor as having gastroenteritis. Ms Donoghue argued that the manufacturer owed her a duty of care not to produce the beer in a negligent manner, especially in a situation where the product left the manufacturer in the

---

[16] Battery cases are very rare as most insurance policies expressly exclude cover for deliberately inflicted injuries. This means that the defendant will be held personally liable. The club will not be held liable. See S. Gardiner *et al.*, *Sports Law* (London: Cavendish Publishing, 2006), at 630. This point was made in the case of *Elliott v Saunders and Liverpool FC*, High Court, unreported, QB, 10 June 1994. Here the trespass case was dropped as Liverpool FC's insurance would not pay out on a battery claim. See also M. James, 'The Trouble with Roy Keane' (2002) 1(3) *Entertainment Law* 72–92, at 81. Elliott proceeded with a negligence claim. Battery has been successfully pleaded in some Australian cases; see *McNamara v Duncan* (1971) 26 ALR 584. While there are very few sporting cases involving intentional torts, there are some examples from Australia, see *Canterbury Bankstown Rugby League v Rogers* (1993) Aust. Tort Reports 81-246 and *McCracken v Melbourne Storm* [2005] NSWSC 107. See also Thorpe and Buti *et al.*, *Sports Law*, at 109–112.

[17] [1932] AC 562; [1932] All ER Rep 1.

form in which it was intended to reach the ultimate customer (i.e. in a bottle). The House of Lords allowed Ms Donoghue to sue for negligence. Lord Atkin, in *Donoghue*, developed the neighbour principle, which is similar to the Christian concept of loving your neighbour.

> The rule that you are to love your neighbour becomes in law you must not injure your neighbour; and the lawyer's question: Who is my neighbour? receives a restricted reply. You must take reasonable care to avoid acts or omissions which you can reasonably foresee would be likely to injure your neighbour. Who, then, in law, is my neighbour? The answer seems to be persons who are so closely and directly affected by my act that I ought reasonably to have them in contemplation as being so affected when I am directing my mind to the acts or omissions that are called in question.[18]

The case of *Donoghue v Stevenson* is important in a number of respects.[19] The case established that the existence of a contract between the parties was not required in order to establish liability in negligence. It also established a general test for liability in negligence. A person owes a duty of reasonable care not to cause injury to those who he or she can reasonably foresee could be injured by his or her act or omission. A person does not owe a duty to the world at large. There must be proximity between the parties, a relationship between the parties is required. Proximity can relate to closeness in distance, time, relationship or some other connecting factor.[20]

The principle established in *Donoghue* has developed to include situations outside of defective products. In assessing whether a defendant is liable in negligence a number of factors must be considered:

1. Duty of care – did the defendant reasonably foresee that by his or her act or omission that the plaintiff would suffer an injury. Once it has been established that a duty of care exists, the next issue to be determined is the extent of this duty, namely, the standard of care
2. Standard of care – the standard of care depends on the circumstances. The test employed by the courts is that of how a reasonable person would have acted in the particular situation. It is an objective test which looks at the general standard of behaviour and not that of the particular individual[21]

---

[18] [1932] AC 562, at 580.
[19] It was adopted by the Irish courts in *Kirby v Burke & Holloway* [1944] IR 207.
[20] Quill, *Torts in Ireland*, at 21. A proximate relationship includes the following: doctor–patient, solicitor–client, priest–parishioner and driver–pedestrian.
[21] Quill, *Torts in Ireland*, at 72.

3. Damage – as a result of the defendant's conduct, the plaintiff has suffered damage. Damage may be a combination of physical injury and economic loss.[22] Damage may also be psychological. In this situation, injury relates to the person's mental state[23]

4. Causation – is there a causal link between the injury suffered by the plaintiff and the defendant's conduct? If there is no causal link then liability will not attach even though the defendant may have acted negligently. Remoteness of damage provides a cut-off point after which the defendant will not be held liable[24]

5. Lack of defence – *volenti non fit injuria* – means that an individual assumes risk. The defence will argue that the plaintiff by his or her conduct or agreement assumed the risk that he or she would be injured. In a sporting situation, participants assume that contact sports carry an inherent risk. If an injury is sustained within the rules of the game, the defendant will not be held liable.

This common law defence is now contained in the Civil Liability Act, 1961. The defendant may also raise the defence of contributory negligence. The plaintiff is considered to be partly responsible for the injury suffered. The plaintiff's lack of care and the defendant's negligent conduct have contributed to the injury. The court will apportion damages and damages will be reduced as the plaintiff has contributed to his or her own injury. For example, the defence could be used in a case where a crash helmet was not worn, or a player did not wear shin guards or other protective clothing or equipment. The defence of contributory negligence is also provided for in the Civil Liability Act, 1961

DUTY AND STANDARD OF CARE: PARTICIPANTS

As mentioned above, it must be established that the defendant owes a duty of care which depends on the circumstances of the case. Duty of

---

[22] Most jurisdictions adopt a cautious approach when a case is based purely on economic loss. See Quill, *Torts in Ireland*, at 53.

[23] Quill, *Torts in Ireland*, at 58–72.

[24] *Overseas Tankship (UK) Ltd v Morts Dock & Engineering Co. (The Wagon Mound)* [1961] AC 388; [1961] 2 WLR 126; [1961] 1 All ER 404. In this case the defendant's employees spilt a large quantity of oil into Sydney Harbour. The oil spread to another part of the harbour where the plaintiff was welding. He stopped welding and resumed on receipt of expert advice that oil would not ignite on water. The oil ignited as some sparks from the welding fell on cotton waste. The wharf was damaged. The court held that harm to the wharf by the oil spill was foreseeable; however, the harm caused by the fire was not foreseeable as oil does not usually ignite on water. The claim for damages for harm

care is succinctly defined by Fleming as 'an obligation recognised by law, to avoid conduct fraught with unreasonable risk of danger to others'.[25] The plaintiff must establish that there is a relationship between him or her and the defendant and that relationship required the defendant to take reasonable care not to cause injury to the plaintiff. In the case of *Condon v Basi*,[26] the English Court of Appeal held that ordinary principles of negligence applied. In holding the defendant liable, the Court of Appeal held that a player owed a duty to exercise the degree of care that was reasonable in the circumstances, which in a game of football were different from going for a walk in the countryside. The referee had considered the tackle to be 'reckless and dangerous' and that it amounted to 'serious foul play'.[27]

The trial court held that the defendant owed the plaintiff a duty of care and his 'reckless and dangerous foul' demonstrated a 'reckless disregard for the plaintiff's safety...which fell far below the standards which might reasonably be expected in anyone pursuing the game'.[28] The trial judge accepted that there was no malicious intent to cause harm but that the defendant had acted in a manner that was a reckless and dangerous.[29]

Court of Appeal in *Condon v Basi*

On appeal, the defendant argued that he did not owe a duty of care to the plaintiff as the plaintiff impliedly consented to risk by virtue of him playing in the game. Basi also argued that the trial judge erred in his application of an objective standard of care. Basi maintained that a subjective test of recklessness more akin to the criminal standard was the more appropriate test to be applied. The Court of Appeal rejected Basi's contention and dismissed the appeal. The Court of Appeal agreed with the findings of the trial judge but instead of using the standard of reckless disregard, the Court of Appeal used ordinary negligence principles.[30]

---

caused by the fire was rejected by the court. The Wagon Mound case was adopted in Ireland, see *Burke v John Paul & Co. Ltd* [1967] IR 277.
[25] J.G. Fleming, *The Law of Torts* (9th ed., Sydney: Lbc Information Services, 1998), at 149.
[26] (1985) 1 WLR 866.
[27] *Ibid.*, at 869.
[28] *Ibid.*
[29] Opie, in his case note on the case, remarks that it is not clear whether the trial judge meant that the defendant did not mean to make contact with Condon or that the defendant did not mean to cause the plaintiff any physical harm. See H. Opie, 'Condon v Basi' (1986) 15 *Melbourne University Law Review* 756–762, at 756.
[30] Gardiner, *Sports Law*, at 631, is critical of the Court of Appeal's approach. He argues

The Court of Appeal was heavily influenced by the earlier case of *Rootes v Shelton*, specifically the judgments of Kitto J and Barwick CJ.[31]

Rootes involved a water-skiing accident. Rootes was severely injured and sued the respondent for negligence for failing to take care in the control of the boat and in failing to warn of the presence of a stationary boat.[32] Barwick CJ (at 386) accepted that there are risks inherent in the sport of water-skiing; however, failure by the driver of the towboat to warn of the presence of a stationary boat and to drive so close to a stationary boat were not inherent risks. The judge (at 384) held:[33]

> By engaging in a sport or pastime the participants may be held to have accepted risks which are inherent in that sport or pastime: the tribunal of fact can make its own assessment of what the accepted risks are: but this does not eliminate all duty of care of the one participant to the other.[34]

Donaldson MR felt that this was a more generalised duty of care which was modified to reflect the fact that participants have impliedly consented to inherent risks in sport.[35]

Kitto J (at 389) held that there is a general standard of care akin to Lord Atkin's neighbour principle.

Donaldson MR favoured the approach of Kitto J, although he admitted that, while both judges had different approaches, the end result was the same. Donaldson MR summarised Kitto J's judgment as follows: 'you are under a duty to take all reasonable care taking into account of the circumstances in which you are placed; which in a game of football, are quite different from those which affect you when you are going for a walk on the countryside.'[36]

Donaldson MR rejected the contention by the defendant's counsel that the standard of care was subjective. He noted that the standard is objective but objective in a different set of circumstances.[37] Donaldson MR

---

that Sir Donaldson MR did little to clarify the legal position. However, Opie, 'Condon v Basi', at 756, applauds the Court of Appeal for not using the cumbersome and confusing standard of reckless disregard.

[31] [1967] HCA 39; (1967) 116 CLR 383.

[32] [1967] HCA 39; (1967) 116 CLR 383, at 384.

[33] (1985) 1 WLR 866, at 867F.

[34] Gardiner, *Sports Law*, at 634, is critical of the approach of Barwick CJ. He notes that players do not consent to risks but rather they consent to contacts that are inherent in the sport and they run the risk of being injured due to such contacts.

[35] (1985) 1 WLR 866, at 867F.

[36] *Ibid.*

[37] Counsel for Basi had submitted that the 'standard of care was subjective to the defendant and not objective, and if he was a wholly incompetent football player, he

concluded that objective would mean something different depending on the circumstances.[38] In applying the objective standard, controversially, the judge added that a higher duty of care would be required from a first division player than from a player in a local league game. However, such an assertion would seem improbable. For example, in the FA Cup, teams from different league levels play each other and if Donaldson's comments were taken to its logical conclusion it would mean that in a match involving a premier league side and a lower division team, the premier side would owe a higher duty of care than their opponents in the same match.[39] Admittedly, there is a different standard of play expected from a professional player than that of an amateur player. However, the same standard of care in the circumstances is expected.

Donaldson MR dismissed the appeal and awarded damages in favour of the plaintiff. His concluding comments were somewhat dismissive. He held that '[i]t is not for me in this court to define exhaustively the duty of care between players in a soccer football game.' Not surprisingly the case caused much confusion and it was left up to subsequent cases to clarify the appropriate standard of care.[40]

The Court of Appeal clearly accepted that a breach of the rules of the game would be needed in order for liability to attach. The Court of Appeal seemed to be suggesting that a breach of the rules is 'virtually a necessary, albeit not a sufficient, requirement for liability to attach'.[41]

---

could do things without risk of liability which a competent football player could not do'. However, Donaldson MR rejected this contention.

[38] Objective means that the standard is based on the reasonable person rather than the individual defendant.

[39] Sir Donaldson's comments conflict with the earlier case of *Nettleship v Weston* [1976] 2 QB 691. In this case, the court held that the standard of care for a learner driver was that which is expected of the ordinary, reasonably careful and prudent qualified driver. The standard is an objective one. However, the driving analogy has its limitations when applied to sport. Every driver owes every other driver the same duty of care, irrespective of the individual skill of the particular motorist. As Gardiner (*Sports Law*, at 636) notes: 'In sport, the analogy only stretches as far as each individual games or at most each individual competition, not each entire sport…however, that does not mean that those at the higher levels of play owe a higher duty of care. A higher degree of skill may still be expected but also would a higher degree of risk taking and the acceptance by all involved of those risks.' See C. Moore, *Sports Law and Litigation* (2nd ed., Welwyn Garden City: CLT Professional Publishing, 2000), at 145. Moore notes that varying standards have been accepted in other fields – medicine, for example.

[40] For criticisms, see Gardiner, *Sports Law*, at 632 and M. James, 'Liability for Professional Athletes' Injuries: A Comparative Analysis of Where the Risk Lies' [2006] 1 *Web Journal of Current Legal Issues* (available online: <http://webjcli.ncl.ac.uk/2006/issue1/james1.html>, last accessed 18 March 2010).

[41] M. Beloff *et al.*, *Sports Law* (Oxford: Hart Publishing, 1999), at para 5.37.

Participants and the Standard of Care

The standard of care has posed some problems for the court. The debate has centred on whether the standard of care should be the standard associated with ordinary negligence or whether a higher threshold for liability is required. The Australian case *Frazer v Johnston* provides an example of the two standards.[42] The case centred on a collision between two jockeys in flat horse racing. The defendant's horse had veered in too close to the plaintiff's in a situation where there was no room to do so. The plaintiff suffered severe injuries as a result of the collision. The plaintiff argued that the standard owed was that of ordinary negligence, citing the cases of *Rootes v Shelton*[43] and *Condon v Basi*.[44] The defendant, on the other hand, argued that the appropriate test was that of reckless disregard, as held in *Wooldridge v Sumner*[45] and *Turcotte v Fell*.[46] The court applied the case of *Rootes*, and in doing so rejected the standard of reckless disregard proposed by the defendant.[47] The court held that Johnston owed Frazer a duty of care and awarded damages of AUS$121,490.

On appeal, the defendant argued that the duty in sporting cases differed from other activities. However, the Court of Appeal rejected this and held that sporting cases should be treated the same as all other negligence cases.[48]

In the aftermath of *Condon*, the test applicable in sporting cases was that of ordinary negligence. Some earlier cases had suggested the use of the standard of reckless disregard.[49] In *Elliott v Saunders*, while ordinary principles of negligence were applied, Drake J, however, held that Saunders had not acted in reckless disregard for the plaintiff's safety.[50]

---

[42] (1990) 21 NSWLR 89.

[43] [1967] HCA 39; (1967) 116 CLR 383.

[44] (1985) 1 WLR 866.

[45] *Wooldridge v Sumner* [1963] 2 QB 43. In this case, the rider at an equestrian event collided with a photographer. The court held that it was an error and not negligence on the part of the rider. The court held that the standard was that of reckless disregard for the safety of others.

[46] 510 NYS 2d 49 (Ct App.) (1986). Turcotte was a professional jockey and during a race the defendant's horse clipped off his horse, causing him to be thrown. The New York Supreme Court in dismissing the case held that there were risks inherent in the sport and that the plaintiff consented to the race but did not consent to intentional or reckless acts.

[47] For a discussion on civil liability and horse racing, see P. Charlish, 'Sports Ordinary Negligence in the Final Furlong' (2005) 4 *Journal of Personal Injury* 314–325.

[48] *Frazer v Johnston* (1990) 21 NSWLR 89.

[49] For example, *Wooldridge v Sumner* [1963] 2 QB 43 and *Turcotte v Fell* 510 NYS 2d 49 (Ct App.) (1986).

[50] High Court, unreported, QB, 10 June 1994. This test has been subject to further

In line with the dicta of Donaldson MR in *Condon v Basi*, Elliott endeavoured to argue that a different standard of care applied in a professional game. Elliott proposed that Saunders owed him, a fellow professional, a higher standard of care in line with that expected of a highly trained and skilled participant. However, Drake J disagreed and held:

> The fact that players are top professionals with very great skills, is no doubt one of the circumstances to be considered, but in my judgment, the fact that the game is in the Premier League rather than at a lower level does not necessarily mean that the standard of care is different; liability on the part of a defendant depends on the facts and circumstances of each individual case.[51]

Saunders counter-sued and argued that Elliott's lunge was intimidatory in nature and that he had instinctively jumped to avoid Elliott, causing him serious injury. The court agreed with Saunders and held that he had not acted in a reckless and deliberate manner as suggested by Elliott. Drake J was heavily influenced by the testimonies of the match officials. Drake J dismissed video and photographic evidence as being two-dimensional and, with modern technology, easy to edit and manipulate.[52]

The lack of success in *Elliott* did not mean that other footballers were dissuaded from bringing tort actions. In a similar case in 1994, Northern Ireland international and Norwich player John O'Neill received a reported £70,000 in damages from John Fashanu of Wimbledon in an out-of-court settlement.[53] Brian McCord, the former Stockport County player, successfully sued Swansea City and its captain, John Cornford, after his career was ended by a tackle during a match.[54] McCord was the first professional footballer to succeed in a negligence case.

---

refinement in subsequent cases, including *Caldwell v Maguire and Fitzgerald* [2001] EWCA 1054. Elliott was the first professional footballer in the United Kingdom to bring a negligence action.

[51] High Court, unreported, QB, 10 June 1994, at 5.

[52] J. Anderson, 'The Practice of Sports Law', seminar to the Professional Practice course, the Law Society of Ireland, Dublin, 11 November 2003. Anderson summarises *Elliott* as follows: 'Thus, in England it seems that from now on, given that the legal principles to be invoked in cases of "sporting" negligence are well settled around the fulfilment of a behavioural standard of reckless disregard, the presented evidence assumes the utmost importance....'

[53] R. Trapp, 'Professional Foul? You'll Be Hearing from My Solicitor. Can a Player Be Held Liable for the Injury of an Opponent? Or Is It all Part of the Game?', *Independent*, 19 July 1995.

[54] *McCord v Swansea City AFC Ltd* [1997] *The Times*, 11 February.

In *Watson v Gray*, the defendant and his club, Huddersfield Town, were found liable for injuries suffered by the plaintiff (he broke his leg) in a match involving Bradford City and Huddersfield Town.[55] Hooper J held that a professional footballer is at risk of being proved negligent if he is shown to have caused injury with an act which a reasonable professional player would know to carry a significant risk of causing serious injury. The tackle in question was considered late, forceful and high. Hopper J was influenced by video evidence which he watched on a number of occasions in slow motion.[56] In *Pitcher v Huddersfield Town Football Club Ltd*[57] the claimant was a professional footballer who was injured in a match by his opponent, Reid. The claimant argued that the defendant was liable in negligence as he had failed to exercise reasonable skill and care and that his standard of football fell below that expected of a professional footballer. Damages was a crucial factor as the injury was career-ending. Hallett J dismissed the claim and held that a lapse in judgment or a mistimed tackle could not be equated with negligence, especially in a fast-paced game such as football. Expert witnesses testified that tackles of this nature occurred on Saturday afternoons up and town the country in the First Division.[58]

Hallett J (at 19) held that the claimant had not shown that the challenge crossed 'the high threshold to take this case from a simple late tackle, albeit one with tragic consequences, to one of negligence'. In applying principles of ordinary negligence, Hallett J noted that certain sports carried inherent risks and the standard of care depended on the circumstances of the case. Pitcher was required to show on the balance of probabilities that Reid's actions had fallen below the standard required of a professional footballer. Hallett J found that the lack of supporting evidence and Pitcher's inability to establish liability on the balance of probabilities required her to find against the claimant.

Caldwell v Maguire and Fitzgerald – The Standard of Care Clarified

Shortly before the *Pitcher* decision, the Court of Appeal heard a similar civil liability case involving jockeys.[59] *Caldwell v Maguire and Fitzgerald* is an important judgment as the court clarified the standard of care in

---

[55] [1998] *The Times*, 26 November.
[56] James, 'The Trouble with Roy Keane', at 82.
[57] [2001] All ER (D) 223 (Jul).
[58] The manager, doctor and physiotherapist did not recall seeing the stud marks on Pitcher's knee.
[59] *Caldwell v Maguire and Fitzgerald* [2001] EWCA 1054.

sporting cases. The trial judge, Holland J, set out five propositions that should be considered when deciding liability. These five propositions were approved by the Court of Appeal:[60]

1. Each contestant in a lawful sporting contest owes a duty of care to each and all other contestants
2. That duty is to exercise in the course of the contest all care that is objectively reasonable in the prevailing circumstances for the avoidance of infliction of injury to such fellow contestants
3. The prevailing circumstances are all such properly attendant upon the contest and include its object, the demands inevitably made upon its contestants, its inherent dangers (if any), its rules, conventions and customs, and the standards, skills and judgment reasonably to be expected of a contestant. In the particular case of a horse race, the prevailing circumstances will include the jockey's obligation to ride a horse over a given course competing with the remaining contestants for the best possible placing, the rules of racing, and the standards, skills and judgment of a professional jockey, as expected by co-contestants
4. Given the nature of such prevailing circumstances, the threshold for liability is in practice inevitably high; the proof of a breach of duty will not flow from proof of no more than an error of judgment or from mere proof of a momentary lapse of skill (and thus care) respectively when subject to the stresses of the race
5. In practice, it may therefore be difficult to prove any such breach of duty in the absence of conduct that in point of fact amounts to reckless disregard for the fellow contestant's safety

The case was appealed to the Court of Appeal. The Court of Appeal approved the five propositions put forward by Holland J and accordingly

---

[60] Academic commentators have welcomed the decision as, in the words of Gardiner *et al.*, *Sports Law*, at 632, the case 'has come closest to defining the true scope of negligence in this area'. Similar comments are made by James, 'The Trouble with Roy Keane', at 82. However, Charlish, 'Sports Ordinary Negligence in the Final Furlong', at 324, is most critical of the decision and argues that the decision has led to more uncertainty and 'stripped away the relative clarity that had been present since *Condon v Basi* and replaced it with an unsatisfactory compromise that is going to need further judicial intervention to settle the appropriate *standard* of care for sports in England and Wales' (italics in original). In *Frazer v Johnston* (1990) NSWLR 89 a similar incident had occurred and the failure to look was deemed to be the reason for the accident, and liability was attached. However, in *Caldwell*, the court held that the failure to look was an error in judgment and liability was not attached.

dismissed the appeal.[61] The Court of Appeal reiterated the point that an error of judgment, an oversight or a lapse of which any participant might be guilty in the context of a race of that kind could not be equated with negligence. Something more serious is required to attribute negligence to the actions of the defendants. Incidents of this nature happened often and were part of what is termed the 'playing culture of the sport'.[62]

The Duty of Care and the Standard of Reckless Disregard

Although an Irish court has yet to be asked to adjudicate on the standard of care in sport, a similar approach to that taken by the trial court and Court of Appeal in *Caldwell* might be adopted in this jurisdiction. The Court of Appeal in *Caldwell* followed the approach taken by Kitto J in *Rootes*. It follows from the *Caldwell* case that there is a generalised duty of care, which is derived from Lord Atkin's neighbour principle. The courts in *Condon* and *Caldwell* applied ordinary negligence principles. A participant is under a duty to take all reasonable care, taking account of the circumstances. However, the court in *Caldwell*, in applying the principles of ordinary negligence, added that the nature of the sport is irrelevant; what are important are the circumstances in which the injury takes place. Following the reasoning of the courts in *Condon* and *Caldwell*, a future court would be advised to take the following into consideration: the rules of the game, the playing culture, the level of play, and the experience and age of the participants.[63] Other factors to consider include: Is the sport contact or non-contact? Is the accident the result of the heat of the moment or has it occurred in the quiet passage of play? Has the level of risk necessarily been accepted as inherent in the sport? What are the cost and availability of precautions?[64]

---

[61] For a discussion on this case, see M. James and I. Deeley, 'The Standard of Care in Negligence Cases: Caldwell v Maguire and Fitzgerald [2001] EWCA 1054' (2002) 1(1) *Entertainment Law* 104–108. James and Deeley, at 106, remark that the court, in dismissing the standard of reckless disregard, 'has ensured that sports participants are judged by the same legal standard as everyone else'.

[62] For a detailed discussion of the playing culture see Gardiner *et al.*, *Sports Law*, at 637–638. James and Deeley, 'The Standard of Care in Negligence Cases', at 106–107, in support of the playing culture, note that 'it concentrates on the playing of the game and its inherent dangers rather than allowing the defendant to show a greater degree of negligence to the claimant before liability is imposed.' However, the inclusion of the playing culture has not gained universal acceptance. If the playing culture developed further it could allow certain fouls to become accepted as an inherent part of the game; such a development would not be welcomed.

[63] Gardiner *et al.*, *Sports Law*, at 634.

[64] These factors are listed by Beloff *et al.*, *Sports Law*, at para 5.38.

If the injury suffered is caused by reasonable contact and of a nature that the participant has accepted as an integral part of the sport, then no liability can be said to attach. For example, body checks in ice hockey are an accepted and lawful part of the sport; however, they would not be acceptable in a sport such as tennis.[65]

Reckless disregard has caused much debate and disquiet among academic commentators and the courts alike. Most of the cases above provide that ordinary negligence principles should apply to sport. Sport should not be treated differently to other activities. Others argue that reckless disregard seems to be more suitable to professional sportspersons as the standard of care is lower since professional players should be taken to have understood and assumed the inherent risks relevant in the particular sport.[66] As reckless disregard is a very high standard, it is more difficult for a participant to breach it. It means that participants can engage in the particular sport in their usual manner without fear of litigation. However, reckless disregard would grant almost total immunity to sports participants.[67] Reckless disregard applies only in situations which involve a high degree of negligent or reckless play. It would seem that most of the comments made in relation to the standard of reckless disregard are *obiter*.[68] It is doubtful that a new standard of care will be developed by the English courts.[69]

LIABILITY OF REFEREES

Referees have been held to owe a duty of care to participants. The role of the referee is not just to enforce the rules of the game to ensure fair play but also to ensure that the sport is played according to the rules for the safety of the participants.

---

[65] Gardiner *et al.*, *Sports Law*, at 634.
[66] S. Gardiner and A. Felix, 'Juridification of the Football Field: Strategies for Giving the Law the Elbow' (1994–1995) 5 *Marquette Sports Law Journal* 189–220, at 208. The writers argue that the better course of action is to hold the clubs vicariously liable for the actions of their players. However, as Drake J pointed out in *Elliott*, the clubs would in turn go after the player to recover the compensation paid out, so the dispute would still end up in the court.
[67] Charlish, 'Sports Ordinary Negligence in the Final Furlong', at 323. Charlish adds that if such a standard was used it would mean that claimants would find it almost impossible to obtain compensation.
[68] *Obiter* refers to comments made by a judge as an aside; such comments are not part of the binding part of the judgment.
[69] For a more detailed discussion, see Gardiner *et al.*, *Sports Law*, at 639–641. In the United States, reckless disregard is used in most states.

In the case of *Smolden v Whitworth and Nolan*, the plaintiff successfully sued the referee for injuries sustained as a result of a collapsed scrum in a game involving underage rugby players.[70] The referee argued that the relevant standard was that of reckless disregard. The referee admitted that he owed a duty of care to the players. The court, however, disagreed and followed the approach of *Condon*, holding that the duty was to exercise such degree of care as was appropriate in all the circumstances. An important factor for the court was the fact that the players were underage. Curtis J held that the referee had not enforced safety requirements set out in the laws of the game, which contained special provisions relating to players aged under nineteen. The trial court found the referee liable in negligence. The case was appealed by the referee. Lord Bingham LCJ observed that this case was the first of its kind in the common law world. Nolan argued that the court should have used the standard of reckless disregard. He endeavoured to rely on the comments of Lord Diplock and Sellers LJ in *Wooldridge v Sumner*.[71] The referee argued that the standard of reckless disregard should apply in order to protect match officials from litigation. A number of referees are volunteers and fear of litigation would mean that such referees would be less likely to offer their services. The Court of Appeal disagreed and held that the appropriate standard of care was to be expressed as follows:

> The level of care required is that which is appropriate in all the circumstances, and the circumstances are of crucial importance. Full account must be taken of the factual context in which a referee exercises his functions, and he could not be held liable for errors of judgment, oversights or lapses of which any referee might be guilty in the context of a fast-moving and vigorous contest. The threshold for liability is a high one. It will not be easily crossed.[72]

The Court of Appeal imposed liability on Nolan, holding that his inability to control the scrummage effectively was a breach of the duty owed to Smoldon. An important point made by the court was

---

[70] [1997] PIQR 133. The game was a colts' game, meaning all the players were under 19 years of age. There was a paternalistic element in the case.
[71] [1963] 2 QB 43. Sellers LJ held: 'If the conduct is deliberately intended to injure someone whose presence is known, or is reckless and in disregard of all safety of others so that it is a departure from the standards which might reasonably be expected in anyone pursuing the competition or game, then the performer might well be held liable for any injury his act caused.'
[72] [1997] PIQR 133, at 134.

that the obligations on the referee differ when he is observing the scrum rules and has taken control over the players and a situation involving fast-paced open play where the referee has limited control over the players. If an injury is sustained during passages of robust open play, then the referee cannot be held liable. In contrast, if the referee has blown the whistle and has time to think out his options and has made the safety instructions clear to the players, failure on the part of the referee to properly enforce the rules may result in the imposition of liability.

It was feared that the decision in *Smoldon* would open up the flood-gates of litigation. However, such fears were unfounded as the next case involving a referee came before the court five years later: *Vowles v Evans and the Welsh Rugby Union*.[73] Vowles suffered a severe spinal cord injury and was confined to a wheelchair after an injury sustained in a rugby match in Wales. The Court of Appeal upheld the decision of the trial court and held that an amateur referee in an amateur match owed a duty of care to the participants. Ironically, Evans was a solicitor who specialised in personal injuries and the court noted that he had provided very detailed notes in his referee's report. Lord Philips MR (at para 28) made an important point in relation to volunteer referees. He noted that at times a referee may not turn up to an amateur match or the referee may be injured in the course of the game and a volunteer steps in. In this situation, the volunteer cannot reasonably be expected to show the skill of one who holds himself out as a referee or to be fully conversant with the laws of the game. However, this did not apply to Mr Evans as he had played rugby for many years and had attended a Welsh Rugby Union (WRU) refereeing course and had been refereeing ever since.

The element of control was a deciding factor for the Court of Appeal.[74] The referee's role is to take control over the players in situations involving scrums. Had the incident occurred in an ordinary passage of play, then the referee would not be held liable as he would have minimum control over the players.[75]

---

[73] [2003] EWCA Civ 318. The Welsh Rugby Union was held to be vicariously liable as it had appointed Evans as a referee.

[74] [2003] EWCA Civ 318, at para 27 of the judgment, Lord Philips MR referred to the discussion in *Smoldon* where it was suggested that the level of skill to be expected of a referee depended upon the grade of the referee, or upon the grade of match he was refereeing. The discussion was inconclusive in the case as the answer to that question did not matter in *Smoldon*. The issue did not apply in *Vowles*.

[75] This would be the position in rugby. However, in sports such as football, players have sustained serious injuries due to tackles which take place in open play. R. Caddell in

Similarly, in the joined cases of *Agar v Hyde* and *Worsley v Australian Rugby Football Union*,[76] an action brought against the International Rugby Football Board (IRFB) was dismissed on the grounds that the board could not be held liable for injuries sustained as a result of rule changes due to the minimalist control each member of the IRFB had over the creation of new rules for rugby.[77] Initially, the claimants were successful but this was overturned by the High Court of Australia. Had the decision been upheld by the High Court it would have exposed the members of the IRFB to thousands of claims.

LIABILITY OF GOVERNING BODIES

In the case of *Agar v Hyde* above, the IRFB was not held liable for injuries sustained by the two claimants. However, in the case of *Watson v British Boxing Board of Control*, the defendant was held liable for the injuries sustained by a boxer.[78] The referee stopped the fight in the final round when Watson appeared to be unable to defend himself. Watson had sustained a brain haemorrhage and lapsed into unconsciousness. It took 7 minutes for the doctor to get to the ring and a further 25–30 minutes before Watson arrived at the hospital. By the time he got there, he had sustained serious brain damage.

The British Boxing Board of Control (BBBC) is the sole controlling body that regulates boxing in the United Kingdom.[79] All fighters, clubs, agents, match-makers and any person involved in the sport of boxing must obtain a licence from the BBBC. The BBBC argued that it did not owe Watson a duty of care. The BBBC further argued that, had the necessary medical equipment and personnel been there on time, it would not have made any difference given the nature of the injuries sustained. Although the BBBC were not directly involved in the fight (i.e. there was no contractual involvement), it was held to be negligent

---

'The Referee's Liability for Catastrophic Injuries – A UK Perspective' (2005) 15(2) *Marquette Sports Law Review* 415–424, notes (at 423) that in cases where there is an undercurrent of violence and the referee fails to assert his authority to prevent certain incidents, a player could take an action against the opponent who caused the injury and the referee for failing to exert adequate control over the match.

[76] (2000) 201 CLR 552; (2000) 74 ALJR 1219; (2000) ATR 81–569.

[77] Both players were left as quadriplegics.

[78] [2001] 2 WLR 1256.

[79] The BBBC is not a statutory body. Counsel for the BBBC argued that liability should not be imposed as the BBBC was not a profit-making organisation and did not carry insurance. However, Lord Philips MR rejected this contention and said it was irrelevant.

in not providing immediate resuscitation at the ring side. As the BBBC had sanctioned the fight, the court held that to be sufficient proximity between Watson and the BBBC.

CIVIL LIABILTY AND COACHES

Like referees and players, coaches can attract civil liability. Coaches owe a duty of care to those they coach, manage or instruct, and if it is found that they have fallen below the standard of care required, liability will be imposed. As with participants and referees, the extent of the duty varies from case to case. In most situations, a coach cannot be deemed to guarantee playing success or safety of the sportsperson under their pupilage, save in situations where it is reasonable to have such an expectation. For example, in some sports that carry inherent dangers, the coach is required to teach the techniques necessary to play the sport safely and to demonstrate how the game should be played to minimise injury.

The main duties of the coach can be summarised as follows:

- The coach must ensure a player is fit to play and play in position in which he or she is picked
- The coach must ensure proper warm-ups, avoid excessive or dangerous training regimes and should not encourage the use of dietary supplements or banned substances
- If the coach confirms the safety of the equipment, then the player should be able to rely on that assertion. If it transpires that the equipment was not safe, this will generate a duty of care on the part of the coach
- Coaching sessions should be run in a manner that does not expose participants to unreasonable risks, or to such risks which could be avoided by conducting the session in a different manner
- It must be recognised that not all risks can be avoided; it is inevitable that accidents will happen
- The coach must act reasonably; this will depend on the age,[80] skill, size and experience of the participant and the nature of the sport[81]

---

[80] There is a higher duty of care owed to children in sport: the coach is said to be *in loco parentis*, which means 'in the place of the parent'. It refers to the legal responsibility placed on an adult who is not the parent of the child but assumes a duty, given the relationship between him or her and the child. The Irish Sports Council has a number on publications on child protection in sport on its website: <http://www.irishsports-council.ie/Participation/Code_of_Ethics/> (last accessed 12 March 2010).

[81] See *Morrell v Owen*, *The Times*, 14 December 1993. The court held that a higher duty

- The coach must ensure that sub-coaches are reasonably competent
- The coach must provide appropriate medical care should the need arise
- The coach should prevent injured athletes from competing
- The coach must ensure, where appropriate, necessary forms have been filled out by the athlete (for example, doping forms)
- The coach is precluded from including a term in a contract where he or she guarantees results[82]
- The coach must keep up to date with the latest developments in coaching and must attend courses
- A coach should not encourage aggressive play[83]

In *Brady v Sunderland FC* the former Irish international Kieron Brady brought an action in contract and negligence against his club on the grounds that the coach and the physiotherapist had failed to diagnose and take seriously his complaint of serious leg pains.[84] Buckley J dismissed the claim, finding that the club was not in breach of contract nor had it breached its duty of care owed to the player. He admitted that the manager's attitude in instructing the player to continue with the training session was 'robust' but this could not be equated with negligence. On appeal, the Court of Appeal upheld Buckley J's decision.

CIVIL LIABILITY AND INSTRUCTORS AND GUIDES

The case of *Woodroffe-Hedley v Cuthbertson* is the leading authority on the duty of care owed by professional instructors to their clients.[85] Cuthbertson was a qualified guide and experienced mountaineer. He was paid £500 by Hedley to escort Hedley on a climb on the Mont Blanc Massif. During their ascent, Cuthbertson feared that the ice would melt as there had been some sun so he decided it would be prudent to move towards an area in the shade in case the ice melted and caused rocks to fall.

---

of care is owed by coaches and organisers to disabled people because of their special needs. In this case the disabled archer was struck by a discus on the temple, which caused permanent brain damage. Both events, archery and the discus-throwing event, were taking place in the same hall and were separated by a curtain. The plaintiff successfully sued the organisers and coaches.

[82] However, it is improbable that an athlete could claim that improper coaching affected his or her playing potential.

[83] A coach could be held criminally liable if he or she encourages such violence in breach of the rules of the game.

[84] [1998] EWCA Civ 1780.

[85] (1997), QBD, unreported.

According to established mountain-climbing practice, when two climbers are connected two screws are inserted into the ice as an anchor and an intermediary point between the two climbers should be created (called a running belay) to lessen the strain. Cuthbertson only inserted one screw and did not set up the running belay. A large sheet of ice broke away causing Cuthbertson to slip and, as the lead climber, he dragged Hedley, who was connected to him. The sole screw could not hold the weight of both men. Hedley fell and was killed. Cuthbertson suffered minor injuries. The Court of Appeal held that Cuthbertson was negligent and that he breached the standard expected of a reasonably competent and careful Alpine guide.[86]

REFORM

There are a number of ways in which a sport can regulate itself so as to avoid costly litigation in the courts. Match officials should take better control of games and interpret the rules properly, as Gardiner notes: '...better a man with a whistle regulating the game than a man with a wig.'[87] Soccer could benefit from the better utilisation of the linesmen, like in rugby. In rugby there are two touch judges who have greater powers to assist the referee than their linesmen counterparts in soccer.[88] In cricket there is a third umpire who sits in the stand and watches the match on a monitor. Tackles from behind in football could be banned and the penalties imposed for infractions of the rules could be increased, for example, in football a red card now not only means an automatic sending off but also a three-match ban.[89]

Often players or participants seek redress in the courts if a sport does not have an adequate compensation scheme. If sports had appropriate compensation schemes and players were properly insured, this would also reduce the need for the intervention of the courts.

---

[86] For a more detailed discussion on this case, see J. Fulbrook, *Outdoor Activities, Negligence and the Law* (Aldershot: Ashgate, 2005), at 132–134. See also, *Affiong Day v High Performance Sports Ltd* [2003] EWHC 197 (QBD). Here liability was not attached as the plaintiff, an experienced climber, had not tied her ropes properly. Her father brought the case against the manager of the leisure centre but lost. The court held that the actions of the defendant were reasonable.
[87] Gardiner and Felix, 'Juridification of the Football Field', at 216.
[88] *Ibid.*
[89] James, *Sports Law*, at 75.

CONCLUSION

The law of tort covers a wide range of issues. Some of the issues are relevant to sport, particularly the liability of participants, referees, coaches, instructors and governing bodies. With regard to participants, a player is under a duty to take all reasonable care taking account of the circumstances. The standard is objective; it is based on the reasonable person rather than the individual defendant. Liability will not attach in situations where there is an error or lapse of judgment. Something more serious is required for the defendant to be held liable. The threshold for liability is high and thus very difficult to reach. While some plaintiffs have been successful, in many of the cases the plaintiff has been unable to demonstrate that the defendant breached the relevant standard of care.

Referees may be subject to liability. However, the courts have given some latitude to volunteer referees. As referees may be held liable, it was feared that volunteer referees would be less likely to offer their services for fear of potential litigation. The element of control is an important factor in these cases. A referee must ensure that the rules of the game are properly adhered to as failure to do so may expose him or her to liability.

Coaches have a number of duties. They must keep up to date with developments and ensure that players or athletes do not compete while injured. The coach must not encourage an athlete to take prohibited substances or be aggressive on the field of play. Guides and instructors owe a duty of care to a client and the relevant standard of care is that of a reasonably competent and careful instructor or guide. Sports such as mountain climbing carry inherent risks (normal hazards) but climbers are not said to assume the risk of their instructor acting negligently. A client is entitled to rely on the expertise of a guide and it is the role of the guide to minimise the risk of injury or death.

CHAPTER 5

Drug Testing and Gender Testing in Sport

INTRODUCTION

Participation in sport is viewed as a privilege and not a right. Sports governing bodies are private organisations that create their own rules and regulations. Elite athletes accept that certain rules and regulations, while being somewhat invasive, are a basic part of their profession. Drug testing has become an integral part of both amateur and professional sport over the last few decades. It is viewed as a fundamental component of maintaining the element of fairness in sport. Drug testing also serves to protect the athlete's health and endeavours to ensure that the image of the sport is not undermined by allegations of drug use.[1]

HISTORY OF DRUGS IN SPORT

The use of drugs in sport is not a recent phenomenon but rather the 'modern manifestation of an old, perhaps even ancient, difficulty'.[2] The use of drugs in sport can be traced back to the third century where athletes in Ancient Greece were reported to have taken substances to enhance their performance.[3] At the Olympic Games of 668 BC it was

---

[1] The relationship between the athlete and the governing body is one of contract and the prohibition of banned substances is an implied term of that contract. Athletes are bound by the rules of their club, which in turn is bound by the national body, which in turn is bound by the international governing body of the sport. By taking a banned substance the athlete is in breach of the rules of the sport. See S. Gardiner *et al.*, *Sports Law* (3rd ed., London: Cavendish Publishing, 2006), at 288.
[2] C.L. Dubin, *Commission of Inquiry into the Use of Drugs and Banned Substances Intended to Increase Athletic Performance* (Ottawa: Canadian Government Publishing Centre, 1990), at 9.
[3] M. Verroken, 'Drug Use and Abuse in Sport' in *Drugs In Sport* (ed. D. Mottram) (2nd ed., London: E & FN Spon, 1996), 18–55, at 18.

claimed that the winner of the 200-metre sprint, Charnis, had been on a special diet of dried figs in order to enhance his performance.[4]

In the mid to late nineteenth century, cocaine and opium were considered to have medicinal properties. These drugs were commonly used in the United States and Britain.[5] By the early twentieth century, the dangers of these drugs became apparent and the British Government enacted the Dangerous Drugs Act in 1920. This Act limited the availability of cocaine and opium to prescription only. The International Association of Athletics Federation (IAAF) in 1928 became the first international federation to ban the use of stimulating substances. Scientists in the 1930s were able to isolate the male hormone testosterone.[6] By the late 1940s, bodybuilders in the United States were using hormones in their endeavours to increase stamina and strength. The Soviet Union weightlifting team resorted to similar measures in the 1950s. Amphetamines were developed to combat fatigue among soldiers during World War II. After the war, amphetamines found a new use among cyclists. It was not until the 1960s that drugs became increasingly associated with modern sport. Danish cyclist Knud Jensen collapsed during a race and died shortly afterwards in a hospital in Rome in August 1960. Tests revealed the presence of amphetamines in Jensen's body.[7]

In the aftermath of Jensen's death, drug use in sport became highly topical.[8] There were rumours of drug use and gender fraud among athletes. In response, the International Olympic Committee (IOC) became the first sporting organisation to establish a Medical Commission (in 1967) that was entrusted with the task of policing the use of banned substances and of verifying gender. In 1968 the IOC carried out drug and gender tests at the Olympic Games in Mexico City.

During the 1970s, allegations of drug use among athletes were rife. Dr Robert Voy, a former chief medical officer with the United States

---

[4] M. Finlay and H. Plecket, *The Olympic Games: The First Thousand Years* (London: Chatto and Windus, 1976). See also P. Lenehan, *Anabolic Steroids and Other Performance-Enhancing Drugs* (London: Taylor and Francis, 2003), at 61.

[5] D.F. Musto, 'Opium, Cocaine and Marijuana in American History' (1991) 265(1) *Scientific American*, 40–47.

[6] E.J. Bird and G.G. Wagner, 'Sport as a Common Property Resource' (1997) 41(6) *Journal of Conflict Resolution* 750–766.

[7] It was announced that Jensen had died of sunstroke. Two of his team mates were also brought to hospital.

[8] In 1886 Arthur Linton, a Welsh cyclist, died from allegedly ingesting strychnine. It was reported that he died from typhoid fever. His coach was banned from sport after it was claimed that his coach had administered the strychnine.

Olympic Committee, wrote of his experience at the Olympic Games. He concluded that 'instead of being a competition and celebration for the human, the Olympics have in some ways become a mere proving ground for scientists, chemists and unethical physicians.'[9] During the 1970s, there were concerns about the change in appearance of some of the female athletes. As will be discussed in the section on gender testing (below), doubt was cast upon the femininity of some of the elite female athletes. It led one commentator to remark, 'anyone looking at these "women" would be hard pressed to remember in them the girl next door (unless you lived next door to the New York Jets of course).'[10]

Throughout the 1980s and 1990s performance enhancing drugs continued to infiltrate sport.[11] In the 1988 Olympic Games in Seoul, Canadian athlete Ben Johnson broke the world 100 metres record in a time of 9.79 seconds and won the Olympic title. Johnson tested positive for the banned substance stanozolol and was stripped of his medal.[12] The positive result and subsequent ban shocked the world as it was (mistakenly) believed that doping was a problem associated with Eastern European countries. As a direct result of Johnson's positive test, the Dubin Commission was established to investigate the use of drugs in sport. The Commission, headed by Charles L. Dubin, was convened in Canada in 1988–1989 to discuss the widespread use of drugs in sport and the methods employed in detecting prohibited substances. Evidence was heard from 122 witnesses, with 48 athletes including Johnson admitting that they had used prohibited substances. The commission found that doping was rife in the higher levels of sport. Cox *et al.* note that the period following the report saw the beginnings of the first period of intense anti-doping practices within sport and at government level.[13]

In 2004, a number of high profile scandals emerged. A number of elite athletes were found to have links with a Californian laboratory,

---

[9] *Drugs, Sport and Politics* (Champaign, IL: Leisure Press, 1991), at xv. He refers to the 1976 Games in Montreal where the head of the East German swimming team was asked about the deep voices of the female swimmers. The official sardonically replied: 'We have come here to swim, not to sing.'

[10] B. Goldman, *Death in the Locker Room* (South Bend: Icarus Press, 1984).

[11] The Council of Europe Convention on Doping is an international convention on doping, which was opened for signatories in November 1989. It has been ratified by 50 states, including Ireland. For more details, see: <http://www.coe.int/t/dg4/sport/Doping/convention_en.asp> (last accessed 24 June 2010).

[12] See Chapter 6 on restraint of trade for a more detailed discussion on the case of Johnson.

[13] N. Cox, A. Schuster and C. Costello, *Sport and the Law* (Dublin: First Law, 2004), at 83.

BALCO (Bay Area Laboratory Cooperative), after a syringe containing a mysterious substance was sent to the United States Anti-Doping Agency (USADA). The substance was identified as the designer drug THG (Tetrahydrogestrinone), which had been heretofore undetectable. Following an investigation, a number of Olympic champions were found to have taken testosterone, human growth hormones and THG.[14] Dwain Chambers and Linford Christie were among those who admitted to having used these designer drugs. The American athlete Marion Jones, who had won five medals at the Sydney Olympics, was found to have lied to a grand jury during the investigation and was sentenced to six months in prison in 2008. Jones was forced to return the five medals. She was also banned for two years from competing in track and field athletics.

The Athens Olympics in 2004 were not without controversy. Two Greek athletes, Kostas Kenteris and Katerina Thanou, had evaded testing before the Games and it was claimed that a motorbike accident had prevented them from providing a test. The two athletes did not compete in the Olympics and the IAAF provisionally banned the two athletes for two years pending disciplinary proceedings. The athletes eventually admitted the offence and were banned for two years. The IAAF had sent the case to the Court of Arbitration (CAS); on both parties reaching a settlement, the CAS allowed for the case to be withdrawn in November 2006.

At the Beijing Games in 2008, six athletes were found to have committed doping infractions. However, a number of other positive tests were recorded when 948 samples were re-tested after new testing technologies were developed by the French anti-doping agency. Five athletes were found to have CERA (Continuous Erythropoietin Receptor Activator) in their B sample.[15] The new technology was also used to detect the use of insulin by non-diabetic athletes. CERA is a new version of Erythropoietin (EPO), which enables the blood to carry more oxygen, leading to the athlete having greater endurance.

---

[14] Jason Giambi, the New York Yankees star batter, initially denied using performance enhancing drugs. He was also implicated in the BALCO scandal. Fraud charges were brought against him, with Giambi admitting to a federal grand jury that he injected HGH and used steroids. See M. Fainaru-Wada and L. Williams, 'Giambi Admitted Taking Steroids', *San Francisco Chronicle*, 2 December 2004 (available online: <http://www.sfgate.com/cgi-bin/article.cgi?f=/c/a/2004/12/02/BALCO.TMP>, last accessed 12 April 2010).
[15] 'Positive Beijing Tests Confirmed', *BBC Sport*, 9 July 2009 (available online: <http://news.bbc.co.uk/sport2/hi/olympic_games/8024828.stm>, last accessed 10 April 2010).

WHY ARE DRUGS BANNED?

The use of drugs, performance enhancing or recreational, can compromise the health of the athlete. Recreational drugs are illegal under the law of the land.[16] The prohibition of drugs ensures a level playing field as it dissuades the use of performance enhancing drugs and it punishes those who use such drugs. Drugs also tarnish the image of the sport. Some drugs are not illegal but are banned as they give an athlete an unfair advantage. Performance enhancing implies that the individual already has skill and ability, but by taking a drug the athlete will be able to reach his or her full potential.[17]

Gardiner contends that drugs are banned due to the paternalistic nature of the governing bodies.[18] It is easy to understand the paternal nature of the governing bodies if minor athletes or children are involved but it is more difficult to justify when it comes to adults.[19] The governing bodies are somewhat inconsistent. If they care about the health of their athletes then they should have a rule that prevents an athlete competing while injured, or they should review sports, including gymnastics, in which there is a high level of arthritis and other diseases among participants in later life.[20]

As stated, drugs are banned as they are a form of cheating and thus constitute an unfair advantage. However, competitive sport is all about one athlete being better than another.[21] Some athletes have a natural advantage, whether it is a physical advantage such as height, or a technological advantage in the form of superior training facilities or diet.[22] Equally, a competitor in bobsledding from Canada has an advantage over a competitor from Ireland. There are merits in these arguments, but the fact remains that performance enhancing drugs are not natural. Athletes could be forced to take them by a coach or a trainer. Drugs undermine the sport and are contrary to the principles of fair play.

It is important to note that there is no single list of prohibited substances automatically applicable to every sport. The World Anti-Doping

---

[16] Some argue that recreational drugs should not be of concern to the sporting bodies. See R. Welch, 'A Snort and a Puff: Recreational Drugs and Discipline in Professional Sport' in *Drugs and Doping in Sport* (ed. J. O'Leary) (London: Cavendish, 2001) 75–90, at 88.

[17] Gardiner *et al.*, *Sports Law*, at 287.

[18] *Ibid.*, at 288–291.

[19] *Ibid.*, at 288.

[20] *Ibid.*, at 288–289.

[21] *Ibid.*, at 286.

[22] *Ibid.*

Agency list (see below) can be adapted to suit the individual sport. Some categories of substances would not be an issue for certain sports. Each sporting federation drafts its own list of prohibited substances. Taking alcohol as an example – alcohol is prohibited in competition only in the following sports: karate, archery, automobile sports, aeronautic sports, modern pentathlon (for disciplines including shooting), motorcycling, nine-pin and ten-pin bowling, and power boating. Beta blockers, which regulate the heart, are prohibited in certain sports, including archery, bobsledding, gymnastics, curling, golf, shooting and power boating.[23]

THE WORLD ANTI-DOPING AGENCY

Until the WADA Code, there was a lack of uniformity when it came to a list of banned substances. The IOC had a list but it was only operational during the Summer and Winter Games. Many sports adopted the IOC list but its shortcomings were well documented. In 1998 a number of positive tests in the Tour de France astounded the sporting world. The IOC was troubled by the fact that various sports bodies and international federations had different definitions of doping, different sanctions and different procedures. The test results in the Tour de France accentuated the need for a new approach to doping.

The IOC held a World Conference on Doping in Sport in 1999 where it called for more cohesion between the national governing bodies (NGBs), the IFs and the IOC, as each organisation had different approaches to doping. As a result, their anti-doping code was revised and a new body, the World Anti-Doping Agency (WADA), a Swiss-based private company that operates under Swiss law with its headquarters in the Canadian city of Montreal, was established to enforce the provisions of the revised code.

WADA set about establishing a universal anti-doping code that would consolidate the doping rules of the various sporting organisations. Out of this came the World Anti-Doping Code, a code that has been accepted by the various IFs, 205 national olympic committees and 193 countries. In Ireland, the code is enforced by the Irish Sports Council (ISC).[24] As many governments cannot be legally bound by a non-governmental document, the code was implemented by way of

---

[23] For a full list see <http://www.wada-ama.org>.
[24] Since 2008, Ireland is also a party to the UNESCO Anti-Doping Convention. The then Minister for Arts, Sport and Tourism, Martin Cullen, ratified the Convention. All national governing bodies in receipt of public funding in Ireland are bound by the WADA Rules and the Council of Europe Anti-Doping Convention.

international treaty which the United Nations Educational, Scientific and Cultural Organisation (UNESCO) drafted. At the UNESCO International Convention against Doping in Sport in October 2005, the first global international treaty against doping in sport was adopted. In 2007, the UNESCO Convention came into effect.[25]

The Irish Sports Council updates its rules whenever amendments are made to the code. The code has been amended on a number of occasions since 2004. The latest version of it came into effect on 1 January 2009.[26] The list of prohibited substances is updated annually. The prohibited list which came into force on 1 January 2010 places pseudoephedrine back on banned list. Pseudoephedrine is commonly found in cold and flu remedies and was placed on the WADA Monitoring Program in 2004. This meant that it was removed from the banned list but would be monitored. If it was felt that the substance was being abused, it would be put back on the banned list. The 2010 list now provides that pseudoephedrine is prohibited when its concentration in urine is greater than 150 microgrammes per millilitre. Changes have also been introduced in relation to salbutamol, which is permitted at a level of under 1,000 nanogrammess per millilitre. Under the 2010 list, its use by inhalation will no longer require a therapeutic use exemption (TUE) but rather a simplified declaration of use. This measure will allow the handling of salbutamol by anti-doping organisations in a more cost-efficient way.[27]

The WADA Code operates according to the athlete whereabouts system. Under this system, elite athletes must provide their IF or their national anti-doping organisation (in Ireland this is the ISC) with information in regard to their whereabouts. Until 2009 athletes were required to select one hour per day, five days a week to be available for no-notice drug tests. These tests can take place at home or at the training ground. The Irish Sports Council has a registered testing pool (RTP),[28] which

---

[25] The IOC will only consider applications to hold the Olympic Games from countries that have ratified the UNESCO International Convention against Doping in Sport.

[26] The code can be accessed online at: <http://www.wada-ama.org/en/World-Anti-Doping-Program/Sports-and-Anti-Doping-Organizations/The-Code/> (last accessed 24 June 2010).

[27] See <http://www.irishsportscouncil.ie/Anti-Doping/TUEs_and_Medicines/> (last accessed 24 June 2010) for the ISC update on the therapeutic use exemption.

[28] Defined by WADA as: '[A] pool of top level athletes established separately by each International Federation (IF) and National Anti-Doping Organisation (NADO) who are subject to both in-competition and out-of-competition testing as part of that IF's or NADO's test distribution plan'. The glossary is available online at: <http://www.wada-ama.org/en/Anti-Doping-Community/Athletes-/Anti-Doping-Glossary/> (last accessed 5 July 2010).

includes the following competitors: elite athletes, those who have qualified for the Olympics and Paralympics, an athlete who is registered in the pool of their IF, athletes who have come back from retirement and were previously in a RPT, any athlete serving a period of ineligibility, and athletes in high risk sports as identified by the ISC. However, on 1 January 2009, this was extended to seven days a week and, unlike the previous system, athletes have to be available for the full hour.[29] The Belgian sports union has challenged the extension of time under Article 8 (right to privacy) of the European Convention on Human Rights. FIFPro (the worldwide representative organisation for all professional football players) has also argued that the extension of time is in breach of employment law provisions. If an athlete has to make themselves available 365 days a year, then this raises questions with regard to holiday entitlements.[30] However, WADA has continually defended the system and holds it to be in compliance with human rights legislation. The whereabouts code still remains a part of the WADA Code.

BANNED SUBSTANCES AND METHODS

Banned List

There are nine divisions of prohibited substances under the WADA Code:

1. Stimulants (in competition)
2. Narcotics (in competition)
3. Cannabinoids (in competition)
4. Anabolic agents (in and out of competition)
5. Peptide hormones (in and out of competition)
6. Beta-2 agonists (in and out of competition)
7. Agents with anti-estrogenic activity
8. Masking agents including diuretics (in and out of competition)
9. Glucocorticosteriods (in competition)

---

[29] WADA includes a question-and-answer section on the website in regard to the whereabouts system: <http://www.wada-ama.org/en/Resources/Q-and-A/Whereabouts/> (last accessed 24 June 2010). For an example of a whereabouts form, see the Athletics Ireland website: <http://www.athleticsireland.ie/content/wp-content/uploads/2009/01/Final%20Version%20-%20Filled%20in%20Version.pdf> (last accessed 10 April 2010). Rules 5.10 and 5.11 of the Irish Anti-Doping Rules 2009 provide detailed provisions on the whereabouts system.

[30] M. Slater, 'Legal Threat to Anti-Doping Code', *BBC Sport*, 22 January 2009 (available online: <http://news.bbc.co.uk/sport2/hi/front_page/7844918.stm>, last accessed 10 April 2010).

The banned list is updated annually. Peptide hormones include EPO and CERA. After peptide hormones it states 'and related substances'; this is to ensure that substances that are not expressly stated but have similar properties are also included. However, 'and related substances' is somewhat vague and it may be difficult to base a doping infraction on this.

In the Atlanta Olympics in 1996 five athletes tested positive for bromantan. Two of the athletes had won medals. When they were found to have committed a doping offence, the two athletes challenged the decision of the IOC before the Ad Hoc Division (AHD) of the CAS.[31] The athletes argued that bromantan was not a prohibited substance as it could only strengthen the immune system and help the athletes cope with the heat at the Games.[32] The IOC argued that the drug was a stimulant under the IOC Medical Code and, as such, would be classified as a banned substance although not expressly stated to be one. The AHD held in favour of the two athletes, opining that the drug could be classified as a stimulant in the future but in the present case the evidence adduced was not sufficient to warrant such a conclusion. Bromantan is now expressly prohibited.

Banned Methods

Doping is not confined to the taking of banned chemical drugs;[33] it also involves more complex scientific methods including blood doping. Blood doping involves the taking of blood out of the athlete's body, re-oxygenating it and pumping it back into the athlete's body.[34] Gene doping is a more recent method of doping and involves the non-therapeutic use of genes, genetic elements and/or cells that have the capacity to enhance athletic performance.

Technological Doping

Although not technically a form of doping, a recent development has been 'technological doping'. Swimming provides an illuminating example. For a number of years swimmers have worn very high-tech swimming suits. A second generation suit was launched in February

---

[31] CAS OG 1996/3-4 Andrei Korneev/IOC & Zakhar Gouliev/IOC.
[32] G. Zorpette, 'The Chemical Games' (2000) 283(3s) *Scientific American Presents, Quarterly* 16–17, at 21.
[33] Defined as pharmacological, chemical and physical manipulation.
[34] Defined as enhancing the transfer of oxygen by blood doping or the administration of products that enhance the uptake, transport or delivery of oxygen.

2008. The LZR Racer swimsuit was made of 100 per cent polyurethane and was impermeable. It was so tight it took up to forty minutes for the swimmer to get into the suit. The suit compressed muscle and added buoyancy. Some commentators claimed that the suits were performance enhancing. In support of this contention, it was found that 108 records set in two years could be attributed to the swimsuit. On 24 July 2009, the world governing body for swimming, FINA, banned the high-tech swimsuit. FINA tried to ban the swimsuits prior to World Championships in Rome in 2009. However, fearing legal action from some swimmers, it was decided to make the ban effective from January 2010. FINA now only allows suits made from 'textiles', including woven material. The swimsuit may not have any fastening devices such as a zipper (drawstrings on male jammers permitted). The ban on the LZR Racer applies only to World Championships and Olympic Games.

DRUG TESTING IN IRISH SPORT

The Irish Sports Council, as established by the Irish Sports Council Act, 1999, carries out drug testing in all Irish sport, both amateur and professional. The Act contains a provision on drug testing, establishing a doping control committee responsible for creating guidelines on drug testing procedures. Under section 6(1)(d) of the Act, the council is empowered 'to take such action as it considers appropriate, including testing, to combat doping in sport'. Section 18(3) of the Act provided for the creation of a:

> Committee to be known as the Anti-Doping Committee of the Irish Sports Council, to (a) assist and advise the Council in relation to the performance of its functions under section 6(1)(d), and (b) exercise such powers and carry out such duties relating to that function as the Council may from time to time delegate to the Committee.

Irish Sport Anti-Doping Disciplinary Panel

The Irish Sport Anti-Doping Disciplinary Panel was established in 2004. The panel is empowered to hear and determine the consequences of any anti-doping rule violation that falls under the Irish anti-doping rules. Three experts attend a panel hearing, one from a legal background, one from a medical background and one from a sports background. In total the panel consists of a chair and four vice-chairs, each of whom must be a registered solicitor or barrister not less than ten years qualified or a retired High Court or Supreme Court judge; five medical practitioners, each of whom must be qualified at least ten years; and five sports administrators or former athletes. Members serve a four-year term which is renewable.

The role of the panel is to hear cases fairly and impartially. When an athlete is alleged to have committed a doping infraction, the ISC refers the matter to the panel to determine whether a violation has occurred. None of the members of the panel can have had any prior involvement in the case, except in a situation where the chair has been involved in an appeal on a decision to impose a provisional suspension. If any member of the panel has been involved, they must notify the chair who will in turn appoint another member. At the hearing a representative of the ISC, WADA or the IF may attend. The standard of proof is whether the national governing body has established the anti-doping rule violation(s) to the comfortable satisfaction of the hearing panel, bearing in mind the seriousness of the allegation that is made. This standard of proof in all cases is greater than a mere balance of probability but less than proof beyond a reasonable doubt. In some cases, the ISC may, on the agreement of the governing body and the athlete, assist the governing body in presenting the case.

In rebutting the charges, the burden of proof on the athlete lies with the balance of probabilities, except as provided in Articles 10.3.2, 10.5.1 and/or 10.8.2 of the ISC Doping Code where the athlete must satisfy a higher burden of proof.[35] It is presumed that the sample was analysed

---

[35] Article 10.3.2 states: 'To justify any elimination or reduction, the *Participant* must produce corroborating evidence in addition to his or her word which establishes to the comfortable satisfaction of the hearing panel the absence of an intent to enhance sport performance or mask the *Use* of a performance enhancing substance. The *Participant's* degree of fault shall be the criterion considered in assessing any reduction of the period of *Ineligibility*.' Article 10.5.1 provides: 'If the *Irish Sport Anti-Doping Disciplinary Panel* determines in an individual case involving an anti-doping rule violation other than violations under Articles 2.7 and 2.8 that aggravating circumstances are present which justify the imposition of a period of *Ineligibility* greater than the standard sanction, then the period of *Ineligibility* otherwise applicable shall be increased up to a maximum of four (4) years unless the *Participant* can prove to the comfortable satisfaction of the hearing panel that he or she did not knowingly commit the anti-doping rule violation.' While Article 10.8.2 provides: 'Where a *Participant* who has been declared *Ineligible* violates the prohibition against participation during *Ineligibility* described in Article 10.8.1, the results of such participation shall be *disqualified* and the period of *Ineligibility* which was originally imposed shall start over again as of the date of the violation. The new period of *Ineligibility* may be reduced under Article 10.4.2 if the *Participant* establishes to the comfortable satisfaction of the *Irish Sport Anti-Doping Disciplinary Panel* that he or she bears *No Significant Fault or Negligence* for violating the prohibition against participation.'

properly in the WADA-accredited laboratory and in accordance with the International Standard for Laboratories. The athlete may rebut and argue that there was a deviation from the accepted standards and practices that caused an adverse analytical finding. In this situation, the burden is placed on the ISC to establish that such a departure did not cause the adverse analytical finding. The panel may draw adverse inferences in a situation where the athlete, who has been given reasonable notice, does not appear at the hearing, either in person or by telephone.

Hearings are held in private and are confidential unless the panel decides otherwise. The panel may conduct the hearing in person, by video or teleconference or by a mixture of the three. Each party has the right to be represented at the hearing. Each party has the right to present evidence, call witnesses, cross-examine witnesses[36] and avail of the services of an interpreter. The panel may request that documentation and other evidence be made available to the other party. If this is not complied with, the panel will take this into account when making its decision. The hearing will still go ahead in the absence of one of the parties. It may be adjoined or postponed and the panel may appoint an expert to advise them on any matter pertaining to the case.

The deliberations of the panel are private. There are no dissenting decisions. One decision is given. No member of the panel may abstain from giving a decision. The decision is written and dated and reasons for the decision are stated. If the ISC or WADA are not party to the proceedings, they are notified of the decision as soon as practicable. The decision is final and binding on all parties, however, it may be appealed subject to the conditions detailed in Article 13.

The national governing body, with the consent of the ISC, may use its own disciplinary panel to determine the case.[37] However, the national governing body is bound by the rules of the panel. If the ISC is of the opinion that the national governing body's disciplinary panel is not adhering to the rules and regulations, the agreement is rescinded and the matter is referred to the panel.

The Annual Anti-Doping Report

The most recent report is from 2008. According to the report, the ISC carried out 1,114 tests in 2008.[38] A total of 982 tests were completed

---

[36] Article 8.6.4: '(subject to the hearing panel's discretion to accept testimony by telephone, written statement or submission, whether by fax, email or other means)'.
[37] Article 8.8.
[38] The total in 2007 was 1,135.

under the national programme, which is the highest number of tests carried out since the establishment of the anti-doping programme. The council also completed 132 tests in 11 sports under the 'user pays' programme.[39] Thirty-seven sports were tested during 2008 and 60 per cent of the tests completed were out of competition tests.

Doping Rules and Procedures in Irish Sport

All national governing bodies are bound by the ISC's anti-doping rules. Participants, by virtue of their membership or affiliation with a national governing body, are bound by the anti-doping rules. The role of the governing body is to ensure that the relevant sport adheres to the anti-doping rules. The national governing body entrusts the ISC with doping control on its behalf. If an athlete is found to have committed a doping infraction, the case is heard and determined by Irish Sport Anti-Doping Disciplinary Panel. It may also be sent to the CAS. The rules also stipulate that an athlete may not initiate court proceedings 'that are inconsistent with the foregoing submission to the jurisdiction of the Irish Sport Anti-Doping Disciplinary Panel and CAS'.[40] It would be illegal and unconstitutional to oust the jurisdiction of the court in all circumstances. However, the courts insist that the athlete has exhausted all the internal disciplinary mechanisms within the sport before seeking redress in the courts.

A doping offence occurs when a prohibited substance is used or its use is attempted. An athlete who refused to provide a sample is also deemed to have committed a doping offence. Doping is defined as a strict liability offence. As long as a prohibited substance is found in the athlete's body, a doping infraction has occurred. It does not matter whether the substance was ingested accidentally or unknowingly, or that the athlete was negligent.[41] Once a prohibited substance is found in the blood or urine sample, a breach of the rules has been committed. The use of the principle of strict liability is in line with the provisions

---

[39] The European Rugby Cup and Irish Water Safety availed of the user pays system. Under the user pays system the governing body elects to have extra testing (outside that of the ISC) and pays for the tests itself. A number of sports availed of the user pays system in addition to tests carried out under the national programme. Among the sporting bodies which availed of dual testing were the Racquetball Association of Ireland, Triathlon Ireland, the Irish Hockey Association, the Irish Rugby Football Union, the Irish Hockey Association, Cycling Ireland and Athletics Ireland.

[40] Provided by Rule 1.2.2.5 of the Irish Anti-Doping Rules 2009 (available online: <http://www.irishsportscouncil.ie/Anti-Doping/Rules/Irish_Anti-Doping_Rules_2009/>, last accessed 24 June 2010).

[41] Rule 2.1.1. of the 2009 rules.

of the WADA Code. In general, if an individual is found to have a prohibited substance from a sample taken in competition, the results of the athlete for that competition are automatically rendered void. In some situations, the governing body may exercise flexibility when it comes to sanctions. If an athlete can demonstrate to the satisfaction of the disciplinary panel that the substance was ingested through no fault of the individual, the sanction may be reduced. The burden of proof is on the athlete.

Therapeutic Use Exemption (TUE)

It is also an offence for an athlete to be in possession of any prohibited method or substance in competition and out of competition.[42] However, if the athlete can establish that the possession falls under the therapeutic use exemption (TUE), then an offence has not been committed. If an athlete has a documented medical condition, he or she may apply for a TUE. If it is granted, it allows the athlete to ingest certain substances which ordinarily would expose them to a doping offence. The individual applies for a TUE from the ISC or the IF.[43] The ISC has a TUE Committee, which comprises three physicians.[44]

In late 2008 the GAA Anti-Doping Committee handed down a decision in the case of Kerry footballer Aidan O'Mahoney.[45] O'Mahoney was found to have exceeded the accepted therapeutic use exemption when he tested positive for salbutamol. The ISC permitted the GAA Disciplinary Committee to hear the case.[46] The player, an asthmatic, had been prescribed the medication in the form of an inhaler. The GAA decided not to ban the player but to give him a warning and reprimand. New WADA rules provide for the principle of *lex mitior* which

---

[42] It is also an offence to administer or attempt to administer or traffic a prohibited substance or method.

[43] Rule 4.1.5 refers to international-level athletes. International-level athletes may only obtain a TUE from their IF or in accordance with the rules of their IF. Other athletes who are competing in an international event may be required to seek a TUE from an IF or a major event organisation. Each IF shall publish a list of international events for which a TUE is required, either from that IF, or in accordance with its rules.

[44] For rules relating to the application procedure, see Rule 4.3; the criteria for granting a TUE, see Rule 4.4; criteria for granting the TUE retrospectively, see Rule 4.5; the expiration of the TUE, see Rule 4.6; and for a review of the decision in relation to the TUE, see Rule 4.7.

[45] For a discussion of the main changes introduced by the 2009 WADA Code and a commentary on the O'Mahoney case, see 'O'Mahoney Has Provisional Drug Suspension Lifted', *Irish Examiner*, 22 November 2008 (available online: <http://archives.tcm.ie/irishexaminer/2008/11/22/story78158.asp>, last accessed 11 April 2010).

[46] Under Article 8.8 of the Anti-Doping Rules.

permits the committee to hand down a sanction which is more favourable to the player.

Testing

Testing can take place either in competition or out of competition. If the event is taking place at national level, the ISC initiates and directs the collection of samples. If it is an international event, the international organisation that is the ruling body for the event initiates and directs the collection of the samples, subject to the right of the ISC to initiate and conduct the testing.[47] The following organisations are permitted to initiate out-of-competition testing: WADA, the ISC, the IF, the IOC or the Olympic Council of Ireland (OCI) and the Paralympic Council of Ireland (PCI), and any other anti-doping organisation that has jurisdiction over the athlete.[48] The ISC may conduct out-of-competition testing on any competitor up to 12 hours before the event.

Minors may be tested with the express permission of their parents or guardians. The parents or guardians, in permitting the minor to participate in the sport, have been deemed to consent to testing.

An athlete, if selected for testing, is required to sign the notification form and must inform the tester if he or she is taking any medications. The athlete is asked to provide a urine sample. In some situations, blood, DNA or genomic profiling is carried out.[49] The athlete is asked by the doping control officer to choose a sealed bottle of water. The athlete may ask for a representative to accompany them while providing the urine sample. Sometimes blood samples are taken. Certain drugs, such as human growth hormone (HGH), are only detectable in blood samples. If an athlete's sample produces a positive result, the ISC will check to see if the individual has a TUE. If the athlete has a TUE for the substance in question, then the athlete may be subject to target testing. If the athlete does not have a TUE, the athlete, the relevant national governing body and the ISC Anti-Doping Disciplinary Panel are notified. The athlete has seven days to request the testing of the B sample. The athlete and/or a representative may attend the opening of the B sample. The athlete may also request a copy of the laboratory documentation package. The athlete has 14 days to admit to the anti-doping violation and the ISC and the Anti-Doping Disciplinary Panel decide

---

[47] Rule 5.5.2.
[48] There should be coordination between the various bodies so that athletes are not tested repeatedly.
[49] Rule 6.4.

the appropriate sanction. The athlete may deny the doping infraction. If the athlete neither admits nor denies the positive result, he or she is deemed to have committed a doping offence.

Once the A sample has been found to have an adverse analytical finding, the athlete is provisionally suspended pending a hearing.[50] If the B sample is found to have no adverse analytical finding, the suspension is removed and if the athlete is taking part in a competition or event, he or she will be reinstated. An athlete who is found to have committed a doping violation is entitled to an expedited hearing.[51]

Pre-Olympic Testing

In the months preceding the 2008 Olympics, the majority of the Olympic and Paralympic team members (with the exception of late qualifiers) were tested three times. The Anti-Doping Unit worked closely with the OCI and the PCI in the preparation of the Olympic team for Beijing, in particular in relation to education and adherence to the whereabouts system during the Games period. The unit also provided WADA with details of any missed tests which had arisen in the previous 18 months for any of the athletes on the Irish Olympic Team.

Availability for Testing

Article 2.4.1 of the Irish Anti-Doping Rules (2009) states:

> An Athlete shall be deemed to have committed an anti-doping rule violation under Article 2.4 if he or she commits a total of three (3) Whereabouts Failures, which may be any combination of Filing Failures and/or Missed Tests adding up to three (3) in total, within any eighteen (18) month period, irrespective of which Anti-Doping Organisation has declared each of the Whereabouts Failures in question.

Five athletes, four in athletics and one in bobsledding and skeleton (a type of tobogganing sport) received a first warning. One athlete (in athletics) received a second formal warning due to unavailability for testing.

Violations in 2008

The ISC worked with the laboratory in King's College London from 1999 to 2008. The council entered a contract with the WADA accredited laboratory in Cologne in January 2008.

---

[50] Article 7.6.1.
[51] Article 7.6.6.

Four athletes were found to have committed doping infractions. A rower tested positive in competition for cannabinoids, resulting in reprimand and a three-week suspension. A member of the Irish Martial Arts Commission (IMAC) received a three-month suspension for failing to give a sample (out of competition). Two other athletes, one in rugby and one in the GAA, positively tested for beta-2 agonist. The rugby player received a reprimand and warning; the GAA player was reprimanded.

Sanctions for Doping Violations

If an athlete fails an in-competition test, any results, titles, medals or points from the competition or event are forfeited.[52] If the athlete establishes that the doping violation was due to no fault or negligence on their part, the results of other competitions are not forfeited unless it was likely that the results were affected by the doping violation. Where an athlete forfeits the results, medals, points and titles, an opponent whose placing is now affected by the doping violation is not entitled to an adjustment in their results unless provision is made for such adjustment in the rules of the IF or in the applicable event or competition rules. All prize money is forfeited and used to reimburse the ISC. The IF rules may provide that the money is to be allocated to other athletes. If so, the ISC is bound by this. If not, whatever money is left over after the ISC has been reimbursed will be allocated in accordance with the IF's rules.

An athlete may be suspended for two years in the case of a first violation. This may be reduced or increased depending on the circumstances.[53] A two-year suspension is imposed on athletes who fail or refuse to give a sample without any justification (Article 2.3 of the Irish Anti-Doping Rules) and those who are found to have tampered or attempted to tamper with any part of the doping control (Article 2.5). For athletes who violate the whereabouts rule (Article 2.4), the penalty is a minimum of one year's to a maximum of two years' suspension, depending on the athlete's degree of fault. An athlete who traffics or attempts to traffic a prohibited substance or method faces a four-year to lifetime ban. A four-year to lifetime ban is also applicable to someone who administers or attempts to administer to an athlete in competition or out of competition any prohibited method or prohibited substance,

---

[52] Article 9.
[53] If there are aggravating factors, the ineligibility may be increased to four years. See Article 10.5.

or assists, encourages, aids, abets, covers up or is involved in any other type of anti-doping rule violation or any attempted violation. The four-year to lifetime ban can be eliminated or reduced in exceptional circumstances, for example, through no significant fault or negligence the athlete admits a doping violation before having received notice of a sample analysis.

Where an individual has given substantial assistance to the ISC or another anti-doping organisation, criminal authority or professional disciplinary body in discovering and establishing doping violations, the sanction may also be reduced.[54] If an athlete can establish two or more of the exceptional circumstances, the ban may be reduced to one-quarter of the period of ineligibility.[55] For a second violation, the period of ineligibility can be reduced or increased depending on the factors outlined in relation to the first violation. There is a chart provided in the Irish Anti-Doping Rules under Article 10.6.1, which provides the appropriate sanctions. For a third violation, the sanctions (depending on the circumstances) can range from eight years to a lifetime ban.

Any athlete who is suspended may not take part in any competition or event during the currency of their suspension. If an athlete participates in a competition or an event, the period of ineligibility starts over again from the date of violation.[56]

Article 11 details the sanctions for team sports where more than one member has been found to have committed a doping infraction. Article 12 provides for sanctions for national governing bodies, which may result in the ISC withdrawing financial and non-financial support. Article 13 provides for the grounds of appeal and appeal procedures from a decision made by the panel. Article 14 outlines the role of the ISC in reporting the granting of the TUE of an athlete to the IF, national governing body and WADA;[57] in reporting to WADA, the applicable national governing body and any other relevant anti-doping agency of whereabouts failures; in reporting to WADA all tests carried out on athletes in and out of competition in the registered testing pool; in reporting information concerning adverse analytical findings and other alleged anti-doping rule violations; in reporting compliance with the WADA code; and the publishing of statistics. The ISC is required, 20 days after the hearing, to publish the name of the athlete who was found

[54] See Article 10.4.3.
[55] Article 10.4.5.
[56] Article 10.8.2.
[57] Article 14.1: '...except where the granted TUE is in relation to an Athlete who is not included in the Irish Sports Council Registered Testing Pool'.

to have committed a doping offence.[58] If the athlete is found not to have committed an offence, he or she may request that his or her name is not published. A summary of the decision may be published.

National Legislation and Doping

Many European countries make the use of certain prohibited substances a criminal offence. Denmark, France, Germany, the Netherlands, Spain and Sweden have national legislation prohibiting doping in sport.[59] In Ireland there is no national legislation that criminalises the use of performance enhancing drugs in sport. However, Anderson argues that the introduction of legislation that would make it a criminal offence for an athlete and others involved in sport to use EPO and growth hormones (save for licensed clinical requirements) would be a 'definitive statement of this State's attitude to doping in sport'.[60]

CONSTITUTIONAL RIGHTS AND DRUG TESTING IN IRELAND

Drug testing is generally accepted by athletes as an integral part of life. As long as the relevant anti-doping agency and governing body do not deviate from the established rules and practices, the testing methods and procedures are not challenged. Traditionally, the public law was loath to interfere in the decisions of sporting tribunals. Participation in sport is seen as a privilege and not a right and governing bodies are private organisations which can create their own rules and regulations. Some athletes have challenged the determinations of governing bodies on the grounds of fair procedures and due process;[61] others have argued that the imposition of lengthy suspensions is an unreasonable restraint of trade.[62] The principle of strict liability has been challenged on the grounds that the athlete's right to the presumption of innocence has been denied.

The Right to Privacy

Article 40.3.3 of the Irish Constitution contains a number of unenumerated rights that have been developed by the courts over the past forty

---

[58] Article 15.
[59] The national legislation is listed on the WADA website (<http://www.wada-ama.org>).
[60] J. Anderson, 'Ignorance of the Law is No Defence', *Irish Times*, 18 December 2004, at 3.
[61] *Quirke v Bord Lúthchleas na hÉireann* (1988) IR 83; (1989) ILRM 129 is discussed in Chapter 8.
[62] This is discussed in Chapter 6.

years. The first case to explore the limitations of this article was *Ryan v The Attorney General*,[63] where the court held that the right to bodily integrity was an unenumerated right as guaranteed by the Constitution. While identifying these rights the courts have always viewed them in light of the 'spirit of the Constitution'. As societal attitudes in Ireland began to change, so too did the court's interpretation of the Constitution. The right to marital privacy was evoked in *McGee*,[64] where it was held by Walsh J that the 'legislature is not free to encroach unjustifiably upon the fundamental rights of individuals or of the family in the name of common good'.[65] By 1987 in *Kennedy v Ireland*[66] this right to marital privacy was extended to include the right to individual privacy, but Hamilton P concluded this right is 'not an unqualified one. Its exercise may be restricted by the constitutional rights of others, by the requirements of the common good and is subject to the requirements of public order and morality.'[67]

As of yet, no Irish court has been called upon to reside over a privacy case involving a sportsperson. As sportspersons are required to urinate in the presence of an official, it raises questions about the level of privacy an athlete can expect. Most professional athletes accept that drug testing is an integral part of the sport and by taking part in a sport they are bound by the rules and regulations of that sport. There have been a few cases in the United States where collegiate and high school athletes challenged the drug-testing policies of their respective colleges or schools. These cases show that the courts are willing to uphold the drug-testing policies on the grounds that they are in the interests of the health and well-being of the student athletes.[68] In *Acton*, the parents of school athletes were required to consent to the random drug testing of their children.[69] If parents refused to consent the student was deemed

---

[63] *Ryan v AG* [1965] IR 294.
[64] *McGee v The Attorney General* [1974] IR 284.
[65] *Ibid.*, at 308.
[66] [1987] IR 587.
[67] *Ibid.*, at 592.
[68] See L. Donnellan, 'The Right to Privacy and Drug Testing: An Irish Perspective' (2002) 10(5) *Sports Law Administration and Practice*, 11–15. See *University of Colorado v Derdeyn* 863 P. 2d 929 (Colo. 1993). In this case, the university drug-testing policy was challenged as it not only tested student athletes but also the cheerleaders, student trainers and managers. The court was of the opinion that the testing was not voluntary and not supported by reasonable suspicion. See also *Hill v NCAA* (1994) 7 Cal. 4th 1; S. Ct of California, 865 P. 2d 633 (Cal. 1994); 18 Cal. App. 4th 1290; 273 Cal. Rptr 402; 1990 Cal. App.
[69] *Vernonia School Dist 47J v Wayne Acton*, 115 S. Ct 2386 (1995).

ineligible to participate in school athletics. Wayne Acton's parents refused on the grounds that it violated their son's constitutional rights under the Fourth[70] and Fourteenth Amendments. The court was of the opinion that, contrary to what the parents believed, there are times when a warrant is impracticable and a 'search unsupported by probable cause' does not render the procedure unconstitutional.[71] Drawing on *Hill* (see note 68), the court (Justice Scallia giving the majority opinion) held that when an athlete chooses to join a team they 'voluntarily subject themselves to a degree of regulation even higher than that imposed on students generally'.[72] The court was of the opinion that the school was acting *in loco parentis* and was only carrying out the random testing for the health and protection of the children. Not only did the court find the urinalysis a minimal intrusion but also that high school students 'have a diminished expectation of privacy in comparison to other individuals'.[73]

The decision in *Acton* caused much disquiet among academics.[74] To many, it signalled the erosion of collegiate athletes' constitutional right to privacy. It was felt that collegiate athletes had fewer rights than their non-sporting counterparts. To sporting enthusiasts the decision spelt the demise of the Bill of Rights, a document once revered for its liberating qualities. While it was thought that there was nowhere to go after *Acton*, the decision in *Todd* further eroded high school athletes' right to privacy.[75] In *Todd*, the court deliberated on the right to privacy of school athletes.[76] Citing *Acton*, the court held that 'the linchpin of this drug testing program is to protect the health of the student involved'[77] and where the school is confronted with disruptive behaviour, which is damaging the school principles, then it is reasonable for it to step in and carry out such testing.[78]

---

[70] The Fourth Amendment concerns the right against unreasonable searches and seizures by public officials.

[71] *Vernonia School Dist 47J v Wayne Acton*, 115 S. Ct 2386 (1995), at 2390.

[72] *Ibid.*, at 2392–2393.

[73] D. Jackson, 'The Constitution Expelled: What Remains of Students' Fourth Amendment Rights?' (1996) 28 *Arizona State Law Journal* 673–698, at 684.

[74] J.M. Ettman, 'Vernonia Case Comment: High School Students Lose Their Rights When They Don Their Uniforms' (1996–1997) 13 *New York Law School Journal of Human Rights* 625–662.

[75] *Todd v Rush County Schools and Ed Lyskowinski*, 133 F 3d 984 (7th Cir. 1998).

[76] It concerned other extra curriculum activities such as the Foreign Language Club and the Student Council.

[77] *Todd v Rush County Schools and Ed Lyskowinski*, 133 F 3d 984 (7th Cir. 1998), at 3.

[78] In 2001 a case similar to *Acton* came before the Tenth Circuit. In *Earls v Board of Education* F 3rd 1264, 1276 (10th Cir. 2001), the court rejected a 'suspicionless' drug-testing

In a number of states in the United States, student athletes and students who engage in extracurricular activities are randomly drug tested. While this has been challenged on numerous occasions, the courts continue to uphold the policies in the interest of student health. In United States high school and collegiate sport, drug testing has become an integral and accepted part of the student athlete's life; a similar development has yet to take place in Ireland. However, an Irish court, if ever countenanced with a privacy action taken by a student athlete, would perhaps uphold the drug testing policy on the basis of the common good.

Professional Athletes and Drug Testing

The reasons behind the drug policies of professional or elite sport are distinguishable from the motivations behind the drug policies in high school and collegiate sport. In cases relating to the latter, the courts have been motivated by the health and welfare of the students and the integrity of the game. Professional sport is motivated by profit.[79] The professional drug-testing policies have been the result of collective bargaining between owners and players' associations.[80] Thus, there have been very few cases brought by professional sportspersons on the grounds of privacy. The courts have been willing to uphold random drug testing in the employment sphere and once they find that employees have agreed to drug testing in collective bargaining agreements, the courts are prepared to hold that agreement as binding.[81]

STRICT LIABILITY

The WADA Code defines doping as a strict liability offence. Once an athlete's sample contains an adverse analytical finding, he or she is automatically deemed to have committed a doping infraction. However, the principle of strict liability seems to be at variance with the right to the presumption of innocence. The 2009 WADA Code allows for more flexibility when it comes to sanctions. If an athlete can

---

policy and held that participation in an activity does not erode a student's privacy expectations. However, the Supreme Court is unlikely to depart from its position. The Derdeyn case (see note 68 above) can be distinguished from *Acton* on the grounds that it was decided by the Colorado Supreme Court, while *Acton* was a United States Supreme Court decision and is thus regarded as the better decision.

[79] S.O. Ludd, 'Athletics, Drug Testing and the Right to Privacy: A Question of Balance'(1991) 34 *Howard Law Journal* 599–632, at 618–619.
[80] *Ibid.*, at 618.
[81] *Ibid.*

demonstrate to the satisfaction of the disciplinary panel that the substance was ingested through no fault of the individual, the sanction may be reduced. The burden of proof is on the athlete. This is a positive development as it recognises that an athlete can innocently ingest a prohibited substance. The CAS has upheld the strict liability in the interests of fair competition. In *Hansen v FEI* the CAS acknowledged that the principle is not inconsistent with Article 6(2) of the European Convention of Human Rights (ECHR) on the right to a fair trial.[82]

In *Foschi*,[83] an American swimmer and Olympic hopeful tested positive for mesterolone, an anabolic steroid banned under the rules of FINA. Even though Foschi denied knowledge of the drug, the United States Swimming Committee (USS), in exercising their jurisdiction, instead of banning the swimmer, merely placed her on probation. The leniency of the United States Swimming Committee seemed contrary to the principle of *nemo judex in causa sua* (nobody shall be a judge in his own case), a principle that is one of the cornerstones of the common law. Considering that Foschi was a talented swimmer, the panel presumably did not wish to furnish her with a suspension and thus deprive the United States of an Olympic hopeful. FINA objected to this leniency and ordered that Foschi be banned for two years.[84] The case accordingly went to the American Arbitration Association.[85] The arbitrators found in favour of Foschi, concluding:

> [T]hat the claimant and all those all those connected with her are innocent and without fault...and the imposition of any sanction on the claimant so offends our deep rooted and historical concepts of fundamental fairness so as to be arbitrary and capricious.[86]

A year after *Foschi*, a case involving the Swiss athlete Sandra Gasser[87] came before a Swiss court. The IAAF had banned Gasser even though,

---

[82] CAS 2009/A/1768, at 38. The CAS referred to the cases of *Salabiaku v France* (1988) 13 EHRR 379, paras 28–29; *Janovic v Sweden*, no. 34619/97, ECHR. 2002-VII, 1 (2004), at para 101.

[83] In the matter of Arbitration Between Jessica Foschi and US Swimming Inc, decision of 1 April 1996 (American Arbitration Association).

[84] Instead, the USS imposed a two-year probation struck off Foschi's times from the 1995 summer nationals and informed her that if she tested positive again she would face a lifetime ban.

[85] The AAA was chaired by three independent arbitrators.

[86] A. Wise, 'Strict Liability Drug Rules of Sports Governing Bodies' (1996) 146 *New Law Journal* 1161–1164, at 1162. The AAA also stated that the FINA regulations turned 'our concept of justice on its head'. FINA imposed a two-year ban on Foschi retroactive to August 1995, the date of her positive test.

[87] *Gasser v IAAF*, Richteramt Bern 111 of 22 December 1987, SJZ 84 [1988] 85.

like Foschi, she had protested her innocence and claimed she had no idea how the substance had been present in her body. The court subsequently revoked her two-year suspension. The matter also came before an English court.[88] Gasser contended, *inter alia*, that the drug test carried out by the IAAF was not in accordance with their rules and regulations and by placing a two-year ban on her it created an unreasonable restraint of trade. Counsel for Gasser had argued that the integrity of the tests depended on the governing body carrying out a test both accurately and with proper controls. It had emerged that the urine sample contained in the A sample had a different steroid profile than that which was found in the B sample. Scott J could not criticise the way in which the doctor had analysed the samples. The judge was of the opinion that the IAAF had not breached their doping rules.

The judge then turned to Gasser's claim of innocence. He deliberated on the submission made by Gasser's counsel that at times an athlete may ingest a banned substance unknowingly, such as if the athlete's coach or medical advisor or a 'malicious prankster' administers the drug without the knowledge of the athlete. However, the judge was in agreement with the defendant's counsel, who had argued on the point of the 'defence of moral innocence' and had concluded that such a defence would open up the floodgates and would thus render the IAAF's attempts at preventing drug taking among athletes ineffective. Counsel for Gasser contended that it was unjust that a morally innocent athlete would have to suffer so that the guilty would not go unpunished. The judge, while sympathetic to this argument, upheld the decision of the IAAF.

The case of Andrea Raducan provides an illuminating example of the strict liability regime at Olympic level. Raducan was a young Romanian gymnast who had received the gold medal in the Women's Individual All-Round Event. She was drug tested after her win and tested positive for the banned substance pseudoephedrine.[89] She argued that her doctor had given her medication and therefore she was not responsible for the positive result. Raducan also argued that the amount detected in her body was so minute that it could not be construed as performance enhancing. The AHD held doping was a strict liability

---

[88] *Gasser v Stinson* [1988] QBD, unreported, 15 June 1988. See also CAS 1994/129 USA *Shooting & Q/International Shooting Union (UIT)*. In this case, a shooter tested positive for a banned substance after taking medication prescribed by his doctor. His doctor had assured him that the medication was safe to take. The CAS admitted that the ban was draconian but it would be unfair on the other athletes not to ban the shooter.
[89] The drug was an ingredient in a cough mixture.

offence and therefore intention was irrelevant. The AHD, while sympathetic to Raducan, nevertheless held that the issue was not whether the banned substance enhanced performance or not but the fact that it was found in the athlete's body was evidence enough to warrant the application of the strict liability regime.[90]

Irish Sport and Strict Liability

Irish swimmer Michelle Smith De Bruin was banned for four years after she was found guilty of manipulating a drug test carried out by FINA. FINA had claimed that De Bruin had used excess amounts of alcohol to mask the presence of drugs. The sample contained such a high level of alcohol that, according to FINA officials, it would have resulted in death had it been a legitimate sample. The swimmer denied that she had taken any banned substances. De Bruin, in defence of the allegations, claimed that a third party had manipulated the samples.[91] De Bruin appealed her suspension to the CAS, which upheld the decision of FINA.[92] The three-member panel, including Michael Beloff, QC, rejected De Bruin's defence that there had been tampering by a third party or that the samples were not hers. The swimmer had also contended that the burden of proof was on FINA to 'eliminate all possibilities other than manipulation by the swimmer'. The CAS also rejected this argument.

GENDER TESTING

At the 2008 Olympic Games in Beijing, a gender verification laboratory was set up at the Peking Union Medical College Hospital. The laboratory was similar to those established for the Sydney and Atlanta Games. The laboratory examined the outward appearance, genes and hormones of female athletes under suspicion using a series of four tests, including blood, gene and chromosome tests. The creation of a specific gender laboratory was quite surprising as the IOC had suspended gender testing at its 112th session in Seoul in June 1999. However, the IOC reserves the right to examine individual athletes if it is suspicious as to the gender of that particular athlete. While the IOC reserves this right, the creation of a specific laboratory implied a more extensive use of testing than a re-application of testing in regard to suspected individuals.

---

[90] Raducan was deprived of her medal and disqualified from competition.
[91] As samples A and B were stored separately, such a claim was unfounded.
[92] The CAS 1998/211 *Smith de Bruin/FINA*, Digest of CAS Awards II 1998–2000 (The Hague: Kluver Law International, 2002), at 255–273.

Gender testing was introduced in the 1960s. At the time all female athletes were gender tested. In Beijing only 'suspect' female athletes were
to be tested.

Gender testing has attracted much criticism from the medical profession as gender is not simply determined by chromosome properties;
other factors must be considered, including the environment in which
the person was raised, the gender identity that the individual presumes
her or himself to have, the external genitalia, and the gender of the individual presumed by others.[93]

Drug testing became an important issue for the IOC in the 1960s.
After the death of cyclist Knud Jensen (see above), the IOC became the
first sporting organisation to establish a Medical Commission (in 1967)
that was entrusted with the task of policing the use of banned substances and of verifying gender. In 1966 the IAAF introduced gender
testing at the European Athletic Championships in Budapest as an
increasing number of female athletes began to compete.[94] All 243 female
athletes were required to take part in 'nude parades' where female doctors inspected them to see if they were biologically female by examining
the vaginal opening. The existence of overlarge clitorises, testes or
penises would have roused much suspicion.[95] All 243 athletes were certified as female.

Around this time, a small number of female elite athletes failed to
appear for examination, citing illness and retirement as the reason.[96]
Two Russian sisters, Irina and Tamara Press, who between them had

[93] A. Ljungqvist, 'Gender Verification' in *Women in Sport: Volume VIII of the Encyclopaedia of Sports Medicine* (ed. Barbara L. Drinkwater; IOC Medical Committee Publication in Collaboration with the International Federation of Sports Medicine) (Blackwell Science Ltd, London, 2000), at 188. Ljungqvist lists eight criteria that are used to determine gender and argues that for some individuals one or two of the criteria may be vague and question the assumed sex of the individual. Most governing bodies use only one of the eight criteria, the chromosome pattern. This calls into question the real reason behind gender testing if the objective is simply to catch men masquerading as women.
[94] Women competed in the Olympics for the first time in 1900. Out of the 1,225 partic-
ipants, 19 were women. Women competed in tennis, yachting and golf. In 1910 the IOC added gymnastics and swimming for women for the 1912 Olympics. In 1960, 611 women competed in Rome. This figure represented only 11.5 per cent of the total par-
ticipation. By 1980, 20 per cent of the participants were women and by 2000, 4,069 women competed out of a total of 10,651 participants (38 per cent). At the Games in Athens in 2004, 44 per cent of the participants were women. For more detail on women in sport, see *Focus: Women in Sport, Olympic Review*, Official Publication of the Olympic Movement, February 2004.
[95] Ljungqvist, 'Gender Verification', at 184.
[96] *Ibid.*, at 183. Ljunguist notes that it is five according to some commentators and six according to others. J.C. Reeser, 'Gender Identity and Sport: Is the Playing Field Level?'

set 26 world records and had won five gold medals, unexpectedly retired at this time. The idea that a female athlete could possess such superiority over her competitors caused much disquiet.[97] Culturally and socially, women had traditionally been viewed as being 'athletically inferior' to men and by excelling in their sport Irina and Tamara's femininity came into doubt. Both sisters were presumably intersexed and were not male impostors.[98] After Budapest, female athletes were subjected once again to physical examination by a gynaecologist in the Commonwealth Games in Kingston, Jamaica in 1967. In 1968 the IOC carried out drug and gender tests at the Games in Mexico City.

Drug testing is non-discriminatory as it applies equally to male and female athletes. However, gender testing is arguably a discriminatory practice that compromises the rights and dignity of intersexed persons. There is no evidence to suggest that intersexed persons have an unfair advantage over other typical females and males.[99] Medical evidence shows that the combination of hormone therapy and surgery eliminates any advantage a transsexual woman would have over natal females.[100]

Men Masquerading As Women

The 1936 Olympics in Berlin witnessed Hermann Ratjen bind up his genitals and compete as a female high jumper called Dora. Ratjen came fourth in the final and his deception was not discovered until 1957. Ratjen argued that he was forced by the Nazi Youth Movement to pose as a woman in the hope of winning the gold medal for Germany.[101] He

---

(2005) 39 *British Journal of Sports Medicine*, 695–699, states that there were six athletes (available online at: <http://bjsm.bmj.com/content/39/10/695.full.pdf>, last accessed 5 July 2010).

[97] J. Duncan, *Sport in American Culture from Ali to X Games* (Santa Barbara, CA: ABC-CLIO, 2004), at 150–151.

[98] Intersex refers to a group of conditions where there is a discrepancy between the external genitals and the internal genitals (the testes and ovaries). For a detailed discussion see: <http://www.nlm.nih.gov/medlineplus/ency/article/001669.htm> (last accessed 5 July 2010). D. McArdle, 'Swallows and Amazons, or the Sporting Exception to the Gender Recognition Act' (2008) 17(1) *Social and Legal Studies* 39–47, at 41.

[99] 'OLL Denounces Sexist Discrimination and Human Rights Violations of Intersexed Athletes in Beijing', press release, Organisation Intersex International, Montreal, 28 July 2008 (available online: <http://www.intersexualite.org/Olympics.html>, last accessed 28 June 2010).

[100] J. Finney Boylan, 'The XY Games', *New York Times*, 3 August 2008.

[101] It has been noted that the segregation of sport into male and female events provides an incentive for an individual to commit sex fraud. People like Ratjen are so desperate for success that they will go to great lengths to win. See Reeser, 'Gender Identity and Sport'.

had competed as a woman for three years, from 1933 to 1936. Ratjen is quoted as finding his three years posing as a woman to be 'most dull' and returned to live as a man after the Berlin Games.[102] Ratjen competed at a time before the advent of drug testing. It would be very difficult in light of current drug testing methods for a male athlete to pose as a woman while urinating in the presence of an official.

Stella Walsh – Mosaicism

Stanislawa Walasiewicz, a Polish sprinter, competed in the 1932 and 1936 Olympics. She moved to the United States and changed her name to Stella Walsh. In 1980 she was accidentally shot during an armed robbery and her autopsy revealed that she had male genitalia. She was found to have both male and female chromosomes, a genetic condition known as mosaicism. She had spent her entire life as woman and everyone else viewed her as a woman. As the fastest woman in the world at one time, Walsh's athletic prowess has been overshadowed by a genetic condition.

Stephens, who beat Walsh in the 100-metre final at the 1936 Games, came under suspicion at the time and had to undergo a sex test. Her record-beating time of 11.4 seconds (to Walsh's 11.7) cast doubt on her gender identity since she could run faster than Walsh, the fastest woman in the world. Ironically, it was Walsh who was declared male by the County Coroner's Office some 40 years later.

The Sex Chromatin Test

Female athletes resented the use of physical examination. In 1967 the IAAF introduced the sex chromatin test at the European Athletics Cup in Kiev. This 'femininity control' test marked a turning point in gender testing.[103] The criteria for assessing a female athlete's gender changed from one of physical examination to a more radical, though less invasive, test.[104] Gender testing assumed a more sinister role. It was no

---

[102] Boylan, 'The XY Games'. According to *Der Spiegel* this version of events is incorrect and this is actually a case of confused sexuality rather than a deliberate plot. See <http://www.spiegel.de/international/germany/0,1518,649104,00.html> (last accessed 11 October 2010).

[103] S. Jenkins, *Sports Science Handbook: The Essential Guide to Kinesiology, Sports and Exercise Science* (Brentwood: Multi-Science Publishing, 2000), at 318.

[104] It was cheaper and also quicker. See C.L. Cole, 'One Chromosome Too Many' in *The Olympics at the Millennium: Power Politics and the Games* (eds. K. Schaffer and S. Smith) (New Jersey: Rutgers University Press, 2000), 128–146, at 129.

longer concerned with men posing as women athletes but with athletes who externally appeared as women but whose genetic properties claimed otherwise. An abnormality in an individual's chromosomes could render a person who has the outward appearance of one sex to be of the other sex. The sex chromatin involves the collection of cells (a buccal smear) from inside the cheek to determine the chromosome properties. Normally, men and women have 46 chromosomes; men have one X and one Y chromosome, while women have two X chromosomes. Only those who were found to have two X chromosomes were deemed to be eligible to compete in women's events.[105] It is estimated that 1 in 500 people have abnormalities when chromatin tested.[106] Some women have what is known as androgen insensitivity and as a result have a Y chromosome. Those affected 'are resistant to androgenic hormones and therefore cannot benefit from the administration (doping) or endogenous presence of such hormones'.[107]

Polish sprinter and Olympic Champion Ewa Klobukowska was gender tested at Kiev and was found to have 'one chromosome too many to be declared a woman for the purposes of athletic competition'. Klobukowska had successfully passed the nude parade the previous year. Klobukowska was stripped of her medals and titles and was banned from competing for life. Medical experts differ in their conclusions in regard to Klobukowska. Alan Ryan, an American gynaecologist and obstetrician, argues that one too many chromosomes could mean that Klobukowska had three X chromosomes.[108] A number of theories

---

[105] This raises the question: if an athlete was registered as male but was suffering from a genetic defect which meant he had two X chromosomes, would this allow him to compete as a woman? Interestingly, Reeser refers to the situation of a male-to-female transsexual who is receiving oestrogen but can still compete as a man, whereas a hormonally treated female-to-male athlete would be prohibited from competing against women 'because the presence of exogenous testosterone would identify them as having "doped", a proverbial "Catch-22" situation' (Reeser, *Gender Identity and Sport*, at 699).

[106] See G. Vines, 'Last Olympics for the Sex Test? The world's biggest sports body has just banned sex tests, branding them unfair and unnecessary. But the old guard at this year's Olympics still insists the practice must go on', *New Scientist*, issue 1828, 4 July 1992, 39–42. Vines notes that genes can swap from one chromosome to another. A woman with a XY complement may physically be feminine but may have conditions known as an androgen insensitivity or testicular feminisation. These women produce more testosterone than an average woman. It would seem that these athletes are at a disadvantage as they can produce more testosterone but they cannot respond to the hormone. If such an individual took an anabolic steroid they would not be able to produce more muscle. As they are classified as male, these physically female athletes are deemed ineligible.

[107] Ljungqvist, 'Gender Verification', at 187.

[108] Cited by Cole, 'One Chromosome Too Many', at 129.

were forwarded to explain what was meant by one chromosome too many. Some argue that she had male genitalia, others argue that Klobukowska had a genetic defect that made her neither XX nor XY but XX/XXY.[109] While there is no definite answer as to her condition, most agree that Klobukowska had a rare genetic condition that gave her no competitive advantage over her fellow competitors. Ironically, Klobukowska gave birth to a child a couple of years after receiving her lifetime ban.

At the Atlanta Games in 1996, eight female athletes failed the test, although all were cleared by subsequent examinations. It was found that seven out of the eight were intersexed and that they did not have any unfair competitive advantage. Edinanci Silva, a Brazilian judo competitor, was born with both male and female organs and had surgery to correct this in the mid-1990s. The IOC allowed her to compete as a woman in the 1996, 2000 and 2004 Olympics, much to the chagrin of her Australian opponent, who constantly referred to Silva as 'he' in press conferences.[110] A mouth swab confirmed that Silva was female.

Attitudes to Gender Testing

Leading medical academics and practitioners have long called for the abolition of gender testing.[111] The test has been referred to as 'unscientific', 'nonsense' and 'morally destitute'[112] and it is claimed that there is no definitive test for determining gender. Questioning a person's gender can have serious repercussions. The Indian middle distance runner Santhi Soundarajan failed a sex test in 2006 after being observed by an official during a urine test for doping.[113] She was stripped of the silver medal she had won in Qatar at the Asian Games. Soundarajan was diagnosed with androgen insensitivity. This is a genetic defect that does not produce testosterone. Therefore, sufferers of this condition do not gain any competitive advantage through increased levels of testosterone. Similarly, in 1988, Spanish hurdler Maria Patino was reinstated after it was discovered she had androgen insensitivity. The Olympic Council of Asia's decision to disqualify Soundarajan is questionable on grounds of both ethics and efficacy. Soundarajan is believed to have

---

[109] Cole, 'One Chromosome Too Many', at 129.
[110] E. Saner, 'The Gender Trap', *The Guardian*, 30 July 2008.
[111] Vines, 'Last Olympics for the Sex Test?'
[112] *Ibid.*
[113] K. Thomas, 'A Lab Is Set to Test the Gender of Some Female Athletes', *New York Times*, 30 July 2008.

attempted suicide as a result of her gender being questioned. However, as a small token, the state government of Tamil Nadu supported her and awarded her 1.5 million rupees (approximately €23,800) for her performance in the Asian Games.[114]

Improved training and sociological changes have been cited as the reasons behind the 'striking improvement in athletic achievement by women'.[115] As women's sport became increasingly popular and accepted in the 1960s, it caused some to question the femininity of these women. Of particular importance was the competition between the United States and the Soviet Union during the Cold War period. The United States placed pressure on the IOC to introduce mandatory gender testing as Soviet athletes were dominating the Games. A number of Soviet athletes and East German athletes were rumoured to be intersexed owing to their masculine physiques. It was later discovered that a number of these athletes were using steroids. A notable example is that of Heidi Krieger, the East German shot putter, now known as Andreas. Her coach put Heidi on steroids and the contraceptive pill at the age of 17. With the combination of the pill and the steroids, Krieger's weight increased, as did her muscle mass. At 19 Krieger became conscious of her urge to become male.[116] In 1997, Krieger had gender reassignment surgery and is quoted as saying that the combination of the drugs and her own confusion in regard to her gender caused her to request a sex change.[117]

The Winter Games in Lillehammer in 1994 were somewhat controversial as Norwegian scientists refused to conduct gender tests as prescribed by the IOC.[118] The IOC had to bring a medical team from Albertville to carry out the tests. In 1995, at the Junior World Championships in Alpine Skiing, the Norwegian medics again refused to carry out the tests. In 1997 a law was enacted that prohibits gender testing in Norway.[119]

Failed Tests in Recent Years

Up until the early 1990s, when an athlete was chosen for a gender test, she would be tested using the chromatin test. If the results were

---

[114] Editorial, 'The Sad Story of Santhi Soundarajan', *Times of India*, 9 January 2007.

[115] M. Genel, 'Gender Verification No More?' (2000) 5(3) *Medscape Women's Health* (available online: <http://www.medscape.com/viewarticle/408918>, last accessed 5 July 2010).

[116] E. Cashmore, *Sports Psychology: The Key Concepts* (London: Routledge, 2002), at 262.

[117] Saner, 'The Gender Trap'.

[118] Ljungqvist, 'Gender Verification'.

[119] *Ibid.*

inconclusive, she would be asked to provide a blood sample. If the blood sample was inconclusive, the athlete would be examined physically. Once the athlete had passed the test, she would be given a sex certificate. The sex chromatin test could result in a failed test in a situation involving a female athlete with the appearance of a woman but who is found to have a Y chromosome. Evidence suggests that the buccal smear does not always present a clear picture.[120] It is estimated that 30 per cent of the cells will be positive and accordingly judged as female.[121] The subjectivity of the examiner is also an important factor to consider.[122]

Testing Methods Reconsidered

In the late 1980s and early 1990s, the IOC and IAAF convened a number of workshops. It was stressed that the objective of gender testing was not to stigmatise women but to prevent male athletes masquerading as women. It was on this tenuous hook that the continued use of the chromatin test rested. Despite its stated objectives, the IOC continued to exclude intersexed athletes and those suffering from androgen insensitivity in situations where there was a perceived competitive advantage.[123]

A group of international professionals attended an IAAF workshop on methods of femininity verification held in Monaco towards the end of 1990. They recommended the discontinuation of gender testing. In 1991 the IAAF duly followed the recommendation and in its place introduced medical examinations for the purposes of checking the health of the athlete, both male and female.[124] In 1992, at a conference held in London, the IAAF discussed the feasibility of continuing with medical examinations. The IAAF decided to dispense with the requirement of medical examinations and opted not to replace it with any other form of screening or examination. It reserves the right to assess an athlete's gender in the event of suspicion arising in relation to an individual; however, it has yet to employ this provision. The IAAF recommends continued health checks although they are not mandatory.[125]

---

[120] *Ibid.*, at 186.
[121] *Ibid.*
[122] *Ibid.*
[123] J.L. Simpson, J.A. Ljungqvist and M.A. Ferguson-Smith *et al.*, 'Gender Verification in the Olympics' (2000) 284(12) *Journal of the American Medical Association*, 1568–1569.
[124] *Ibid.*
[125] Ljungqvist, 'Gender Verification', at 188.

The IOC remained committed to gender testing and introduced at the Albertville Winter Games in 1992 a DNA-based method called polymerase chain reaction (PRC) to detect Y chromosomal properties.[126] PRC allows scientists to produce unlimited copies of a DNA strand in a very short space of time. This new method replaced the chromatin test and was first used at the 1992 Winter Games in Albertville. If the results were found to be abnormal, the athlete had to undergo a gynaecological examination.

The PRC method, while believed to be a more conclusive method of testing, was not without its critics. The supposedly sophisticated method excluded as many female competitors as its chromatin predecessor. Initially, the PRC method was supposed to 'identify uniquely male DNA sequences', however 'further investigation revealed that at least one of the DNA sequences used to prime the PCR was in fact not specific to males, and may have contributed to an unfortunate number of false positive test results'.[127]

In the aftermath of the 1996 Games, an increasing number of medical organisations were calling for the abolition of gender testing.[128] The organisations included the American Medical Association, the American College of Physicians and the American Society of Human Genetics.[129] The organisations made the point that the clothing worn by athletes and the direct supervision of officials in observing urination for doping purposes made it impossible for men to compete in women's events.[130] It was concluded that gender testing was expensive, unnecessary and futile.[131] At its 112th Session in 1999, the IOC decided to abandon its policy of gender testing. It still reserves the right to investigate suspect individuals. It is still used in national and regional events.

In August 2009 at the Berlin World Championships, Caster Semenya, the South African 800 metre world champion, was gender tested. The IAAF announced in July 2010 that Semenya is cleared to re-enter competition against other female athletes with immediate effect. The results of her gender verification test have not been disclosed.[132] Reports

---

[126] Genel, 'Gender Verification No More'.
[127] Reeser, 'Gender Identity and Sport'.
[128] *Ibid.*
[129] *Ibid.*
[130] *Ibid.*
[131] *Ibid.*
[132] A. Kessel, 'Caster Semenya May Return to Track this Month after IAAF Clearance', *The Guardian*, 6 July 2010 (available online: <http://www.guardian.co.uk/sport/2010/jul/06/caster-semenya-iaaf-clearance>, last accessed 11 October 2010).

have suggested that she is a hermaphrodite: she is believed to have internal testes and a womb but no ovaries. The young athlete has been allowed to keep the medal she won at Berlin.[133]

TRANSSEXUAL ATHLETES

The IAAF had first introduced gender testing in the 1960s and the IOC followed suit. The IOC continued with the practice until 1999. However, in 2004 the IOC introduced provisions allowing transsexuals to compete subject to certain criteria, while the IAAF has continued to deal with transsexuals on a case-by-case basis. The IAAF provides for similar guidelines as the IOC in regard to transsexuals who have surgery prior to puberty; however, the IAAF leaves it up to the relevant medical body within the sport's organisation in question to decide on cases involving post-puberty gender reassignment.[134]

The Supreme Court of New York decided the legal status of a transsexual athlete in 1977.[135] In 1934 Renee Richards was born male and called Richard Raskind. In 1975 Raskind had a gender re-assignment operation and changed his name to Renee Richards. Richards had a successful career as a tennis player and in 1976 was refused entry as a female competitor into the US Open by the United States Tennis Association (USTA). Richards refused to be physically examined to verify her biological gender. She successfully challenged the decision of the USTA with the Court holding that there was overwhelming medical evidence that supported the contention that Richards was in fact female. The USTA compared the position of transsexuals to 'drug cheats' and 'female impersonators' and 'impostors'.[136] The Court rejected this comparison, and held 'there to be very few biological males, who are accomplished tennis players, who are also either preoperative or post-operative transsexual[s]'.[137]

McArdle notes that in the 30 years since the judgment in Richards, there have been no transgender athletes competing at elite level.[138] The

---

[133] J. Longman, 'South African Runner's Sex-Verification Result Won't Be Public', *New York Times*, 19 November 2009 (available online: <http://www.nytimes.com/2009/11/20/sports/20runner.html>, last accessed 11 October 2010).
[134] Ljungqvist, 'Gender Verification', at 188.
[135] *Richards v US Tennis Assn.*, 93 Misc. 2d, 713, 400 NYS 2d 267 (Sup. Ct, NY, 1977).
[136] *Ibid.*, at 269.
[137] *Ibid.*
[138] McArdle, 'Swallows and Amazons, or the Sporting Exception to the Gender Recognition Act', at 43.

fears that athletes would change their gender in the hope of 'a shortcut to sporting glory' have proved unfounded.[139] There are a number of health risks associated with hormone therapy and where the patient is not under medical supervision or is sharing needles, the risks increase even more.[140] A person undergoing hormone treatment is advised to take exercise to minimise the effects of weight gain and to maximise bone density.[141]

The Gender Recognition Act, 2004

While transgender persons have expressed a willingness to compete in sport, sport remains 'hostile' and almost homophobic.[142] A recent example can be seen in the the United Kingdom Gender Recognition Act, 2004. Under this Act an exemption has been given to sporting bodies (who would seem to be public bodies for the purposes of the Human Rights Act, 1998) under section 19. Section 19 provides that transgender persons can be restricted from participation in sport on the grounds of 'competitive fairness' and 'safety'. Medical opinion has shown that a male-to-female transsexual would not pose any competitive advantage. In the example of Renee Richards, she had moderate success as a female tennis player and is perhaps better known for coaching Martina Navratilova.

Participation in sport is beneficial for both physical and mental health and denying a transsexual individual from participating raises concerns among advocates of human rights.[143] While section 19 may not impact upon elite-level sport, it has the potential to affect participation in low-level recreational sport. It is questionable whether unfair advantage and indeed safety can be reconciled with such low-level sport. Ironically, the 2004 Act was enacted to address previous cases where it was found that the United Kingdom had breached Articles 8 and 12 of the European Convention on Human Rights.[144] Under the ECHR a transgender person has the right to be recognised as their postoperative sex.

Neither the House of Lords nor the Joint Committee on Human Rights (JCHR) voiced any objections to section 19.[145] It was argued that

---

[139] *Ibid.*, at 44.
[140] *Ibid.*
[141] *Ibid.*
[142] *Ibid.*
[143] *Ibid.*, at 40.
[144] See *Goodwin v United Kingdom* (2002) 35 EHRR 18 and *Bellinger v Bellinger* [2003] 2 AC 467.
[145] McArdle, 'Swallows and Amazons, or the Sporting Exception to the Gender Recognition Act', at 46.

the new clause does not prevent transsexuals in general from partici-pating, only those who present an unfair advantage or a threat to the safety of others.[146] Section 19(4) provides that a sport is a gender-affected sport if the physical strength, stamina or physique of average persons of one gender would put them at a disadvantage to average persons of the other gender as competitors in events involving the sport. This sub-section largely replicates section 44 of the Sex Discrimination Act, 1975.[147] McArdle notes that section 44 was considered 'dead law' and its replication in the form of section 19 'heralds an unwelcome return to the concept of the "average" person in legislation otherwise concerned with affording opportunity rather than denying it'.[148]

Recognition of Transsexuals by the IAAF and IOC

In the wake of the *Richards* decision there were no clear rules in regard to athletes who had changed their sex. In 1990, the IAAF became the first IF to recognise that the gender assumed after the sex change was the gender of the athlete. However, those who had undergone post-pubescent surgery posed problems, as a former male could still have the hormone levels of a man, which could result in an unfair advantage when com-peting with women. The IAAF decided that in post-pubescent cases the individual would be assessed on a case-by-case basis.[149] As yet there are no clear guidelines for post-pubescent transsexuals.

On 17 May 2004, the IOC approved proposals recommended by the IOC Medical Commission in relation to athletes who had changed sex.[150] If a pre-pubescent male undergoes gender reassignment to become female, she will be considered female. The same applies to a pre-pubescent female who became male: he will compete as a male. For athletes who change sex after puberty, a number of conditions must be fulfilled:[151]

- The individual concerned has completed the surgical anatomical changes, including external genitalia changes and gonadectomy[152]

---

[146] *Ibid.*

[147] *Ibid.*, at 47.

[148] *Ibid.*

[149] For more details see: <http://multimedia.olympic.org/pdf/en_report_904.pdf> (last accessed 29 June 2010).

[150] An ad-hoc committee was convened by the Medical Commission, which met on 28 October 2003 in Stockholm. The committee included Professor Arne Ljungqvist.

[151] For more details see: <http://multimedia.olympic.org/pdf/en_report_905.pdf> (last accessed 29 June 2010).

[152] This involves the surgical removal of the gonads.

- Legal recognition of their assigned sex has been conferred by the appropriate official authorities
- Hormonal therapy appropriate for the assigned sex has been administered in a verifiable manner and for a sufficient length of time to minimise gender-related advantages in sports competitions

An individual will not be eligible to compete for at least two years after the removal of the gonads. If an individual's sex is questioned, the medical committee of the relevant sport will be permitted to carry out further tests to determine the gender.

Men are typically taller than women and male-to-female transsexuals may have an unfair advantage when it comes to sports where height is an important factor, such as volleyball, netball and basketball.[153] As a precautionary measure, some international associations, including the IOC and the IAAF (as shown above), distinguish between pre- and post-puberty surgery. If a male has surgery after puberty, he may have 'residual testosterone induced attributes [that] could influence performance capacity'.[154] It thus follows that, in this case, the decision on participation should be decided on a sport-by-sport basis.[155] In general, female volleyball players are on average taller than non-volleyball-playing females.[156] Olympic volleyball players are taller than the previous generation of players.[157] Height, while being an important factor, is not the only requirement. Studies reveal that physiological factors can be as important as psychological factors.[158] Although 'whether or not these performance and success related traits are hormonally mediated remains to be seen.'[159]

Mianne Bagger, a Danish golfer, became the first transsexual to play at a professional golf tournament (the Australian Open), in 2004.[160] The Australian Ladies Professional Golf Association (ALPGA) changed its conditions that required a player to be 'female at birth', thus allowing Bagger to compete.[161] In 2005, a number of golfing associations dispensed

---

[153] Reeser, 'Gender Identity and Sport'.
[154] *Ibid.*
[155] *Ibid.*
[156] *Ibid.*
[157] *Ibid.*
[158] *Ibid.*
[159] *Ibid.*
[160] 'Transsexual to Compete in Australian Women's Open', *Associated Press*, 3 March 2004.
[161] Bagger was born male. In 1992 he underwent hormone therapy and in 1995 had surgery to become a woman. She resumed playing golf in 1998.

with the female-at birth criteria, including the United States Golfing Association (USGA), Ladies Golf Union and the European Ladies Tour, and Bagger became the first transsexual to avail of this change in policy.[162] Bagger's competitors, including Laura Davies, had no issue with Bagger competing. Bagger maintains that she has no physical advantage over her competitors as her hormone therapy caused muscle loss.

Since the 2004 IOC rules, no transsexual athlete has competed in the Olympics, or at least no athlete that is open about his or her transsexuality. Kristen Worley, a Canadian cyclist, narrowly missed out on qualifying for the Beijing Olympics. Had she qualified she would have been the first transsexual to compete under the new rules. Given that the IOC recognises the right of transsexual athletes to compete, why was a gender lab created at Beijing?[163] The presence of the laboratory is even more questionable in light of the frequency of erroneous results in gender testing.[164]

Legal Status of Transsexuals in Ireland

The sporting world has made some strides in recognising transsexual athletes. While confusion still pervades, this is understandable in light of differing medical opinion on transsexuality.[165] Aside from settled medical opinion, some legal systems have been slow to recognise the legal status of transsexuals. The legal position of transsexual individuals has been the subject of recent litigation in Ireland. In the case of Lydia Foy, the High Court ruled that the Irish state was in breach of the European Convention of Human Rights (ECHR) by failing to recognise Foy's sex change.[166] The Court held that it was a basic human right for an individual to 'develop his being as he sees fit; subject only to the most minimal interference of the State being essential for the convergence of the common good'.[167]

---

[162] J. Ireland, 'He Shoots, She Scores', *In These Times*, 27 July 2007 (available online: <http://www.inthesetimes.com/article/3232/he_shoots_she_scores/>, last accessed 29 June 2010).
[163] Boylan, 'The XY Games'.
[164] *Ibid.*
[165] Ireland, 'He Shoots, She Scores'.
[166] *Foy v An t-Ard Chláraitheoir and Ors* [2007] IEHC 470.
[167] *Ibid.*, at para 118. Judgment delivered by McKechnie J on 19 October 2007. The Irish Government subsequently challenged the High Court declaration. However, it dropped its challenge and must now introduce legislation that recognises the right of a transgender individual to obtain a new birth certificate. See 'Government Withdraws

CONCLUSION

Drug testing and gender testing were introduced in the 1960s. Drug testing is an accepted part of an athlete's life. As long as a governing body adheres to its own rules and procedures, there is less room for the athlete to challenge a positive result. Gender testing was originally introduced to prevent men from masquerading as woman. In pre-drug-testing days, it was possible for a male to pose as a woman athlete. With the advent of drug testing and light sportswear used by competitors, a person's gender can easily be assessed.

The IOC's approach to transsexuals and intersexed persons is para-doxical. The IOC accepts transsexual athletes, who in most cases are male to female, but has disqualified a number of female athletes who have a Y chromosome. These athletes are female except for a slight genetic defect. One could argue that transsexuals have a competitive advantage over intersexed persons, as men are generally taller and stronger than women.[168] Yet, the IOC has focused on unfounded evidence that increased testosterone levels in an intersexed person or sufferer of androgen insensitivity gives an unfair advantage. Doctors and scientists argue that, while these athletes have increased testosterone, their body does not respond to it.

Drug testing not only tests for prohibited substances but can also detect genital abnormalities. More importantly, it is a more sensitive method of dealing with athletes suffering from genetic conditions.

Transgender Appeal', *RTÉ News*, 21 June 2010 (available online: <http://www.rte.ie/news/2010/0621/foyl.html>, last accessed 21 June 2010).
[168] Female athletes are generally taller than the average woman. For a more detailed discussion on gender testing, see L. Donnellan, 'Gender Testing at the Beijing Olympics' (2008) 16(1) *Journal of Sport and the Law* 20–28.

CHAPTER 6

Commercial Issues in Sport

INTRODUCTION

Modern sport is a multi-billion-dollar global business.[1] Sport has become increasingly commercialised, with the bulk of the revenue generated being sourced from sponsorship and broadcasting deals and not from the traditional medium of gate receipts and prize money.[2] As sport becomes more professionalised and commercialised, the issue of contracts, agents and media rights assumes even greater importance. As society has become more litigious, individuals have become more aware of their rights; if an individual feels their rights have been unduly compromised, he or she will seek redress in the courts. Sport has been unable to remain immune from such developments. As the law has a role to play in sport, the nature of relationships between those involved in sport has begun to change. Up until the 1960s it was common practice for a club to hold on to a professional football player's registration after his contract expired. However, in the case of *Eastham v Newcastle United*[3] this practice was challenged, with the court holding that the 'retain and transfer' system was an unlawful restraint of trade. Similarly, there was very little regulation of football agents. On 10 December

---

[1] N. Cox, A. Schuster and C. Costello, *Sport and the Law* (Dublin: First Law, 2004), at 304. See also I. Blackshaw, 'Regulating Sport Globally' (2000) 150 *New Law Journal* 617–619. Blackshaw refers to the increased number of people who incorporate more leisure time into their lives, including playing and watching sport.
[2] Cox, Schuster and Costello, *Sport and the Law*, at 304. See also C. Connolly, 'The Sponsorship Contract as a Mechanism of Safeguarding and Influencing the Level of Return on Investment in Sport Sponsorship' (2005) 12(8) *Commercial Law Practitioner* 199–206. S. Gardiner *et al.*, *Sports Law* (3rd ed., London: Cavendish Publishing, 2006), at 399, notes that a three-year exclusive sponsorship of the English Premier League costs £48 million.
[3] [1964] Ch 413.

2000, Fédération Internationale de Football Association (FIFA) passed its Licensed Players' Agents Regulations.[4]

Sport is not just a business, but also a product. Given the amount of money that is at stake, sports bodies will want to protect their product from exploitation. This is where media rights are important. The regulatory and judicial response has forced those involved in sport to rethink their views in regard to the relationship between the law and sport. This chapter will examine a number of commercial issues that are of relevance to sport. Beginning with a brief look at contract law, the chapter will proceed to look at the doctrine of restraint of trade. The latter part of the chapter will discuss the regulation of football agents and media rights in Irish sport.

CONTRACT LAW

A contract is a legally binding agreement between two or more parties. Contract law falls under the branch of law called private law. Private law regulates relationships between individuals. Every day individuals make contracts, often without realising it, for example, buying groceries in the supermarket involves a contractual agreement. A person buying a house will enter into a contract of sale. An employee who works for a regular wage or salary will have a contract of employment.[5] The role of the law of contract is to identify binding agreements, and to interpret and enforce them. Not all agreements are legally binding, for example, promises, favours, gifts and moral obligations can never be the subject of a contract. Contracts to defraud the Revenue Commissioners or commit a crime are illegal and can never be enforced.

Every contract has four essential elements:

1. Offer – must be clear and unambiguous, an interested party must be able to understand exactly to what the contract relates.[6] An offer can

---

[4] These regulations have been amended since 2000.

[5] The Terms of Employment (Information) Acts, 1994 and 2001 provide that an employer is obliged to present an employee with a written statement of terms of employment within the first two months of the commencement of employment.

[6] For example, a seller says that he will sell his car for 'around €5,000'. That is unclear and ambiguous. However, if the seller says he will sell the car for €5,500, there is no ambiguity and is thus clear enough to constitute a contract. It is important to distinguish an offer from an invitation to treat. An invitation to treat is something that invites the potential purchaser to treat themselves by buying the goods. The goods could be advertised in a catalogue or brochure, newspaper, magazine or a shop shelf or window. It could be a kitchen in a showroom that is arranged in a particular manner. The display is not usually for sale and is only indicative of how the kitchen could look. See R.J.

be oral, written or by conduct[7]

2. Acceptance – only the person to whom the offer was made can accept the offer. The offer can be accepted by word or conduct[8]
3. Consideration – the price paid under a contract. It distinguishes a contract from a promise.[9] Something of value must be exchanged, either money or money's worth.[10] Consideration must be sufficient (i.e. regarded by the law as being good or acceptable) but need not be adequate (i.e. of full economic value)[11]
4. Intention to create legal relations – by entering into the contract, it can be inferred (or is implied) that the parties intend to create legal relations

A contract is formed when an offer made by one party has been accepted by the other and is supported by consideration. The parties must intend to create legal relations and in some instances evidentiary formalities are required (i.e. the contract must be in writing).[12] The parties must be regarded by the law as having the capacity to enter into a contract.[13]

Friel, *The Law of Contract* (Dublin: Round Hall, 1995), at 23–24. Such goods are not offers but invitations to treat.

[7] For example, the consumer picks up a bar of chocolate and goes to the checkout and hands the appropriate money to the cashier.

[8] Note: counteroffer – this is a rejection because it varies the terms of the offer. For example, a seller offers to sell her car for €10,000 and the buyer says he will give her €8,500; this counteroffer is effectively a no to the original offer and thus terminates the original offer.

[9] The only instance when an agreement without consideration can be binding is if it is a deed under seal which must be in writing and clearly state that it is legally binding.

[10] An undertaking to confer a benefit on the other party or to suffer a detriment can amount to consideration.

[11] For example, an agreement to sell a Porsche for €10 is a valid contract. In this situation the consideration is sufficient and thus satisfies the legal requirement. However, the €10 is not adequate, but that is of no concern to the law. Note, however, inadequacy might be evidence of fraud, duress or undue influence, which would justify setting the contract aside.

[12] In general, contracts may be either written, oral or a combination of both. The Statute of Frauds (Ireland), 1695 provides that certain contracts are enforceable only if they are evidenced in writing, i.e. the principal terms of the agreement must be noted and signed by both parties. The following must be in writing: contracts for the sale of land; contracts for the sale of goods worth over £10 (section 4 of the Sale of Goods Act, 1893); contracts of guarantee; and contracts which are to be performed more than 12 months after the date of the agreement. Section 2 of the Statute of Frauds has been replaced by section 51 of the Land and Conveyancing Reform Act, 2009.

[13] See R. Clark and B. Clarke, *Contract Cases and Materials* (3rd ed., Dublin: Gill & Macmillan, 2004), 664–684.

The Role of Contract in Sport

In regard to sport, Beloff remarks that the law of contract 'is the legal tool with which the stage designers of sport create the scene; and it contains the script used by the sporting actors to play to the public'.[14] In the sporting realm, contracts are between a player and a club, a sportsperson and a sponsor, and a sportsperson and an agent or a manager. If a coach is hired to train a team, there will be a contract between the club and the coach to give legal effect to the relationship. When Giovanni Trapattoni became the manager of the Irish national team, a contract was signed between him and the Football Association of Ireland (FAI). Initially, the contract was for two years, 2008–2010. In September 2009, the contract was extended by a further two years to 2012.

Contracts may be used in situations involving the right of access to sporting competitions.[15] The rules of a sporting body, once accepted by the club or individual, form the basis of a contract between the body and the club or individual. A referee is contractually bound to enforce the rules of the sport as set by the governing body. A contract will also form the basis of an agreement to grant media rights. For an event manager or a governing body to secure exclusive broadcast rights over a sporting event, a contractual agreement must be negotiated with the owner of the venue and the spectators.[16] This agreement will provide that only the official broadcaster can gain access to the venue for the purpose of broadcasting the footage of the event in question.

Contractual Relationships in Sport

For those who are members of a club or association that is unincorporated, once the membership form is signed (either expressly by signing a form or impliedly by conduct) a contractual relationship has been entered into and the member has accepted the rules and regulations of the club. Often clubs will amend their rules. Such rule changes are

---

[14] M. Beloff *et al.*, *Sports Law* (Oxford: Hart Publishing, 1999), at para 2.18.
[15] *Ibid.*, at 39–52. At paras 3.25–3.26 Beloff gives the example of a third division team that wins the Third Division Championship. The team has a contractual right to compete in the second division the next season on the basis of a pre-existing contract between an individual or club and a sporting body. The club has a contract of membership with the league and the league will have terms in that contract, for example the automatic promotion to the higher league of the team that comes first in the league that season. If the league tried to stop the promotion it would be a breach of contract unless there was some rule entitling it to prevent the winning team from being promoted to the higher division.
[16] Cox, Schuster and Costello, *Sport and the Law*, at 364.

permitted so long as the club follows the proper constitutional procedures. Any changes validly introduced are binding on the members.
There is no need for the club to contact each member to inform them of
the change.

An unincorporated club or association is one that is voluntary and
non-trading. It involves the coming together of individuals (members)
who have a common purpose. Unincorporated clubs are relatively
simple to set up and there is no requirement to make public or file the
accounts or returns of the club. An unincorporated club does not have
to comply with the formalities that an incorporated company has to
under the Companies Acts, 1963–2009. Most local clubs who have little
property or staff are unincorporated. The main drawback for these
organisations is that they do not enjoy the principle of separate legal
personality. Separate legal personality means that the company and the
human agents are separate. The company has a legal personality similar to that of a person or individual. When an incorporated company
with limited liability is being wound up, each member is only liable for
the amount unpaid on their shares.[17] If their shares are fully paid up,
then there is no further liability. However, with an unincorporated club
or association, in the event of the company being wound up, the members can be held jointly and severally accountable for all of its debts and
obligations without any limitation. Most local sports clubs in Ireland
are unincorporated. However, most large sports clubs and governing
bodies would be limited liability companies.

If an individual is a member of an unincorporated club or association, there is a contractual relationship between each member. Each
member is in a contractual relationship with every other member.
There is what Beloff refers to as 'a horizontal matrix of contracts binding each member to all other members'.[18] As the unincorporated club
has no legal existence, there is no contract which binds the members to
the club.

An individual may attend a local sporting centre, for example, a gym
or a bowling alley. These organisations are set up as commercial enti-
ties and are usually companies with limited liability. The individual
pays a casual user fee or has a subscription in return for the use of the
facilities. While there is a contract between the individual and the club
or gym (a vertical contract), there is no contract between the various
members except to the extent that the rules so provide.

---

[17] *Salomon v Salomon & Co.* [1897] AC 22.
[18] Beloff *et al.*, *Sports Law*, at 23, para 2.21.

Capacity

In Ireland, minors are generally deemed to lack the capacity to contract. A minor is someone under the age of 18. In general, contracts involving minors are voidable and can be made invalid at the decision of the minor. However, there is an exception in situations where the contract is for *necessities* – goods and services which in some way are essential or beneficial to the minor's condition in life, for example, food, clothing, shelter, educational services and apprenticeship.[19] As the minor athlete or player may be required to sign a contract, the issue has arisen whether the contract is voidable or should be upheld by the court.

There are some early case examples. In *Roberts v Grey*, a contract to enable a minor to receive instruction and earn a living as a professional snooker player was held valid.[20] In this case, damages were awarded against a minor who broke a contract to accompany a professional snooker player on a world tour in order to receive training and develop experience. In *Doyle v White City Stadium*, the plaintiff minor was a heavyweight boxer.[21] He was granted a licence by the British Boxing Board of Control (BBBC) to box. The licence stipulated that if the boxer was disqualified he would forfeit his share of the purse. The plaintiff was disqualified for hitting below the belt. He argued that the forfeit provision did not bind him. However, the court held that as the term was for his general benefit, in encouraging clean and fair fighting, he was bound by it although it operated in this case against him. The court held the contrary in the case of *De Francesco v Barnum*.[22] The minor was released from her seven-year contract as a professional dancer. The defendant was under no duty to find her work, she was unable to accept other work and, if she decided to get married, she would have to resign.

These three cases were cited more recently in the case of *Proform Sports Management Ltd v Proactive Sports Management Ltd*.[23] Proform Sports had contracted British soccer player Wayne Rooney when he was 15 years old. The plaintiff alleged that Proactive Sports had induced Rooney to breach his contract with Proform. Proactive Sports argued that a contract between a minor footballer and an agent was voidable as it did not provide necessities for the footballer, and thus the court was

---

[19] See section 2 of the Sale of Goods Act, 1893.
[20] [1913] 1 KB 520.
[21] [1935] 1 KB 110.
[22] (1890) 45 Ch D 430.
[23] [2006] EWHC 2903 (Ch); [2007] Bus LR 93; [2007] 1 All ER 542; [2007] 1 All ER (Comm) 356; (2006) 156 NLJ 1723; *The Times*, 13 November 2006.

not required to consider if the contract was for the benefit of the minor. As the contract was voidable, there could be no liability imposed on a third party for inducing a breach of that contract. In distinguishing the case of *Doyle v White City Stadium*, where the plaintiff had to sign a contract in order to earn a living as a professional boxer, Hodge J held that a contract between a footballer and an agent was not a necessity. Rooney was already contracted to Everton Football Club so there was no need for a contract to represent him as a professional footballer. Once Rooney reached the age of 17 he would be in a position to earn his living via a contract with Everton or any other club. He would not need an agent for two years. Hodge J held that a football management and agency agreement between a minor footballer (aged 15) and a company was not a contract for necessities or analogous to a contract of apprenticeship, education or service. Judgment was given in favour of the defendants.

Contractual Terms and Their Interpretation

A contract will contain the following terms:

- Express terms – terms that are explicitly stipulated by the parties, for example, the salary and the duration of the contract[24]
- Implied terms – terms that have not been explicitly stipulated but are read into the contract by necessary implication. A contract might not state that a player is confined to playing for just one club; the courts would imply such a term.[25] The court uses the *officious bystander* test[26] to determine whether a term is implied

An implied term was read into the contract in the case of *Bournemouth AFC v Manchester United*.[27] Bournemouth AFC had transferred a player to Manchester United for a stipulated sum. A term of the contract provided that an extra sum would be paid if the player scored 20 goals

---

[24] Where the contract is written the express terms are confined to those set out in the contract document. The parol evidence rule prevents evidence of other terms being adduced.

[25] The courts are reluctant to imply terms on the grounds that a contract represents a consensus reached by the parties. It is up to the parties to agree on the terms and the role of the court is merely as an enforcer of those terms.

[26] The definition of the officious bystander test states that when a court is faced with a contract dispute involving an implied term, the court will decide if the inclusion of the term is necessary for the effectiveness of the contract.

[27] *The Times*, 22 May 1980.

for the new club. Manchester United transferred the player before he had reasonable time to score the goals. The court held that the defendants were in breach of an implied term that the player would be given a reasonable time period in which to score the goals.

Similarly, in *Madison Square Garden Boxing Inc. v Shavers*, heavyweight fighter Earnie Shavers entered into a contract to fight Muhammad Ali in a championship bout.[28] As there was no term in the contract that prevented Shavers from engaging in other fights, Madison Square Garden Boxing Inc. sought an injunction to prevent Shavers from participating in any other fights prior to the Ali fight. The Court held that Shavers could not participate in any other fights for eight weeks prior to the Ali fight. The judgment was based on industry practice and the fact that a period of eight weeks would be needed to train for a championship contest. In general, a court will not imply a non-competition covenant if it will result in undue hardship on the party.

Terms (express and implied) can be further broken down into:

- Condition – if the parties intend that a breach of a term will result in the contract being set aside, that term is a condition. If a condition is breached, the innocent parties may have the contract set aside and may receive damages
- Warranty – a term of minor importance, the breach of which does not entitle the innocent party to set aside the contract; however, the innocent party would be entitled to damages in the event of a breach. If the parties intend that a breach will result in damages only, then the term is a warranty
- Innominate – a term that cannot be classified as a condition or a warranty. If there is a breach of an innominate term the innocent party is entitled to compensation. The contract will not automatically be voidable at the request of the innocent party. It depends on the gravity of the breach, for example, a fundamental breach would entitle the innocent party to have the contract set aside

Exclusion Clauses and Waivers

Exclusion (or exemption) clauses attempt to exclude or restrict the liability of one party in a specified circumstance. It protects the party (usually the one who has drafted the contract) from being sued by the

---

[28] 562 F. 2d 141, 144 (2d Cir. 1977). See P. McCutcheon, 'Negative Enforcement of Contracts in Sports Industries' (1997) 17 *Legal Studies* 65–100, at 78.

other party for a breach of contract, damages, loss or negligence, or it may limit the party's liability. For example, a term of the contract may stipulate that liability is restricted to a fixed sum or it may require that the innocent party bring an action within a stipulated time, or it may state that the party is not liable for any damage howsoever caused. The courts do not favour exclusion clauses and if there is any ambiguity the clause is read *contra proferentem*, i.e. it is read in favour of the party against whom the clause operates.[29]

Standard Form Contracts in Sport

Standard form contracts are used in many professions. A standard form contract is printed and has blank spaces which will later be filled in by the parties to the contract. Standardised contracts are often used in professional sports. The contract will contain provisions relating to the player's salary, the duration of the contract, the club's obligations (i.e. provides medical treatment and pays a player's basic wage while he is injured; ensures that the rules and regulations of the relevant sport are adhered to; provides transport and accommodation when a player is on club business; provides training and professional coaching and services), the player's obligations (i.e. doesn't play for another club during the currency of the contract; attends all training sessions and matches as required; maintains his physical fitness and health; doesn't take part in another profession or sport that would be likely to affect his fitness or ability to play for the club without the club's permission; wears appropriate safety equipment such as shin guards or mouth guard), player secondment or loan, conditions under which the contract would be terminated, incapacity (due to illness or injury), disciplinary rules and grievance procedures, and hours of work and holidays.[30]

A standard form contract may be terminated if the player commits a criminal offence which results in a custodial sentence, is found to have committed a doping infraction or has failed to give a sample when requested, is unable to play due to excessive alcohol or drugs, or has brought the game or club into disrepute. The contract may also be

---

[29] Exclusion clauses in consumer contracts are common. However, such a clause is only valid if it is specifically brought to the consumer's attention and only if it is fair and reasonable.

[30] Given the nature of the player's employment as a professional player, there are no set hours of work. The contract would require the player to make himself available (subject to advance notification) to play and train on any day of the week, including Sundays and bank holidays. The player would be entitled to at least one day of rest per week. A player would also be entitled to a number of days' holidays a year.

terminated if the player seriously breaches one of the terms of the contract. The term 'bring the sport into disrepute' may include extramarital affairs, the taking of recreational drugs, being involved in a brawl outside a night club or on-field violence. Standard form contracts are often criticised as there is a lack of negotiation on the part of the player. However, there can be some advantages. If a contract is drawn up by the governing body, this contract will have the interests of the player and the club in mind.[31] A standard form contract eliminates the need to negotiate every minor detail and thus leaves more time to negotiate the more important terms.[32]

Contract Disputes

Contract disputes are not specific to players or clubs. In a recent case, *Manchester City Football Club PLC v Royle*, a former manager challenged the amount of compensation given to him on the termination of his contract with the club.[33] Joe Royle's contract was for a period of four years (from 1 June 2000). At the time the contract was signed, Manchester City had just been promoted to the English Premier League. The season finished on 19 May 2001 and Royle was dismissed two days later. Royle contended that under the terms of the contract he was entitled to compensation based on club performance. The contract provided that Royle's wages would be increased if the team was promoted from the first division of the league to the premier division. A term of the contract further stipulated that if Royle was dismissed before the end of his contract and the team were playing in the Premier League, he should be paid one year of the higher salary; he would be paid six months of the lower salary if he was dismissed while Manchester City was in the first division. At the end of 2000–2001 season, Manchester City was relegated to the first division after finishing in the bottom three teams. Royle argued that he should receive the higher salary since on 21 May the team was still in the premier division, as the share transfer that would bring membership of the premier division to an end had not yet taken place. Kershaw J of the Mercantile Court of Manchester held in favour of Royle; however, on appeal, the Court of Appeal disagreed and set aside Kershaw's order. The Court of Appeal held that, as the team would be playing in the

[31] D. Healey, *Sport and the Law* (4th ed., Sydney: University of New South Wales Press, 2009), at 70.
[32] *Ibid.*
[33] [2005] EWCA Civ 195 *The Times*, 14 March 2005.

lower division the next season, Royle was only entitled to compensation based on the lower salary.

Contract of Employment

The legal status of professional athletes should be noted. In general, athletes in team sports are held to be employees. In *Walker v Crystal Palace FC* the applicant was a footballer who played for Crystal Palace.[34] Walker was injured during a match and the club paid his wages for the remainder of the season. At the end of the season, Walker applied for compensation for permanent incapacity. He was held to be a worker for the purposes of the Workers Compensation Act, 1906. Cozens-Hardy MR held: '[The player] is bound according to the express terms of his contract to obey all general directions of the club, and I think in any particular game in which he was engaged he would also be bound to obey the particular directions of the captain or whoever it might be was the delegate of the authority of the club for the purpose of giving those instructions.'[35]

Individual athletes such as boxers, golfers, tennis players and track and field competitors are not employees but rather independent contractors. Such individuals are usually contracted for a particular event or competition. In most cases, there is standardised agreement between the individual and the tour or event.

Restraint of Trade

At common law the courts developed the doctrine of restraint of trade. It was developed by the courts to protect individuals from being restricted from earning a livelihood. Initially the doctrine operated to invalidate contract terms which unduly restricted the parties' freedom to contract.[36] Over time, the courts extended the doctrine to

---

[34] [1910] 1 KB 87.

[35] At the time the appropriate test was the control test. An individual would be considered to be an employee if it could be shown that the employer had the right to control not only what was done but also how it was done by the worker. It was argued that skilled workers (including professional athletes) were not under the control of the employer. Cozens-Hardy MR rejected this contention and held that Walker was an employee. Nowadays, the test is the mixed test. The mixed test looks to see if the individual receives a wage and if tax is deducted at source by the employer, if the employer provides tools and equipment and if he or she has the exclusive service of the individual. If the answer is yes to these questions, the individual will be deemed to be an employee.

[36] In Ireland, the doctrine was acknowledged by the court in *Murtagh Properties v Cleary*

non-contractual cases whether imposed voluntarily or involuntarily. Any agreement which restricts trade is *prima facie* void; however, if it is considered reasonable and in the interests of the parties as a whole, the court may uphold the agreement. In a general business context, the law seeks to protect the freedom of competition and to eliminate anti-competitive practices and arrangements. In Ireland competition is regulated by the Competition Act, 2002. Section 4 deals with restrictive agreements and section 5 with abuse of a dominant position. These sections are largely based on Articles 101 (formerly 81) and 102 (formerly 82) of the Treaty on Functioning of the European Union (TFEU).[37]

The burden is placed on the party supporting the restrictive clause to prove that it reasonable and thus should be upheld by the court. However, the party arguing that it is an unreasonable restraint of trade will endeavour to prove that the clause cannot be justified in the public interest. Restraint of trade clauses are often used in business. When a business is sold, a term will often be included in the contract of sale that provides that the vendor will not open a similar business in that area for a stipulated number of years. The role of the courts in restraint of trade cases is to decide if the restraint is reasonable and enforceable, or unreasonable and thus void.

Restraint of trade has been used in a number of sporting cases. It has been used by athletes who have been suspended due to doping violations. Others have used the doctrine to challenge wage ceilings,[38] salary caps, exclusionary rules,[39] nationality rules, the transfer fee system which operated in European football,[40] and the retain and transfer system which operated in English football.[41]

Reasons behind Anti-Competitive Agreements

Clubs and governing bodies will justify anti-competitive agreements on the grounds that they protect and enhance the particular sport. Taking

---

[1972] IR 330 where Kenny J relied on Article 40.2.1 of the Irish Constitution. See also *Landers v AG* [1973] 109 ILTR 1, where Finlay J dismissed the plaintiff's claims, although he acknowledged that 'to prepare and follow a chosen career' was an unenumerated right.
[37] For a discussion on European law and sport, see Chapter 7.
[38] *Johnston v Cliftonville* [1984] NI 9.
[39] *Nagle v Feilden* [1966] 2 QB 633.
[40] C-415/93 *Union Royal Belge des Societes de Football Association ASBL & Others v Jean-Marc Bosman* [1995] ECR I-4921.
[41] *Eastham v Newcastle United FC* [1963] 3 All ER 139.

salary caps as an example, the argument is that if there are maximum levels set in the particular sport it will mean that richer clubs cannot monopolise the playing talent by offering more attractive wages.[42] Prior to the Bosman case (see note 40), a quota system operated in European football.[43] The quota system, which restricted the number of foreign players in domestic and European club games, was justified by the Union of European Football Associations (UEFA) and the clubs on the grounds that the 3+2 rule prevented the top clubs from employing all the leading players, and that there was a bond between club and country which preserved national identity in European competition.[44] In *Bosman*, the quota system was struck down by the European Court of Justice.

Evolution of the Doctrine of Restraint of Trade

One of the earliest cases to examine the doctrine was the 1894 case of *Nordenfelt v Maxim Nordenfelt Guns and Ammunition Co Ltd*,[45] where the Court of Appeal stated that there were three elements to be satisfied for a restraining agreement to be justified: 'If the restriction is reasonable …reasonable that is in the interests of the public, so framed and so guarded as to afford adequate protection to the party in whose favour it is imposed, while at the same time it is no way injurious to the public'.[46] Nordenfelt manufactured a type of gun and sold the business to the defendant for £287,500. Two years later, the defendant merged with another company and thus formed a much bigger company. The plaintiff was employed as a managing director of the company and paid £2,000 per month. A clause of his contract stated that Nordenfelt could neither directly nor indirectly trade as the manufacturer of guns for a period of 25 years. The court held that the clause was enforceable given the specialist nature of the business.

When faced with a restraint of trade case, the court is required to perform a balancing act. The court must reconcile the interests of both parties and also consider the effect on the public interest. It is interesting to note that the courts have not always been receptive to restraint of

---

[42] *Johnston v Cliftonville* [1984] NI 9 and *Adamson v NSWRL* (1991) 31 FCR 242.
[43] *Bosman* is discussed in detail in Chapter 7.
[44] 3+2 rule: a team could only field three foreign players and two assimilated. Assimilated referred to players who were not from the country of the team but had come up through the youth ranks in that particular country, For example, a number of Scottish or Welsh players would have come to play club football in England at the age of 14 and would have played for a few years in the youth teams.
[45] [1894] AC 535.
[46] *Ibid.*, at 565.

trade cases involving sporting organisations. In *McInnes v Onslow Fane*, the court showed its disdain for intervention in the decisions of sporting bodies 'even where those bodies are concerned with the means of livelihood of those who take part in those activities'.[47]

Restraint of Trade Clauses and Employment Contracts

In general, a lot depends on the nature of the restraint of trade clause in an employment contract. It is a central tenet of the employment relationship that an employee provides exclusive service to their employer. A clause that stipulates that the worker has to work solely for the employer and not for a rival employer would be deemed to be valid. However, a clause which states that an employee could not work for another business after the termination of the employment could arguably be deemed invalid and an unreasonable restraint of trade.

Modern Interpretation of Restraint of Trade

The doctrine of restraint of trade was given a more modern interpretation in *Esso Petroleum v Harpers Garage (Stourport) Ltd*[48] where the court set out three criteria:

1. Does the restraint go further than necessary to afford adequate protection to the party in whose favour it is granted?
2. Can it be justified in the interests of the party who is restrained?
3. Can it be justified in the public interest?

In this case, Harpers Garage owned two garages and had entered into a solus agreement with Esso in respect of each garage.[49] Harpers agreed to buy all its motor fuel from Esso, to keep the garages open at all reasonable hours and not to sell the garages without ensuring that the purchaser entered into a similar agreement with Esso. Esso agreed to allow a rebate on all fuels bought. The agreement in relation to one garage was to last for four years and five months and in relation to the other for twenty-one years. The agreement for 21 years was not redeemable before the 21 years were up. This garage was mortgaged to Esso in return for £7,000.

---

[47] [1978] 3 All ER 211, at 223.
[48] [1968] AC 269.
[49] A solus agreement is where an oil company advances money to help with the purchase or development of a garage and/or offers a rebate on the price of fuel, and the garage owner undertakes in return to sell only the company's products at the garage. Similar agreements happen in other trades.

The House of Lords deemed both agreements to be within the ambit of the doctrine of restraint of trade. The Lords held that the 21-year agreement, which was covered by way of mortgage, did not exclude the doctrine. The agreements were *prima facie* void and could only be enforced if they were reasonable. The Lords held that the agreement for four years and five months was reasonable; however, the agreement for twenty-one years was not and was declared void. In a sporting setting, restraint of trade can arise in a number of situations, for example, the retain and transfer system and salary caps. Similar to the above cases, the court will decide whether the restriction is reasonable or unreasonable, taking into account the effect the particular restriction has on the parties (i.e. the players, the clubs and the league) and the general public.

Retain and Transfer System

The retain and transfer system operated for many years in English football.[50] Under the system, when a player was out of contract the club could hold on to his registration after the termination of the contract. The player could be prevented from moving to a new club unless a fee was paid to the previous club. Even though the player was out of contract, the previous club could effectively prevent him from moving and earning a livelihood with a new club. While it had a far more draconian effect on the player, it also affected clubs as they were restricted from signing out-of-contract players.

In essence, the system inhibited the free labour market in professional players. As mentioned above, *Walker* established that footballers are employees. If a similar system operated in any other labour market it would have been deemed unlawful. However, the practice existed for a number of years in professional football. In the *Kingaby* case from 1912, the requirement that a fee be paid for an out-of-contract player was considered, although the court ruled that the terms of the contract permitted the imposition of a fee.[51] The clubs took this case to mean that the retain and transfer system was lawful. The issue of restraint of trade had not been discussed in *Kingaby*.

George Eastham successfully invoked the doctrine of restraint of trade when he challenged the retain and transfer system in 1960s.[52]

---

[50] It was introduced in 1885 by the Football Association (FA). A maximum wage of £4 had been introduced in 1901. There was also a ban on the payment of bonuses.
[51] *Kingaby v Aston Villa* (1912) *The Times*, 28 March 1912.
[52] *Eastham v Newcastle United FC* [1964] Ch 413. In *Aldershot FC v Banks* (4 Nov 1955)

Eastham was employed as a professional footballer and had a yearly contract. At the end of the 1961 season, Eastham requested a move to another club but was refused by Newcastle and told that he would be retained for another year on his existing wage. Eastham refused to re-sign and was informed by the club that he was being retained as permitted by the Football Association (FA) rules. He appealed the deci-sion to the league management committee but his request was declined. Eastham decided to challenge the decision in the courts and sought a declaration that the agreement was an unreasonable restraint of trade. Wilberforce J declared the system to be an unreasonable restraint of trade as it 'imposed excessive fetters' on a footballer who was out of contract with his club and was seeking a transfer to another club.[53] The court held that the league, association and constituent clubs could not legitimately justify the system.

While the court declared the retain system to be an unlawful restraint of trade, the transfer system continued, albeit in modified form. The club could offer the player a new contract with terms as favourable as the expired contract in order to retain his registration. If the club decided not to renew the contract, the player was deemed a free agent. However, transfers were still at the discretion of the selling club and if a club was willing to maintain the player at the previous wage, he was obliged to stay with that club.[54] Wages inflated as a result of Eastham. Johnny Haynes, who captained England and played for Fulham, saw his wages inflate by 400 per cent when his wages were increased to £100.[55] In response, the clubs began to employ fewer players; by the 1967 season there were 2,700 fewer professional players employed.[56]

In 1978 changes were made to the transfer system in English football. Players were deemed to have freedom of contract, but there were still restrictions.[57] If a club offered a player a new contract that was as favourable as his expired contract and he refused it, the new club would be required to pay a transfer fee. The fee was to be decided by the two clubs, but if this proved impossible, the compensation fee would be decided by a FA tribunal. An out-of-contract player faced a number of obstacles. He would have to find a club that was either willing to agree

---

restraint of trade was raised in the case but the case was not ruled on on this ground.
[53] [1964] Ch 413, at 418.
[54] S. Dobson and J.A. Goddard, *The Economics of Football* (Cambridge: Cambridge University Press, 2001), at 91–92.
[55] *Ibid.*
[56] *Ibid.*
[57] *Ibid.*, at 93.

to a compensation fee with the old club or, if agreement was not reached, would be willing to have the fee decided by a FA tribunal.[58]

In *Buckley v Tutty*, a similar case in Australia, the retain and transfer system in rugby was challenged.[59] The High Court held that the retain and transfer system was an unlawful restraint of trade and that restraint went further than necessary to protect the reasonable interests of the league. In *Buckley*, the court went further than its English counterparts in *Eastham*.

Restraint of Trade and Doping Cases

The above cases involved a club's rules on the transfer system. The courts had no reservations about declaring the rules to be unreasonable restraints of trade. However, reconciling an athlete's right to earn a livelihood after being suspended following a doping infraction has not always met with universal approval. Suspensions can range from three months to life depending on the drug and the number of offences committed. In *Gasser v Stinson*, the plaintiff argued that the IAAF's policy of strict liability and their imposition of a mandatory suspension constituted an unreasonable restraint of trade.[60] The IAAF defended the ban on the grounds that the athletes were 'amateurs' and that they 'did not and could not under IAAF rules earn their daily bread as athletes'. Although the athletes received money from sponsors, the IAAF contended that these sponsorship contracts were between the national federation and the sponsors; therefore the athletes were not privy to these contracts. Scott J rejected this argument:

> I would accept that restraint of trade law would not be applicable to activities that were undertaken for no financial reward at all (for example, school sport) ... But, in a sport which allows competitors to exploit their ability in the sport for financial gain, which allows that gain to be a direct consequence of participation in competition, a ban on competition is, in my judgment, a restraint of trade.

Next the court had to establish if the restraint was unreasonable. Scott J held the restraint to be reasonable. He agreed with the IAAF that the rules on drug testing were in the interests of both the sport and the public. The court dismissed Gasser's action on the strict liability issue and the restraint of trade issue, with Scott J concluding that the 'courts

---

[58] *Ibid.*
[59] (1971) 125 CLR 353.
[60] [1988] QBD, unreported, 15 June 1988.

should be slow to interfere in the manner in which an association governing a particular branch of sport administers the sport'.[61]

The English High Court in *Wilander and Novacek v Tobin* rejected claims by tennis players that the International Tennis Federation (ITF) rules on doping were contrary to the Treaty of Rome under the following: Article 48 (now 45) on the free movement of workers, Article 59 (now 66) on the freedom of establishment, Article 60 (now 57) on the freedom to provide a service, Article 85 (now 101) on restrictive agreements and Article 86 (now 102) on an abuse of a dominant position.[62] The players, who had tested positive for a banned substance at the 1995 French Open and as a result had been eliminated from competition, claimed, *inter alia*, that the doping rules of the federation and their subsequent suspension were an unreasonable restraint of trade. The applicants also challenged the fact that the burden of proof had been placed on them, in a reverse of the situation that usually applies. Neill J found the shifting of the burden of proof 'troublesome' but, in considering the procedure as a whole, he held that the procedures did not amount to a restraint of trade. The decision was appealed by the players, with Mr Justice Lightman upholding the doping procedures.

The issue of restraint of trade was also raised by Dwain Chambers.[63] Chambers won the 100 metre sprint at the Olympic trials. Usually, the winner of an Olympic trial would be deemed eligible to compete in the Olympics. The British Olympic Association (BOA) refused to deem Chambers eligible for the Beijing Olympics on the grounds that he had previously been suspended for a serious doping infraction. The BOA based its decision on the controversial Bye-law 25 of the BOA, a provision which was introduced in 1992.[64] Chambers subsequently applied to the High Court to obtain an interlocutory injunction. He

---

[61] This argument was raised by Denning LJ in *Lee v The Showmen's Guild of Great Britain* [1952] 2 QB 329, [1952] 2 ALL ER 1175.
[62] [1996] EWCA (20 December 1996), High Court, unreported, 26 March 1996.
[63] *Chambers v British Olympic Association* [2008] EWHC 2028 (QBD).
[64] This bye-law has been challenged on a number of occasions. Most recently, show jumper Michael Whitaker successfully appealed his ban from competing in the 2012 Olympics. The BOA Appeals Panel held that the doping infraction was minor and there was no evidence to suggest that Whitaker or his groom had deliberately administered the prohibited substance to the horse. There have been 27 successful challenges since the rule was introduced in 1992. The rule has attracted sharp criticism from former athletes and Dick Pound, the former chairman of WADA. See D. Mackay, 'Whitaker Becomes Latest Banned Briton to Overturn BOA Doping Bye-law', *Inside the Games*, 17 March 2010 (available online: <http://www. insidethegames.bizlast>, last accessed 7 July 2010).

argued that the bye-law constituted an unreasonable restraint of trade. He argued the case under the common law doctrine of restraint of trade and also under the competition provisions of the then Articles 81 and 82 of the EC Treaty (now Articles 101 and 102 of the TFEU). He also argued that the court had the right to set aside the bye-law as part of its supervisory jurisdiction. The High Court did not pursue the case under European law.

On the issue of restraint of trade, the court held that it would be difficult for Chambers to prove that his ability to earn a livelihood had been affected. The court noted that the Olympic Games was only one competition and those who qualify for the Olympics and win medals are not rewarded financially. On this ground, the court rejected the application for an interlocutory injunction.

On the issue that the court had the power to set aside the rule as part of its supervisory jurisdiction, the court cited with approval the case of *Stevenage Borough v Football League Ltd*.[65] In *Stevenage*, the plaintiffs (the club) had delayed in bringing the action and as a result the court dismissed the action, holding that even if there was a restraint of trade it was immaterial in light of the delay. Stevenage knew of the rules of the competition from the start of the season and by waiting until the end of the season to challenge the rules it was prejudicial to another team, Torquay United, which had been promoted in the meantime. Similarly, Chambers knew of the bye-law when he returned from his suspension and by leaving it until 72 hours before the BOA sent its team selection to the International Olympic Committee (IOC), Chambers had delayed in bringing an action and such action justified the court not granting the interlocutory injunction.

The above decisions demonstrate the English courts' reluctance to interfere in the determinations of internal tribunals in doping cases.[66] This position can be contrasted with that of Australian and Canadian courts which have overturned the decisions of governing bodies to suspend an athlete on grounds of it being unreasonable restraint of trade. In one Australian decision, *Robertson v Australian Professional Cycling Council Incorporated*, the court held that it was a matter of law whether

---

[65] [1996] EWCA Civ 570 (6 August 1996).

[66] The English courts have also been more stringent in their application of the strict liability standard in sporting cases. In Gasser's native country, Switzerland, the Swiss Court refused to uphold the principle of strict liability and a similar situation arose in the case of Katrin Krabbe, where a German Court upheld her ban only because she had knowingly taken the drugs. See L. Donnellan, 'Strict Liability in Drug Cases?' (2002) 10(6) *Sports Law Administration and Practice* 13–16.

the restraint was unreasonable.[67] This case concerned a professional cyclist who tested positive for nandrolone and was disqualified from holding an Australian Professional Cycling Council (APCC) licence for two years. Robertson appealed to the APCC executive but his claim was dismissed. He brought an action to the courts arguing that, as a professional cyclist, he would be unable to cycle for two years and thus this restraint was unreasonable.[68] Waddell CJ first established that the activities of a professional cyclist should be regarded a trade.[69] The court then held the withholding of the licence to be a restraint of trade.

The next issue to decide was whether the restraint was reasonable. Robertson had argued that the defendant had given two other competitors less stringent sanctions while they had been competing in Germany. The APCC defended this decision by asserting that the two competitors were subject to the rules of their organisation's world governing body, Union Cycliste Internationale (UCI); the plaintiff's doping infraction, however, occurred in Australia. The APCC followed the anti-doping policy of the Australian Sports Commission (ASC). However, this policy provided for a 'more draconian penalty' than that of the UCI.[70] Waddell CJ, holding in favour of the plaintiff,[71] concluded, 'there is no evidence as to why it is that more drastic penalties are needed in the interests of the proper conduct of the professional cycling industry in Australia than in European and other overseas countries.'[72]

Ben Johnson, a Canadian athlete, also brought proceedings against the IAAF on the basis that his suspension amounted to an unreasonable restraint of trade.[73] Johnson had served a two-year ban after testing

---

[67] Unreported, Supreme Court of New South Wales, Equity Division, 26 August 1992.
[68] Robertson also claimed that it was beyond the defendant's powers as the APCC had enacted rules of certain international cycling organisations which provided for less stringent sanctions.
[69] The High Court in *Buckley v Tutty* [1971] 125 CLR 353 had regarded the activities of a professional footballer as a trade. Waddell CJ in *Robertson* cited *Buckley* with approval.
[70] The UCI had imposed a three-month deferred suspension and other penalties on the two competitors in Germany. The approach of the APCC may have been due to financial reasons as the ASC would deny funding and other assistance to governing bodies that breached the ASC's doping rules. See T. Buti and S. Fridman, 'Drug Testing in Sport: Legal Challenges and Issues' (1999) 20(2) *University of Queensland Law Journal* 154–185, at 165.
[71] It had been Robertson's first offence and he was taking the drug to increase his body weight but had found it ineffective. He subsequently stopped taking the drug but mistakenly believed that all traces would be gone by the time the event was to take place.
[72] The defendants had declined to take part in the proceedings and so the court made the point that their conclusion had been drawn from the evidence and, had the defendant taken part, it may have resulted in a different conclusion.
[73] *Johnson v IAAF*, 41 OTC 95, 1997.

positive for the anabolic steroid stanozol. He returned to competition but was banned for life after committing a second doping offence.[74] In the Ontario Court, Madam Justice Caswell contended that the IAAF had not followed the correct procedures, but, while she considered this to be inherently unfair and a deprivation of natural justice, Johnson had failed to exhaust all remedies within the domestic tribunal.[75] The judge held that his life ban was a restraint of trade but was reasonable in the circumstances.

The case was subsequently appealed,[76] but the court upheld Madam Justice Caswell's decision. Johnson brought a final case[77] before an adjudicator seeking reinstatement. Under section 11 of the Canadian Doping Control Standard (SOP)[78] an athlete can apply for reinstatement if exceptional circumstances warrant such a reinstatement.[79] The IAAF is not bound by the decision of an adjudicator and, even if the athlete is reinstated, he or she remains ineligible until reinstated by the IAAF Council.[80] The adjudicator presented evidence put forward by the plaintiff that he had not been afforded the proper procedures in accordance with IAAF rules.[81] Mew, the adjudicator, made the point that partaking

---

[74] Under Rule 60 of the IAAF Doping Control Rules and Regulations, a second offence renders the athlete ineligible for IAAF-sanctioned events for life. Athletics Canada also follows this rule.

[75] The IAAF Doping Commission had refused to permit the plaintiff's counsel and expert to appear and make representations at a meeting held on 5 March 1993 in Paris.

[76] *Johnson v Athletics Canada & IAAF*, 114 OAC 388, 1998.

[77] In the matter of an adjudication under section II of the Doping Control Standard Operating Procedures of the Canadian Centre for Ethics in Sport: Category 11 reinstatement application by Ben Johnson (April 19, 1999) Graeme Mew, adjudicator (unreported).

[78] The Canadian Centre for Ethics in Sport is an independent, non-profit-making and national body supported by the Canadian Government that works in association with the Royal Canadian Mounted Police. The CCES was established in 1991. Originally it was named the Canadian Anti-Doping Organisation and subsequently the Canadian Centre for Drug Free Sport. The organisation was created to encourage a drug-free environment in sport and to act as a protection agency for athletes' rights in drug-testing procedures.

[79] Under sections 11(2) and (3). These exceptional circumstances include age, remorse, circumstances surrounding the infraction, any factors that may have caused or contributed to the applicant's diminished capacity, the applicant's experience in the sport and their contribution to the sport. This list is not exhaustive. After Johnson was suspended he had no other source of income besides his trust fund.

[80] The IAAF also operates a 'contamination rule' which prevents other athletes from competing with a banned athlete in events organised by the governing body. This rule is arguably a restraint of trade on the other athletes. In recent years, the IAAF has relaxed the rule. It is rarely, if ever, used nowadays but at the time of the Johnson case the rule was in use.

[81] In 1993 Johnson was informed that he had a right to appeal under IAAF Rule 59.3.

in athletics may be considered a privilege and not a right, but 'once the privilege is acquired, it should only be taken through a process which is objectively fair.' He considered Johnson's age and his post-infraction behaviour and granted him a reinstatement, subject to a number of conditions.[82] The adjudicator held Johnson's life ban to be an unreasonable restraint of trade.

Restraint of Trade and Part-Time Professionals

Part-time professionals may also invoke the doctrine of restraint of trade. In *Johnston v Cliftonville* the plaintiff was a part-time professional footballer whose 'main' employment was as a civil servant.[83] The English High Court in *Gasser v Stinson* held that the doctrine applied to 'amateur' athletes who were permitted to have payments made into a trust fund, which would be available to them on their retirement.

Restraint of Trade and Wage Restrictions

The issue of wage restrictions was also considered in *Johnston v Cliftonville*.[84] Johnston was a part-time footballer who was given a signing-on fee in excess of that permitted by the Irish Football League rules. The league regulations specified maximum payments for wages, signing-on bonuses and match bonuses in league competitions. Clubs were obliged to adhere to these restrictions as failure do so could result in a fine and deduction of points. The plaintiff challenged these rules on the grounds that they were an unlawful restraint of trade. The court accepted that the rules were a restraint and that the restraint was unreasonable. The court found that the league had failed in its attempts to justify the restraint as being reasonable. The restriction was defended on the grounds that the wealthier clubs would monopolise the playing talent which could threaten the financial viability of some of the smaller

---

However, the rule stated the word 'appeal' but contained a notice of a hearing. Johnson maintained that had he been told that he could avail of an independent review by a private arbitrator within 60 days for less than $100,000 to $200,000, he would have availed of such.

[82] He had showed an eagerness to work with young people and disadvantaged groups in the community. Johnson had to be available for out-of-competition testing at his own expense three times a year for three years, he had to be there within 24 hours when called for testing, and he was prevented from competing in Canada until the IAAF had lifted his ban. The adjudicator gave Johnson four months to apply to the IAAF for reinstatement. Athletics Canada was bound by the decision.

[83] [1984] NI 9. *Johnston* was cited with approval in *Buckley v Tutty* (1971) 125 CLR 353.

[84] [1984] NI 9.

clubs. The court rejected both arguments and held that the restrictions were an unreasonable restraint of trade.

Wage ceilings are sometimes used by sports with limited financial resources. In order to protect the league, player wages are capped. For example, the American Women's National Basketball Association (WNBA) limits the wage a player can receive to $120,000 per year.[85] As no player has ever challenged the ceiling, the restriction continues to operate.[86]

Restraint of Trade and Salary Caps

In Australia, the Australian Football League (AFL), the National Rugby League (NRL), A-League soccer and the National Basketball League (NBA) use salary caps.[87] While wage ceilings restrict the amount an individual player can earn, salary caps set a limit on the earnings of the players collectively.[88] Salary caps remain legal in Australia (and indeed in some American sports) as no court has ever formally commented on the lawfulness of the practice. In *Adamson v NSWRL (No. 2)*, the draft system was challenged. However, some comments on salary caps were made *obiter*.[89] Thorpe notes, 'the comments were inconclusive and opinions vary as to whether these statements support the validity of a salary cap or not'.[90] The purpose of a salary cap is to ensure the economic viability of clubs and to ensure parity between clubs so that the richer clubs cannot buy all the best players and thus dominate competition.[91] Recently, rugby in England has introduced salary caps in the top level leagues.[92]

Restraint of Trade and Player Drafts

Player drafts are used in a number of sports in the United States, Canada and Australia. The draft provides that the team that placed last

---

[85] D. Thorpe and A. Buti et al., *Sports Law* (South Melbourne: Oxford University Press, 2009), at 292.

[86] Thorpe and Buti *et al.*, *Sports Law*.

[87] Salary caps are also used by the National Football League (NFL) in the United States.

[88] Thorpe and Buti *et al.*, *Sports Law*, at 292.

[89] (1991) 31 FCR 242, at 294.

[90] Thorpe and Buti *et al.*, *Sports Law*, at 292.

[91] See A. Caiger and S. Gardiner, *Professional Sport in the European Union: Regulation and De-Regulation* (Cambridge: Cambridge University Press, 2000), at 8.

[92] See P. Rees, 'Salary Cap for England's Premiership Clubs to Be Increased to £4 Million', *The Guardian*, 5 January 2008 (available online: <http://www.guardian.co.uk/sport/2008/jan/04/rugbyunion.premiership>, last accessed 10 March 2010).

in the previous season is given the first choice of available players from a pool. The draft works in reverse order with the top team being the last to pick available players. The process is repeated for a second round, third round and so on.[93] The draft system remains legal as it is deemed to be in the interests of sport (and in the public interest) that the richer teams do not monopolise the player talent.

For the player, it has been argued that there is an element of restraint of trade in this. However, after two years the player is a free agent and can move to another team. In the National Football League (NFL) in the United States, the 32 teams in the league select new eligible college players. The draft for 2010 took place on 22–24 April. The rules provide that players must be out of high school for two-and-a-half years and they must have three years' experience playing at college level. In order to be allowed in the draft, the player must first sign with an agent. A rookie draft player's salary is capped for the first year. The wages also depend on whether the player is drafted in the first or last round. A player drafted in round one will be paid more than a player drafted in round seven. It is a huge event in the NFL calendar, with fans obtaining tickets to attend the draft.

Restraint of Trade and Exclusionary Rules

In *Nagle v Feilden*, the plaintiff, a race-horse trainer, was refused a trainer's licence from the Jockey Club (the governing body) on the grounds that the club had an unwritten practice of refusing to give licences to female trainers.[94] The head lad in her stable had been given a licence and Nagle bypassed the ban by using this licence. She sought a declaration that refusal was contrary to public policy. The trial court struck out her statement of claim, saying that it disclosed no cause of action (i.e. the court ruled in effect that no known legal wrong had been alleged by the plaintiff). The Court of Appeal overruled the trial court and remitted the case to hearing. The Court of Appeal stated that there was an arguable case that in common law there is a right to work at one's profession without being arbitrarily or unreasonably excluded by anyone having governance of it; to exclude a woman from being a horse trainer by reason of her sex would be capricious and unreasonable and therefore the practice of the defendants was contrary to public policy.

---

[93] C. Davis, 'The Draft System in Professional Team Sports and the Restraint of Trade Doctrine: Is the AFL Draft Distinguishable from the NSWRL Draft?' (2006) 1(1) *Australian and New Zealand Sports Law Journal*, 80–102, at 81.
[94] [1966] 1 All ER 689.

Restraint of Trade and Governing Body Rules

In *Greig v Insole* the International Cricket Conference (ICC) placed restrictions on cricketers playing in competitions not sanctioned by it.[95] The ICC placed a retrospective ban on cricketers who agreed to join the Kerry Packer World Series Cricket. Packer was a private promoter who organised a number of test cricketers to play in an autumn and winter series in Australia. The ICC, as the controlling body of test cricket, had the exclusive power to regulate the qualification rules for cricketers to play in test matches. In response to the Packer agreement, the ICC retrospectively changed the qualification rules for test cricketers so that no player could play in a match not approved by the ICC unless the ICC gave express permission. The Test and County Cricket Board (TCCB) (the body that regulates county cricket) planned a meeting and it was believed that a similar ban would be introduced. Before this meeting took place, three of the cricketers brought proceedings against the TCCB and ICC, seeking a declaration that the rules were in restraint of trade. The promoter also sued the defendants for unlawful inducement to breach of contract. Both claims were heard in the same case by Slade J. Holding in favour of both sets of plaintiffs, Slade J held that the rule changes by the ICC and proposed change by the TCCB were unreasonable restraints of trade. While the court accepted that the rule changes were introduced to protect the sport and were in the public interest, they were disproportionate and thus unlawful.

A similar decision was made by the Western Australian Cricket Association (WACA) in the case of *Hughes v Western Australian Cricket Association*.[96] The plaintiff was banned from professional cricket for his part in a rebel tour to South Africa. The defendants would not recognise any match not sanctioned by them. The court found in favour of Hughes and held the restriction to be an unreasonable restraint of trade.

In *Watson v Prager*, the plaintiff, a professional boxer, entered into an agreement with the defendant to act as his manager and promoter for a three-year period.[97] The agreement involved a conflict of interest as the roles of manager and promoter have different aims. A manager has a duty to organise events and negotiate on behalf of the boxer. A manager should act in the best interests of the boxer. However, as a

---

[95] [1978] 3 All ER 449.
[96] (1986) 69 ALR 660.
[97] [1991] 3 All ER 487.

promoter, the individual has a personal and financial interest in events he or she is promoting. The agreement was the standard form prescribed by the BBBC – professional boxers and managers would only be licensed if they signed the standard form contracts and the only term left open to negotiation was the duration. The contract contained an option to extend the length of the contract if the boxer won one of a number of championships. Watson won the Commonwealth title and the defendant purported to extend the contract for a further three years. The court held the contract to constitute an unreasonable restraint of trade because it tied the boxer to fighting on promotions in which the manager had a direct financial interest and on terms unilaterally imposed by the manager; the boxer could not negotiate his own fight terms.

In *Newport AFC v Football Association of Wales*, the plaintiffs sought a declaration that the decision of the Football Association of Wales (FAW) to prevent Welsh clubs playing in English leagues was an unreasonable restraint of trade.[98] The object of this prohibition was to promote the League of Wales. The three plaintiff clubs resigned from the FAW and joined the English FA. The FAW objected to the clubs playing home matches in Wales and the FA honoured that objection by insisting that the clubs play home matches within the territory of England. The plaintiffs suffered a decrease in revenue from their home gates and sponsorship also decreased.

The plaintiffs asked the FAW to reconsider their position but were refused. A declaration was sought by the plaintiffs that the decision to exclude them from playing home games in Wales was void as being an unreasonable restraint of trade. The plaintiffs also sought injunctions to prevent the defendant acting in unreasonable restraint of trade. As the plaintiffs wanted to play their home matches in Wales in the following season, they applied to the court for an interlocutory injunction in the hope a full trial would be heard before the season started. The court granted the interlocutory injunction on the basis that the clubs had shown that there was a serious issue to be tried,[99] i.e. there was a strong case to be made that they were subject to an unreasonable restraint of trade. The FAW failed to establish that its rule was no more than was necessary to protect the legitimate interests of the Welsh FA.

---

[98] [1995] 2 All ER 87.
[99] *American Cyanamid Co v Ethicon Ltd* [1975] 1 All ER 504; [1975] AC 396; [1975] 2 WLR 316, HL.

Restraint of Trade and Irish Sport

There is one Irish case on restraint of trade in sport. In *Macken v O'Reilly* the international show jumper Eddie Macken challenged the rules of the Equestrian Federation of Ireland (EFI) (now Horse Sport Ireland).[100] The EFI, the national governing body, was affiliated with the Fédération Equestre Internationale (FEI). Consequently, the FEI rules were binding on the EFI. Article 100, Rule 1 of the FEI General Regulations provided that the regulations were established so that competitors would compete on fair and equal conditions. The EFI passed a resolution that required Irish competitors in international competitions to ride Irish-bred horses.

Macken challenged the resolution on two grounds. In the first instance, the resolution constituted an unlawful restraint of trade and, second, it prevented Irish competitors from competing under fair and equal conditions, in accordance with Article 100. The Supreme Court ruled in favour of the defendants and upheld the validity of the resolution. It was considered to be reasonable, necessary and fair; it was needed to assist building the Irish horse breeding industry in the interests of equestrian sport generally in the country.

THE LAW OF AGENCY

Agency is a common law creation and was used for practical and commercial considerations to allow a party to act through an agent.[101] The law of agency is based on the following maxim: *qui facit per alium facit per se* (he who acts through another is deemed to act in person), in other words a principal is liable for the acts of his agent. An agent is a person employed to bring the principal into contractual relations with a third party. Therefore the agent is in a fiduciary relationship with the principal. The central feature of the relationship is that the agent has power to make a binding contract between the principal and a third party without the agent becoming a party to the contract. Once the agent has performed the contracted task, the agent departs and the principal and third party continue with the contract. Generally, the law does not require any particular formalities to be observed in the appointment of an agent.[102]

---

[100] [1979] ILRM 79.

[101] See L. Donnellan, 'The Regulation of Football Agents in Ireland' in *Player's Agents Worldwide: Legal Aspects* (eds. R. Siekmann and R. Parrish *et al.*) (The Hague: TMC Asser Press, 2007), 295–308.

[102] H. Ellis, *Modern Irish Commercial and Consumer Law* (Bristol: Jordons, 2004), at para 38.3.

The appointment may be made orally, in writing,[103] by deed[104] or by conduct.[105]

Duties of an Agent

Most of the law pertaining to agency is judge-made.[106] The focus is on the actions of an agent which bind the principal to the third party and in this area the following are of importance: actual, usual and ostensible authority and also the doctrine of restraint of trade.[107] The agent must carry out the instructions given by the principal. In the case of *Turpin v Bilton*,[108] the defendant was an insurance broker who was employed to arrange insurance for the plaintiff's ship. However, the agent failed to insure the ship, which was subsequently lost at sea. The agent was held liable for damages.

The agent must also exercise a certain standard of care and skill; however, the level depends on whether the agent is getting paid. In *Chariot Inns v Assicurazioni Generali SPA and Coyle Hamilton Phillips*,[109] the plaintiff company employed insurance brokers as agents who advised them not to disclose relevant information on the proposal form relating to a previous fire claim. A serious fire occurred at the premises in Ranelagh and the insurance company repudiated liability on the grounds of the non-disclosure of the claim in respect of the Leeson Street property. The court held the agents to be held liable for negligence.

An agent is also under a duty to perform the task personally and not to delegate without authority from the principal;[110] the agent must avoid a conflict of interests,[111] and may not make a secret profit.[112]

---

[103] *Ibid*. If the agency agreement is in writing, the agent is usually appointed by way of a written document or letter of appointment. Ellis notes that this is not always necessary unless required by statute.

[104] This would be used in the appointment of a universal agent who is appointed under a power of attorney. A universal agent is one who performs all acts and duties which the principal is empowered to perform. The universal agent is appointed under a power of attorney, a legal document which allows the agent to act on behalf of the principal.

[105] Here an agency appointment is implied from the conduct of the parties involved.

[106] M. Forde, *Commercial Law* (3rd ed., Haywards Heath: Tottel Publishing, 2005), at para 1.069.

[107] Forde, *Commercial Law*. For a comprehensive discussion, see Ellis, *Modern Irish Commercial and Consumer Law*, Chapter 38.

[108] (1843) 5 Man. & G. 455.

[109] [1981] IR 199; [1981] ILRM 173.

[110] Unless he obtains the implied or expressed consent of the principal. See *De Bussche v Alt* (1878) 8 Ch D 286 (CA).

[111] *Aberdeen Railway Co. v Blaikie Bros* (1854) 1 Marq 461.

[112] *Lamb v Evans* [1893] 1 Ch 218.

Principal's Duties

An agent may receive remuneration, commission or a lien.[113] An agent may only claim remuneration where there is an express or implied term to that effect contained in the contract. The amount depends on the terms of the contract. If there is no agreed sum, a reasonable sum is payable. Where an agent carries out extra work in addition to that outlined in his or her contract, the principal is under an implied duty to pay the agent for this extra work.[114] In a situation where the agent is a professional person and there is no express agreement as to remuneration there is a presumption that he or she is entitled to receive reasonable remuneration for his or her services.[115] Reasonable remuneration may be assessed according to what is customary in the business.[116]

Commission

In general, an agent will only be entitled to commission if he brings about the desired result. Agents will not be entitled to commission in the following circumstances:

- They act outside the scope of their actual authority
- They act in a manner which they know, or ought to have known, is unlawful or dishonest
- They commit a serious breach of their duties as an agent[117]

Termination of Agency

Agency may be terminated by acts of the parties or by the operation of the law. The relationship may be terminated as the contract has been performed, it may be ended by agreement between the parties or there may be a fundamental breach of a condition which renders the contract void. In the latter instance the principal may also sue for damages.

Agency is automatically terminated on the bankruptcy, liquidation, death or insanity of the agent or principal, or the agency may have simply been created for a limited period and that time has now lapsed.

---

[113] An agent may hold on to his principal's property to secure payment of any money owed to him by the principal.
[114] Ellis, *Modern Irish Commercial and Consumer Law*, at para 38.29.
[115] *Ibid.*
[116] *Ibid.*
[117] *Ibid.*

Irish Football and Football Agents

The Football Association of Ireland (FAI) is the governing body for football in Ireland. There are very few professional footballers in Ireland. The majority of agents resident in Ireland represent clients in England, as there is very little agent activity in Ireland. Most Irish-based agents represent players in the English leagues and these agents are regulated by the FA in England. There are currently 18 licensed Irish-based football agents. While these agents have a licence from the FAI, most would not be engaged by Irish-based footballers. Clubs do not engage the services of an agent and players do not earn enough money to pay the agent fees.

The procedure for obtaining a licence is relatively straightforward. Applicants must satisfy the FAI that they have an impeccable reputation. On fulfilling this requirement, they must sit a written examination consisting of twenty questions, five of which are set by the FAI.[118] Once they have passed the examination and have obtained professional liability insurance, they receive their licence from the FAI. The FAI then draws up a list of its licensed agents and sends it to FIFA after every examination date. Once the agent has passed the examination and has satisfied the minimum criteria required by FIFA, he or she is permitted to offer his or her services throughout the European Union (EU) and European Economic Area (EEA).[119]

Apart from these formalities, player agents in Ireland are not subject to any statutory provisions.[120] If the agent is a solicitor, he or she may act as an agent in the course of his or her work as a solicitor. A solicitor who acts as football agent is not only bound by the terms of the agency contract but also by the lawyer–client relationship. Under Irish law, solicitors are governed by their professional body, the Law Society of Ireland. Solicitors are regulated by a number of Acts,[121] statutory instruments and the Law Society guide to professional conduct.[122] However,

---

[118] The exam takes place in FAI headquarters in Dublin. There is a fee of €125 to sit the exam and the applicant is notified of the impending exam around a month in advance. The fee is payable on the morning of the exam.

[119] The rules were introduced in 2001 and revised in 2005 and 2008. The most recent rules are available online: <http://www.fifa.com/aboutfifa/federation/administration/playersagents/regulationstatustransfertsplayers.html> (last accessed 16 August 2010).

[120] If the agent is a solicitor he would also be regulated by the Law Society of Ireland.

[121] For an interesting discussion of the merits of engaging the services of a lawyer over a non-lawyer, see N. Rose, 'Agent of Change?' (2005) 102(31) *Law Society Gazette* 18–20.

[122] *A Guide to Professional Conduct of Solicitors in Ireland* (2nd ed., Dublin: Law Society of Ireland, 2002).

for agents that are not in the legal profession, there is little regulation outside the terms of the agency agreement and the FIFA regulations.

MEDIA RIGHTS

Media Rights in Ireland

Irish law, like its English counterpart, does not recognise a property right in a sports event itself or in the news emanating from the event.[123] This was confirmed in the Australian case of *Victoria Park Racing and Recreational Grounds Co Ltd v Taylor & Others*, were Latham CJ held that '[a] "spectacle" cannot be "owned" in any ordinary sense of that word.'[124] A judge in a common law country like Ireland or England could apply this ruling also.

For an event manager or a governing body to secure exclusive broadcast rights over a sporting event, a contractual agreement must be negotiated with the owner of the venue and the spectators.[125] This agreement will provide that only the official broadcaster can gain access to the venue for the purpose of broadcasting the footage of the event in question.[126] When the proprietary right in question concerns a private individual, who privately owns a sports ground, the situation is quite straightforward. The matter becomes more complicated when an event takes place outside the confines of an enclosed venue; for example, a marathon, motor rally or ocean yacht race.[127] In this situation, an event owner may find it difficult to invoke proprietary rights

---

[123] See L. Donnellan, 'TV Rights in Irish Football' in *TV Rights in Europe* (eds. R. Siekmann and Professor I. Blackshaw) (The Hague: TMC Asser Press, 2009), 373–387.

[124] (1937) 58 CLR 479. This case was an appeal from a judgment for the defendants handed down by the Supreme Court of New South Wales. The defendant, Taylor, owned land near the racecourse. He placed an elevated platform on his land. From this platform he was able to see what took place on the racecourse and was able to read the information which appeared on notice boards on the course as to the starters and the winners of the races. The other defendant, the Commonwealth Broadcasting Corporation, placed a wooden structure on the platform on Taylor's land and through a telephone proceeded to comment and give results from the racecourse. The Commonwealth Broadcasting Corporation held a broadcasting licence under the regulations made under the Wireless Telegraphy Acts, 1905–1936. Victoria Park Racing argued that the activities of the defendants prevented people from going to the races and paying for admission. This was based on evidence that some spectators preferred hearing the races from the adjoining land than attending the racecourse. Victoria Park Racing brought an action against the defendants for nuisance and an unnatural use of the elevated platforms ('angles') on Taylor's land. Latham CJ rejected the appeal and held in favour of the defendants.

[125] Cox, Schuster and Costello, *Sport and the Law*, at 364.

[126] *Ibid.*

[127] D. Griffith-Jones, *Law and Business of Sport* (London, Edinburgh, Dublin: Butterworths, 1997), at 304.

against a broadcaster who sets up in the vicinity of the event (such as a neighbouring property) and whose actions do not give rise to an actionable obstruction.[128]

A more problematic situation arises where there is a series of events that all occur in different locations and are owned by different bodies or individuals, most notably a league, a championship or a related competition.[129] Accordingly, if matches are to be played in different locations involving different participants, then the question of proprietary rights should be addressed at the time the league or competition in question is being set up.[130] Identifying and delineating proprietary rights by those involved at the outset will arguably prevent future strife and will, most importantly, maximise the overall value of any grant of broadcasting rights.[131]

Broadcasting Rights

While it would appear that Irish law does not recognise broadcasting rights *per se* in a sporting event, a broadcaster will hold the copyright for any broadcasts that are produced.[132] There are, however, two limitations to this right, namely, the principle of 'fair dealing' and 'off-tube' coverage.[133] Off-tube coverage involves a radio commentator sitting in front of a television screen and watching footage of an event that is being transmitted by the broadcaster. The commentator describes the action and communicates this to the listener. Often the off-tube coverage will lack the ambiance associated with a sporting event and in response will often simulate noises, such as crowd noises, that have been obtained from a different match. The case of *BBC v Talksport* provides an illuminating example of this.[134] The BBC had exclusive broadcast rights to transmit live radio coverage of the European Football Championships in 2000. Talksport, a licensed British radio broadcaster that allots much of its airspace to sporting matters and events, broadcasted coverage of Euro 2000 'off tube'. The commentators were watching the matches

---

[128] *Ibid.*
[129] *Ibid.*
[130] *Ibid.*
[131] *Ibid.* Griffith-Jones gives the example of problems that arose for the English Rugby Football Union and its deal with BSkyB, which resulted in England being excluded from the Five Nations Championship in 1997–1998.
[132] Cox, Schuster and Costello, *Sport and the Law*, at 364.
[133] The Copyright and Related Rights Act, 2000 defines fair dealing for the first time. The original Copyright Act, 1911 provided for the defence of fair dealing. Fair dealing was also a defence in common law. See Forde, *Commercial Law*, at 402.
[134] BBC v Talksport [2001] FSR 53; [2000] All ER (D) 831 Ch D.

from hotel rooms in Belgium and, in order to entice listeners, the commentators advertised the matches as 'live' and included simulated crowd noises to add ambiance and authenticity to the matches. The BBC sought injunctive relief, as it argued that Talksport was incorrectly representing the nature of the coverage it was providing, and incorrectly representing itself as the holder of live broadcasting rights.[135] While sympathetic to the BBC's claims, Mr Justice Blackburne dismissed the action for an interlocutory injunction, holding that the balance of convenience did not favour its granting.[136] The BBC argued that the actions of Talksport constituted passing off; however, Blackburne J, while finding 'it deceptive and therefore wrong', did not consider that it gave the BBC a cause for action under the tort of passing off.[137]

There are no case examples of 'off tube' coverage under Irish law; nor are there any statutory provisions. The defence of fair dealing, on the other hand, is recognised under Irish law: first under the Copyright Act, 1911 and more recently under the Copyright and Related Acts, 2000, by virtue of sections 50 and 51. Fair dealing allows extracts from the copyrighted material to be used in general news programmes and genuine sporting news.[138] Under section 50, 'fair dealing means the making use of a literary, dramatic, musical or artistic work, film, sound recording, broadcast, cable programme, non-electronic original database or typographical arrangement of a published edition which has already been lawfully made available to the public, for a purpose and to an extent which will not unreasonably prejudice the interests of the owner of the copyright.'

The fair dealing exception arises where the work is used for private study or research, or for the purpose of criticism or review and is accompanied by sufficient acknowledgement. According to section 51(3), 'sufficient acknowledgement' means an acknowledgement identifying the work concerned by its title or other description and identifying the

---

[135] *Ibid.*, at para 12.

[136] The event was going to be over in two weeks and Blackburne J felt that the disadvantages of granting the interlocutory injunction outweighed the advantages such as loss of ambient sound. He felt that an injunction would cause Talksport to end altogether its further off-tube broadcasting of the Euro 2000; this would threaten Talksports' commercial well-being and revenue. See paras 39–40 of the judgment.

[137] Cox, Schuster and Costello, *Sport and the Law*, at 364–365, note that Talksport agreed in a subsequent settlement that in the future it would make it clear that its broadcasts were not in fact live. 'Passing off' involves the use by a trader or company of a business name or brand that is very similar to another business or brand, which then causes confusion in the minds of the public.

[138] *Ibid.*, at 364.

author. This requirement is waived in the case of a work which has been lawfully made available to the public, and was made so anonymously; and, if the work has not been made available to the public, it is not possible for a person without previous knowledge of the facts to ascertain the identity of the author of the work by reasonable enquiry.[139] The defence was upheld in the case of *British Broadcasting Corporation v British Satellite Broadcasting Ltd*,[140] where the BBC had obtained the rights to transmit live coverage of the World Cup in 1990. The defendant broadcasting company used short extracts consisting of 14–37 second snippets from the BBC live broadcasts to show highlights of the matches on Sky News. The court acknowledged that the snippets consisted mainly of the goals, and held that the defendant could rely on the defence of fair dealing, as it acknowledged the BBC as the source for each snippet that was transmitted.[141]

Traditionally, broadcast rights involved the sale of the exclusive rights to a single company. With developments in modern technology, rights can now be divided into 'sub packages', consequently giving rise to the possibility of 'a far more sophisticated exploitation of the potential in an event'.[142] The owner of the event will want to obtain the highest revenue possible from all the 'sub packages', while setting out the rights and obligations of all parties involved in the broadcasting contract.[143] The broadcasting contract will include standard contractual clauses including payment, the term and termination of the agreement,[144] and options to renew.[145] More importantly, the contract will deal with issues of ownership of the rights; exclusivity; the nature and extent of the coverage;[146]

---

[139] For more details, see Forde, *Commercial Law*, at 400–402. See also F. White, *Commercial Law* (Dublin: Thomson Roundhall, 2002), at 695.

[140] [1992] Ch 141. For other examples of the defence, see *Ashdown v Telegraph Group Ltd* [2002] Ch. 149 (CA) and *Hyde Park Residence Ltd v Yelland* [2001] Ch. 143.

[141] In response to this case, the 'Sports News Access Code of Practice' was established and this code regulates the use of excerpts by the major broadcasters from sports broadcasters. See S. Gardiner *et al.*, *Sports Law* (3rd ed., London: Cavendish Publishing, 2006), at 412.

[142] Cox, Schuster and Costello, *Sport and the Law*, at 365. For example, as Cox *et al.* list, live TV and radio coverage, 'as live' rights, extended highlights coverage, mobile telephone rights, news footage rights, magazine programme rights and 'new technology' rights.

[143] *Ibid.*

[144] The event may be a one-off event, thus the broadcasting contract will be for the duration of that specific event. For ongoing or continuing events, the contract may be for a fixed term or for an indeterminate term, terminable by notice. See Griffith-Jones, *Law and Business of Sport*, at 312–313.

[145] Cox, Schuster and Costello, *Sport and the Law*, at 365. These may raise competition law issues.

[146] Is the match live, deferred, highlights or other?

quality of the coverage; promotional and advertising obligations; obligations to event sponsors; the timetabling and content of advertising breaks in the coverage of the event; issues relating to copyright and future use of the broadcast material; statutory and regulatory requirements;[147] territorial rights;[148] capacity to sub licence; resolution of disputes;[149] insurance against the event being cancelled; and measures to be taken to prevent ambush marketing.[150]

Television Without Frontiers Directive

Television broadcasts were held to constitute tradable services within the meaning of Articles 49 (now Article 57 of the TFEU) and 50 (now Article 58 of the TFEU) of the European Community Treaty.[151] The European Community realised the need to develop legal provisions necessary to establish a common market for television broadcasting.[152] Out of this came the Television Without Frontiers Directive (TWF Directive).[153] The original directive was introduced in 1989 and amended in 1997.[154] The amended directive presents a number of anomalies in that a member state cannot restrict the transmission of broadcasts emanating from other member states; however, a member state may draw up a national list of protected sporting events that must be made available to the public on free-to-air television.[155] While a member state may draw up such a list,[156]

---

[147] For example, the agreement must adhere to the Broadcasting Acts, 1960–2009 and, where appropriate, the Television without Frontiers Directive, Council Directive 89/552/EEC, as amended by 97/36/EC, and the Broadcasting Commission of Ireland's codes and practices.

[148] This is an important consideration for international matches.

[149] The contract should outline the ways of resolving disputes. For example, the contract may provide for arbitration, including the Court of Arbitration for Sport, based in Lausanne, Switzerland.

[150] For more details, see J. Anderson, '"These Boots Are Made for Advertising" – Ambush Marketing, Sport and the Law' (2005) 12(8) *Commercial Law Practitioner* 207–213. See also S. Bhattacharjee and G. Rao, 'Tackling Ambush Marketing: The Need for Regulation and Analysing the Present Legislative and Contractual Efforts' (2006) 9(1) *Sport In Society* 128–149.

[151] C-155/73: *Italy v Sacchi* [1974] ECR 409 and C-52/79: *Procureur du Roi v Debauve* [1980] ECR 833.

[152] R. Parrish, *Sports Law and Policy in the European Union* (Manchester: Manchester University Press, 2003), at 169.

[153] Council Directive 89/552/EEC, as amended by Directive 97/36/EC.

[154] Member states had up until December 1998 to adopt the amended directive.

[155] Article 3a of the directive. The list must be drawn up in a clear and transparent manner in due and effective time.

[156] The directive lists, for example, the Olympic Games, the FIFA World Cup and the UEFA European Championships.

the list must be non-discriminatory and proportionate to the objective the member state seeks to achieve. The lists are communicated to the European Commission, who in turn must seek the opinion of the 'Contact Committee' under Article 3a(2). This committee comprises representatives from all the member states and its role is to assess the compatibility of the national measure with EU law. Once the committee has approved measures, they are published in the *Official Journal of the European Union*.[157]

The broadcaster is obliged either to broadcast the listed material freely on air, or else it may share its broadcasting rights with a free-to-air channel for a fair market price.[158] Member states must also exercise appropriate control of broadcasters operating within their territory.[159] Such control must comply with European Union law in general and the terms of the directive.

The TWF Directive and Irish Law

The TWF Directive was transposed into Irish law by the Broadcasting (Major Events Television Coverage) Act, 1999.[160] The Act implemented Article 3a of the directive, which allows member states to designate particular events as being of major importance to society, and thus allows steps to be taken to ensure that such events can be watched on free television services.[161] This was in response to the increase in subscription and pay-per-view events in the 1980s.[162]

The directive was originally introduced in 1989 and was amended in 1997 to reflect two major objectives.[163] The first objective stipulated that,

---

[157] Article 3a(2).

[158] Cox, Schuster and Costello, *Sport and the Law*, at 367. Cox *et al.* add that this is a huge disadvantage for a broadcaster who obtains the rights to an event for a specialist sports channel and whose popularity is derived from having exclusive rights to a particular event. See the case of *R. v Independent Television Commission ex parte TV Danmark Ltd* [2001] 1 WLR 1604 and see commentary by Cox *et al.*, at 367–370.

[159] Cox, Schuster and Costello, *Sport and the Law*, at 367, give the example of a company established in France that wishes to broadcast a listed sporting event; that company would be bound by the laws and regulations of France.

[160] Amended again by the Broadcasting (Major Events Television Coverage) (Amendment) Act, 2003.

[161] See M. McGonagle, *Media Law* (2nd ed., Dublin: Thomson Roundhall, 2003), at 416–423.

[162] Cox, Schuster and Costello, *Sport and the Law*, at 366.

[163] In December 2005 the Commission submitted a proposal to revise the directive: 'Proposal of 13 December 2005 for a Directive of the European Parliament and of the Council amending Council Directive 89/552/EEC on the Coordination of Certain Provisions Laid Down by Law, Regulation or Administrative Action in Member States Concerning the Pursuit of Television Broadcasting Activities' [COM(2005) 646]. See

in the interests of fair competition, broadcasting packages should be split or unbundled. This meant that if a broadcaster was granted the right to live coverage of the event, then another broadcaster should be awarded the right to show the highlights of the event. Second, that special provision should be given to member states to protect (without breaching competition provisions) sporting or other events of 'major importance for society' to be shown as either live coverage or deferred coverage on free-to-air television. The 1999 Act was amended by the Broadcasting (Major Events Television Coverage) (Amendment) Act, 2003.[164] The 2003 Act was introduced in response to the FAI–Sky deal. In July 2002 the FAI sold the exclusive rights to live coverage of the Republic of Ireland's home competitive games to the satellite broadcaster Sky for €7.5 million, which appeared likely to make the games available on a pay-per-view basis only.[165] Irish viewers would only be able to view the live international games on a subscription basis, while the matches would be available on free-to-air an hour after the match would finish.[166]

FAI–Sky Deal

Under the 1999 Act, the Minister for Communications was delegated the task of drawing up a list of designated major events that would be shown on free-to-air channels.[167] This list was not drafted until October 2002.[168] Its promulgation was prompted by the decision of the FAI to sell the rights of Ireland's home internationals to Sky, a subscription television channel. Minister Dermot Ahern introduced the Broadcasting (Major Events Television Coverage) (Amendment) Act, 2003 to augment existing legislation and to prevent retrospectively the FAI–Sky deal.[169]

---

also 2006/952/EC: Recommendation of the European Parliament OJ 2006L378/72 and Directive 2007/65/EC.

[164] Section 9 of the 2003 Act provides that a review must be taken not later than three years after the enactment of the Act in relation to section 2, which concerns events of major importance to society. A review was conducted in 2006, see <http://www.dcmnr.gov.ie/Broadcasting/Review+of+the+Television+without+Frontiers+Directive> (last accessed 14 June 2007).

[165] European Championship and World Cup Qualifiers. The deal was for four years. TV3 acquired the rights in a separate deal to show delayed coverage of the matches. See F. McAnally, 'FAI Defends €7m Sky Deal for Soccer Ties', *Irish Times*, 6 July 2002.

[166] TV3 obtained the rights to show the matches an hour after the end of the game. This was much to the chagrin of RTÉ.

[167] Section 2 of the Broadcasting (Major Events Television Coverage) (Amendment) Act, 2003.

[168] See McGonagle, *Media Law*, at 421, n 168.

[169] See section 2 of the Act.

Section 4 of the Act gives a pivotal role to the High Court in ensuring the proper implementation of the Act. A qualifying broadcaster[170] (free-to-air channels such as RTÉ and TV3) may apply to the High Court for an order to allow them to provide coverage of a designated event on free television services upon terms fixed by the High Court.[171] If the qualifying broadcaster and event organiser cannot agree on the amount to be paid for the rights to the event, either party may appoint an arbitrator to determine reasonable market rates for the acquisition of the rights.[172] Reasonable market rates are determined either by the arbitrator or by the High Court in relation to the following: previous fees (if any) for the event or similar events; time of day for live coverage of the event; the period for which rights are offered; the revenue potential associated with live or deferred coverage of the event; the purposes of Article 3a of the TWF Directive; and such other matters as may appear to be relevant.[173]

RTÉ subsequently issued proceedings under section 4 of the Act. The contract was amended and Sky was awarded joint rights with RTÉ to show all of Ireland's remaining European Championship games and an ongoing exclusive right to Ireland's friendly international matches.

The list of major sporting events includes Ireland's home and away soccer matches in the European Championship and World Cup qualifiers and finals, and Ireland's games (if any) in the finals of such tournaments (also the opening games, semi-finals and finals of such tournaments); All-Ireland Gaelic football and hurling finals; the Olympics; the Irish rugby team's matches in the Six Nations[174] and Rugby World Cup; The Nations' Cup at the Dublin Horse Show; and the Irish Grand National and Irish Derby. It is interesting to note that the Irish Open Golf Championship, Eircom League football matches, rugby matches involving Irish teams in the Celtic League or Heineken European Cup, the Dublin City Marathon, and the Irish Masters Snooker Championships are not listed as sporting events of national importance.[175]

---

[170] A qualifying broadcaster is defined as one who provides near-universal coverage of a designated event, consisting of free television services to at least 95 per cent of the population of the state. See section 1(2) of the 1999 Act.

[171] McGonagle, *Media Law*, at 422.

[172] Section 5 of the 2003 Act.

[173] Section 6 of the 2003 Act.

[174] The Six Nations is listed as an event for which the qualifying broadcaster must be given at least the right to show deferred coverage of the matches. See Cox, Schuster and Costello, *Sport and the Law*, at 375.

[175] See Cox, Schuster and Costello, *Sport and the Law*, at 375. In a speech on 5 April 2006, Minister for Communications Marine and Natural Resources Noel Dempsey stated:

Developing Areas: New Media Platforms

The above discussion examines the traditional means of sports broadcasting. No discussion is complete without looking at new developing areas, simply entitled 'new media'. New media concerns electronic communication, most notably the internet and mobile phones. The development of these new forms of media will undoubtedly have a huge impact on sports broadcasting. In 2000, the IOC convened a special World Conference on Sport and New Media. Dick Pound, the then vice-president, announced: 'new media has the potential to fundamentally alter the way the world relates to and consumes sports as entertainment.'[176]

The IOC established a TV Rights and Media Commission to prepare and implement future IOC broadcasting deals. In 2004 the Commission concluded an agreement with 51 countries (excluding Italy who decided to negotiate directly with the IOC) for the broadcast rights to the Vancouver Winter Games in 2010 and the London Summer Games in 2012. The agreement was ratified by the European Broadcasting Union (EBU) at its general assembly held on 1–2 July 2004. The contract covers a wide range of media categories, including for the first time multi-media and mobile telephony.[177] The contract is worth €614 million (US$746 million).[178]

Mobile phones are being increasingly used to access the web. In the future, such phones may replace the use of the computer as a means of accessing the internet. WAP and 3G mobile phones enable the user to receive the latest scores from sports events and some of the more sophisticated models (smartphones) enable the user to watch the match on the handset. Such developments raise a number of intellectual property issues, which will need to be addressed by individual countries.

CONCLUSION

Sport has had to move with the times and has become increasingly commercialised and professional. As sport has become more

---

'My Department also received many submissions proposing the designation of games involving Irish teams in the European Rugby Cup and of provincial games in the All Ireland Football and Hurling Championships. The report concluded that while there was a major "interest" in such events there was not a sufficient case for these events to be categorised as being of major "importance" to society.' See <http://www.dcmnr.gov.ie/Broadcasting/Designation+of+sporting+events/> (last accessed 19 June 2007).
[176] Blackshaw, 'Regulating Sport Globally', at 424.
[177] See <http://www.olympic.org/uk/organisation/commissions/tv_and_internet/full_story_uk.asp?id=917> (last accessed 20 July 2007).
[178] This is an increase of around 40 per cent from the previous contract.

commercialised, sportspersons have become inclined to seek redress in the courts to protect their interests, most notably in cases involving commercial issues. Sportspersons have challenged the rules of sports governing bodies on the grounds of restraint of trade. Restraint of trade has been used in cases ranging from the retain and transfer system to doping cases. The role of the court is to determine whether the restraint is reasonable or unreasonable. The law of contract has assumed greater importance for sportspersons as it regulates the relationship between the sportsperson and their agent, the sportsperson and their club and so forth. Minor athletes need to be aware of the limits with regard to their capacity to contract. The more recent case involving Wayne Rooney highlights the need for clubs and agents to be aware of a minor's lack of capacity. Football agents are not only bound by FIFA's rules but also by the law of agency. The International Rugby Board (IRB) has regulations concerning player agents. The regulations provide that each union is responsible for the authorisation and regulation of player agents. In Irish rubgy, the relevant union is the Irish Rugby Union. Each player agent must be registered with the IRB. The Irish Rugby Union Players Association (IRUPA) provides information on player agents.[179] A list of recommended agents is available on that website but it is restricted to members only. In Ireland, and indeed in other countries, rugby agents do not require any training or qualifications. There have been calls for the introduction of an agents accredited system (such a system is used in Australia). However, as yet, a move has not been forthcoming.[180] In this situation, the law of agency assumes greater importance.

Contract, agency and broadcast rights have become more associated with sport. The increased involvement had resulted in more regulation. Much of the regulation has been the result of the European Union and it is this issue, the impact of European law on sport, that the next chapter will discuss.

---

[179] See <http://www.irupa.ie>.

[180] Some Irish rugby players use the services of World in Motion Sports Management, see <http://www.worldinmotion.co.uk/site/>. Another company used by Irish rugby players is Global Sports Management, see <http://globalsportsmgmt.com/Home_Page.php>. Platinum One provides athlete representation services, see <http://www.platinumonegroup.com>.

CHAPTER 7

European Law and Sport

INTRODUCTION

Since its inception in 1957, the European Union (EU) has been based on four principles: the free movement of goods, persons, services and capital.[1] These four freedoms form the cornerstones of European integration. The European Economic Community (EEC) Treaty of 1957 included two important competition provisions: a prohibition on restrictive agreements and abuse of a dominant position. The EEC Treaty set about creating a common market in which there would be free movement of goods, persons, services and capital between the six original member states of France, Germany, Italy, Belgium, Luxembourg and the Netherlands.[2] All obstacles to trade were to be eliminated. While

---

[1] The first European Community treaty came into force in 1952, the European Coal and Steel Community (ECSC) Treaty. In 1957 the EEC Treaty and the EURATOM Treaty (the treaty establishing the European Atomic Energy Community) were signed. The EEC Treaty is commonly referred to as the Treaty of Rome. The three treaties were collectively referred to as the Communities. The ECSC Treaty was given a 50-year life span, which expired on 23 July 2002. The Single European Act of 1987 was the first treaty to overhaul the Communities. This treaty created the Court of First Instance and renamed the Assembly the European Parliament. The next treaty, the Treaty on European Union (TEU or Maastricht), introduced a number of substantive amendments, including the establishment of the Three Pillar structure. The TEU also changed the name of the EEC to the EC, dropping the economic part to show that the Community was more than economic. The EC was also a political entity. In 1998, the Treaty of Amsterdam made further amendments. In 2002, the Treaty of Nice was ratified after Ireland held a second referendum. The most recent treaty is the Lisbon Treaty. Lisbon consists of two Treaties, namely, the Treaty on the Functioning of the European Union (TFEU), which amends and replaces the European Economic Community Treaty, and the Treaty on European Union, which amends and replaces the original Treaty on European Union (or Maastricht) of 1993. Lisbon came into force on 1 December 2009.
[2] There are now 27 member states. Ireland joined in 1973 along with Britain and Denmark.

subsequent treaties have amended the scope of the original EEC Treaty, the four freedoms and competition provisions remain very much at the core of the European Union (EU). The freedoms and competition provisions have a wider application than perhaps first envisaged.[3]

As long as sport constitutes an economic activity, European law applies to sportspersons and governing bodies. Governing bodies come within the definition of 'undertaking' for the purposes of Article 101 of the TFEU (formerly 81 of the EC Treaty) on restrictive agreements[4] and Article 102 of the TFEU (formerly 82 of the EC Treaty) on abuse of a dominant position.

EUROPEAN UNION AND SPORTS POLICY

The European Union, until the Lisbon Treaty came into effect on 1 December 2009, had no legal competence to develop a sports policy. Article 26(2) of the TFEU provides that the aim of the Union is to establish an area where goods, persons, services and capital can freely circulate and where competition is not distorted. Accordingly, sport is an area of commercial importance and thus sports bodies must not engage in activities that would breach these treaty provisions.[5] Up until

---

[3] See S. Weatherill, 'Fair Play Please! Recent Developments in the Application of EC Law to Sport' (2003) 40 *Common Market Law Review* 51–93, at 55–56.

[4] It is important to note that an abuse of dominant position is never permitted. It is not an offence for an undertaking to be in a dominant position, Article 102 only applies if the dominant undertaking is abusing its position.

[5] There were also a number of reports published by the European Parliament. Mr James Van Raay was the rapporteur in the A2-415/88 Report of the Committee on Legal Affairs and Citizens' Rights on the freedom of movement of professional footballers in the community, 1 March 1989. In 1994, A3-0326/94 Part A (27/4/94) Part B (29/4/94) *Report of the Committee on Culture, Youth, Education and the Media on the European Community and Sport* (also known as the Larive Report after the rapporteur Mrs J Larive) was published. This report was convened prior to the decision in *Bosman* (see later in this chapter). It examined EC legislation and sport, the role of the union in encouraging active participation in sport, combating hooliganism in sport and fostering a European identity through sport. Under the category of EC legislation and sport, the following EC treaty provisions were discussed: the free movement of persons, the free movement of goods, competition provisions and the freedom to provide a service. The report also referred to legislation on the involvement of animals in sport and the protection of minors in sport with regard to working hours and conditions of work. The rapporteur referred to the restrictions on foreign players (3+2 rule) (discussed later in this chapter) and called for the abolition of any restrictions on the free movement of workers in sport. After the Bosman decision, the *Pack Report* was published. This report was entitled *The Report on the Role of the European Union in the Field of Sport* and was more positive than the *Larive Report* as a number of changes occurred after the Bosman decision. The following reports were also published: the *Helsinki Report on Sport* (on

the Treaty of Amsterdam, there was no mention of sport in the treaties. The drafters of the Amsterdam Treaty found themselves under increased pressure to include a specific article on sport. In response to this, a declaration was attached to the treaty. The declaration emphasised the social and cultural significance of sport in its role in integrating the people of Europe. This was seen as timid move by some, as it seemed to be leaving the regulation of sport to the individual member states.[6] While the declaration acknowledged the specific character of sport, it seemed somewhat aspirational. This is noteworthy considering that sport in the EU is a multi-million-euro industry.

After the declaration, the European Commission published the *European Model of Sport* consultation document. This document sought to determine the essential characteristics of sport in Europe. It called for the comments of the member states and sporting bodies on three important areas, namely, the organisation of sport in Europe; the relationship between sport and television broadcasting; and sport and social policy. The conclusions were then presented in the *Helsinki Report on Sport* in 1999. The report acknowledged that certain developments in sport (such as violence, doping and commercialisation) were denigrating the important social and educational functions of sport. The use of drugs in sport was also addressed, with the report advising the member states and the Union institutions to work together to eradicate doping in sport.

In December 2000, a 'Declaration on the Specific Characteristics of Sport' was annexed to the Treaty of Nice. The declaration recognised that sport has 'social, educational and cultural functions' which combined to make sport 'special'. The declaration not only looked at social aspects, including social inclusion, the protection of children in sport, and the promotion of sport among people with disabilities, it also looked at issues that caught the attention of the Commission in the past, most notably the ownership by one party of a stake in more than one club, the sale of broadcasting rights and the transfer systems in sport, particularly in football.

The ill-fated Constitutional Treaty provided sport with a treaty basis for the first time under Article III-182. This article merely reiterated earlier rhetoric as it did not provide for the harmonisation or

---

safeguarding current sports structures and maintaining the social function of sport within the community); the *Report of the European Parliament on Professional Sport in the Internal Market*; and the *Belet Report* (report on the future of professional football in Europe).
[6] N. Cox, A. Schuster and C. Costello, *Sport and the Law* (Dublin: First Law, 2004), at 13.

approximation of sport at EU level. Nevertheless, it acknowledged the importance of sport in the further integration of the European Union, both socially and culturally.

The Constitutional Treaty formed the basis of the Lisbon Treaty, which came into force on 1 December 2009. Articles 6 and 165 emphasise the importance of sport in Europe and give the Commission a formal competence on sport.[7] Article 165 gives the EU a 'soft' competence on sport, meaning that the Commission will be empowered to develop a specific EU sports programme, which will be supported by a budget. The competence also allows for better promotion of sport in other EU policy areas and programmes, including health and education. The EU will represent all the member states with regard to sport at international forums and also in its discussions with non-EU member states (third countries). All the sports ministers from the 27 member states will begin attending official Sports Council meetings.[8]

Article 165(1) provides that the EU will 'contribute to the development of quality education by encouraging cooperation between member states and, if necessary, by supporting and supplementing their action, while fully respecting the responsibility of the member states for the content of teaching and the organisation of education systems and their cultural and linguistic diversity'.[9] The EU action will, according to Article 165(2), be aimed at promoting education, the mobility of students and teachers and the recognition of diplomas, cooperation between educational establishments, youth exchanges, cooperation between the EU and third world countries and 'developing the European dimension in sport, by promoting fairness and openness in sporting competitions and cooperation between bodies responsible for sports, and by protecting the physical and moral integrity of sportsmen and sportswomen, especially the youngest sportsmen and sportswomen'. By virtue of Article

---

[7] Article 6: 'The Union shall have competence to carry out actions to support, coordinate or supplement the actions of the Member States. The areas of such action shall, at European level, be: (a) protection and improvement of human health; (b) industry; (c) culture; (d) tourism; (e) education, vocational training, youth and sport; (f) civil protection; (g) administrative cooperation.'

[8] The Sports Council had an informal meeting on 20 April 2010 in Madrid. Two main themes were discussed: the first on structuring and strengthening dialogue between sports movement and governments and the second looked at setting up the new EU working party on social inclusion and equality, updates on health and sport, and issues related to doping.

[9] The Union shall contribute to the promotion of European sporting issues, while taking account of the specific nature of sport, its structures based on voluntary activities, and its social and educational function.

165(4), the Parliament and Council will be permitted to adopt incentive measures in the area of sport. The Council, on a proposal from the Commission, shall adopt recommendations. Article 165 has been welcomed by both the IOC and FIFA. The EU's first sports programme is expected to come into force in 2012.[10]

In 2007, the Commission published the *White Paper on Sport*. The paper was the first comprehensive initiative on sport.[11] It was the result of discussions over a two-year period between the Commission, member states, the IOC and other sports federations and stakeholders. The White Paper, while recognising the social and economic importance of sport, emphasised the need for sporting bodies and member states to respect the requirements of EU law. Although Article 165 has provided sport with a treaty basis, the White Paper remains at the core of the Commission's sports policy.

SPORT AS AN ECONOMIC ACTIVITY

Although sport could (depending on the circumstances) be classified as an economic activity, the EC was initially reluctant to become involved in the regulation of sport. It was largely left up to the individual member states to regulate sport at national level. While the Council of Ministers, the Commission and the Parliament (then the Assembly)[12] did not intervene in matters of sport, the then European Court of Justice (ECJ)[13] showed more of a willingness to apply the EEC Treaty to sport.[14]

In the 1970s, the ECJ handed down two important judgments in the cases of *Walrave and Koch v Association Union Cycliste Internationale*[15] and *Doná v Montero*.[16] In *Walrave*, the respondents challenged a rule that required the pacemaker (the person who sets the pace in a race) to be the same nationality as the stayer (long distance cyclist) on the grounds that

---

[10] See <http://www.euractiv.com/en/sports/lisbon-treaty-gives-eu-sports/article-187812>, (last accessed 1 May 2010).

[11] See <http://europa.eu/rapid/pressReleasesAction.do?reference=IP/07/1066>, (last accessed 1 May 2010).

[12] The Assembly was renamed the Parliament by the Single European Act, which came into force on 1 July 1987.

[13] The European Court of Justice was renamed the Court of Justice of the European Union (CJEU) by the Lisbon Treaty. All references prior to 1 December 2009 will refer to the ECJ.

[14] The EEC Treaty was renamed the European Community Treaty by the Treaty on European Union (TEU). The TEU is also known as the Maastricht Treaty and came into force on 1 November 1993.

[15] C-36/74, *Walrave and Koch v Association Union Cycliste Internationale* [1974] ECR 1405.

[16] C-13/76, *Doná v Montero* [1976] ECR 1333.

it was a form of discrimination based on nationality and contrary to the free movement of workers and the freedom to provide a service. The ECJ held that sport was subject to European law insofar as it constituted an economic activity within the meaning of Article 2 of the EEC Treaty. However, the ECJ noted that the prohibition on discrimination did not apply to the composition of sport teams, in particular national teams, as the formation of such teams was a question of purely sporting interest and, as such, had nothing to do with economic activity. Similarly, in *Doná*, the ECJ held that professional footballers enjoyed the benefits of the treaty provisions on freedom of movement of persons and of provision of services.[17] However, the ECJ added that in some circumstances the application of nationality restrictions to those who played on national teams would be a 'non-economic' issue and therefore exempt from the EEC Treaty's provisions. Advocate General Trabucchi, in his opinion, argued that a sporting exception outside of discrimination based on nationality could be justified. The Advocate General was suggesting that more categories of restrictions could be permitted and that the sporting exception could be used to justify restrictions even in situations involving economic activities. The ECJ did not embrace the Advocate General's expansive approach and instead adopted a more narrow construction of the sporting exemption. The ECJ held that restrictions on foreign players could be permitted in 'certain matches'.

The Significance of *Walrave and Koch* and *Doná*

Walrave and Koch and *Doná* are significant as the ECJ held that the EEC (as it was at the time of *Walrave*) Treaty applied to sport so long as it constituted an economic activity. As a corollary, the ECJ created a sport exception to the application of European law. If an activity is of 'purely

---

[17] The chairman of an Italian football club instructed Mr Doná, a sports agent, to seek top foreign professionals to play on the club's team. Doná arranged a number of offers and asked for payment of his expenses. The club refused to pay the agent as there was a restriction on the number of foreign players that could be fielded on a domestic team. Doná argued that the restriction was discriminatory and contrary to the free movement of workers and the freedom to provide a service. The case was referred from the Italian national court to the European Court of Justice under the preliminary reference procedure. The preliminary reference allows a national court to refer a matter to the European Court of Justice (and the lower court, the General Court, since the Treaty of Nice) in situations where the national court is unsure as to how to interpret or apply a provision of European law. While the preliminary reference is being heard, the case in the national court is delayed. The preliminary reference is found under Article 267 TFEU (ex 234 EC Treaty). The Court of First Instance was renamed the General Court by the Lisbon Treaty.

sporting interest' and 'has nothing to do with economic activity', then the EC Treaty had no application.[18] For example, in *Donà*, the ECJ held that nationality restrictions on foreign players playing for national teams in international competitions would fall within the sporting exception.[19] However, national teams playing in international games 'have direct economic consequences,'[20] although this is something the ECJ did not consider in the judgment. The decisions have been the source of much criticism.[21]

The ECJ, while cautious in its approach, recognised that European law could apply to sport. The Commission was more reluctant to become involved in the regulation of sport. Until the 1990s, the development of European sports law was largely attributed to the decisions of the ECJ. The decision in *Bosman* in 1995 forced the Commission to become more involved.[22] The Commission recognised its role in enforcing the provisions of the EC Treaty in sport.[23] The treaties began to give cognisance to the role of sport in society, namely, its cultural importance and its ability to promote social cohesion and equality.

EUROPE AND THE FOOTBALL TRANSFER SYSTEM

The Bosman Case

Jean-Marc Bosman was a Belgian professional football player who played for RC Liège, a Belgian first division club. Before his contract was about to expire, in April 1990, Liège offered Bosman a new one-year contract at a lower salary than his previous contract. Bosman rejected the offer and was placed on the transfer list. A compensation fee was attached to his contract. French club USL Dunkerque expressed an interest in Bosman and were willing to pay the transfer fee. Liège and Dunkerque negotiated a transfer for one year. Bosman would play for Dunkerque and, after a year, the club could obtain the services of Bosman in return for an additional fee.

---

[18] *Walrave and Koch v Association Union Cycliste Internationale* [1974] ECR 1405, at para 8.
[19] The Advocate General proffered that restrictions on foreign players in national teams could be justified 'so as to ensure that the winning team will be representative of the State of which it is the champion team', Opinion of Advocate General Trabucchi, at 1344.
[20] Weatherill, 'Fair Play Please!', at 56.
[21] R. Parrish and S. Miettinen, *The Sport Exception in European Union Law* (The Hague: TMC Asser Press, 2008), at 85.
[22] C-415/93, *Union Royale Belge des Societes de Football Association ASBL & Others v Jean-Marc Bosman* [1995] ECR I-4921.
[23] As the Bosman case was post TEU, the EEC became known as the EC.

The transfer fell through as Liège had reservations about Dunkerque's solvency and thus would not authorise the Belgian Federation of Sport to forward the necessary documentation to allow for the transfer. Liège suspended Bosman, resulting in him being unable to play for the season. Bosman initiated legal action claiming that the Belgian Football Federation and FIFA–UEFA transfer rules had prevented his transfer to Dunkerque. He brought an action against RC Liège and later against the Belgian Football Federation and UEFA. He sought a declaration from the national court that the transfer rules and nationality clauses were incompatible with the Treaty of Rome rules on competition (then Articles 85 and 86) and the free movement of workers (then Article 48).[24] The Belgian National Court referred the issue to the ECJ under the preliminary reference procedure.[25]

Prior to *Bosman*, a quota system operated in European club football. Clubs were permitted to limit the number of foreign players (including EU citizens) who could play in the domestic league, and in European competitions clubs could limit the number of non-national players. UEFA implemented the 3+2 rule whereby each club could field three foreign players and two assimilated players. Assimilated players were defined as players who played in a country for an uninterrupted period of five years, three of which had been spent at youth level. For example, a club like Manchester United could only field three non-English players and two assimilated players, leaving places for six domestic players. A transfer fee was also required in respect of out-of- contract players.

These agreements had been sanctioned by a gentleman's agreement between the Commission and UEFA.[26] A gentleman's agreement is an anti-competitive (or restrictive) agreement which falls under Article 101 of the TFEU (or Article 85 at the time of *Bosman*).[27] A restrictive

---

[24] Now Article 45 of the TFEU. Article 45 provides: 'A worker from one member state is free to take up employment in another member state, free from restrictions which do not apply to nationals of the state in which it is sought to work.'

[25] See note 17 for details on the preliminary reference.

[26] EC Commission Press Communiqué of 18 April 1991 regarding the 'Gentleman's Agreement' in soccer. In Chapter 5, the common law doctrine of restraint of trade was examined. The statutory provisions (Articles 101 and 102 of the TFEU and the Irish Competition Act, 2002) have supplemented and in some situations overtaken the common law provisions.

[27] Article 101 prohibits any agreements which purport to restrict the supply of products, agreements which restrict market access, price fixing agreements and any collusion to manipulate the market. Section 4 of the Irish Competition Act, 2002 is based largely on Article 101. Section 5 of the 2002 Act is largely based on Article 102.

agreement is void (Article 101(2)); however, it may be saved under sub-section 3 if it can be shown that the agreement will be of benefit to the consumer, aid economic or technical progress and the restriction is proportionate to the aims which it seeks to achieve. It was very difficult for sportspersons to challenge these restrictive measures, as the 'Commission was effectively sanctioning discriminatory practises'.[28] Both the transfer system and the quota system were challenged by Jean-Marc Bosman.

Arguments Made by UEFA and FIFA in *Bosman*

Both UEFA and FIFA maintained that the transfer system merely regulated the business relationship between clubs and did not affect players. However, the ECJ rejected this contention as it was satisfied that the effect of the system was to impede football players' free movement as workers. It was further argued that the transfer system provided a measure of economic equilibrium within football. In support of this, reference was made to the nursery clubs that received a transfer fee in return for training and developing the talent of a young player. The ECJ accepted that there was a legitimate interest in maintaining a sporting and financial balance; however, the use of a transfer system for out-of-contract players was not appropriate to secure that objective nor was it suitable for maintaining youth development schemes. An important factor for the ECJ was the fact that the transfer fees under the transfer system were not related to the costs of training young players. Often the fee paid was disproportionate to the cost of training the player. The more wealthy clubs could pay more than a smaller club.

On the issue of the 3+2 rule, UEFA and FIFA contended that such a requirement ensured that there was a bond between club and country and preserved national identity in European competition. Unconvinced by this argument, the ECJ pointed out that there were no rules which restricted a club to fielding players from its town or district in national competitions. The ECJ held that a restriction on the number of foreign players violated the free movement of workers under Article 48 of the EC Treaty and also under Council Regulation 1612/68, which prohibits provisions that restrict the employment of foreign nationals (EC nationals) in an undertaking or activity by number or percentage.[29] The ECJ

---

[28] R. Parrish, *Sports Law and Policy in the European Union* (Manchester: Manchester University Press, 2003), at 92.

[29] Article 4(1) of Regulation (EEC) No. 1612/68 on freedom of movement for workers within the Community, 15 October 1968.

also rejected the contention that the 3+2 rule prevented the top clubs from purchasing the services of the leading players.

Decision of the ECJ and Transfer System and Quota Rules

The transfer system for out-of-contract players was struck down by the ECJ in *Bosman*.[30] The ECJ held that Article 48 of the EEC Treaty (now Article 45 of the TFEU) guaranteed the free movement of persons within the member states and ruled that the requirement that a fee be paid for an out-of-contract player moving from one club in the EU to another EU club was a breach of the treaty. The ECJ also held that the quota system imposed by UEFA was a breach of the treaty.

Since *Bosman*, a club in the EU may field as many EU players as it wishes. A transfer fee is still required for players who are still under contract. The decision applies only to EU players; there are still restrictions with regard to non-EU players.[31] The decision has affected both clubs and players. Clubs are now signing players on longer contracts to prevent a player from being able to move to another club on a free transfer. In return, the clubs are paying higher wages to the players. Some smaller clubs who have trained a player through the youth ranks are liable to lose that promising talent to a new club for free.

Smaller clubs find it very difficult to sign players on a longer contract as they do not have the money to pay the higher wages. It has been argued that is the players themselves who have benefited most from the Bosman ruling.[32] Some clubs are in huge debt due to the rise in salaries. Manchester United has an estimated debt of £700 million, while Liverpool FC is reported to have debts of £237 million.[33] In order to counteract the increase in wages, pay-per-view television has become increasingly popular. Teams are increasing the prices of tickets and merchandise. Before *Bosman*, teams would change their strip

---

[30] Case C-415/93, *URBASFA v Jean-Marc Bosman*. For a detailed discussion, see R. Blainpain and R. Instone, *The Bosman Case: End of the Transfer System* (London: Sweet & Maxwell, 1996) and A. Campbell and P.J. Sloane, *Discussion Paper No. 97-02: The Implications of the Bosman Case for Professional Football* (Aberdeen: University of Aberdeen/Dept of Economics, 1997).

[31] The decision operates at EU level, but includes EEA countries (i.e. Norway, Liechtenstein and Iceland); it also applies to many non-EU states in Eastern Europe and North Africa that have association agreements with the EU.

[32] S. Camatsos, 'European Sports, the Transfer System and Competition Law: Will They Ever Find a Competitive Balance' (2005) 12 *Sports Law Journal* 155–179, at 174.

[33] S. Wilson, 'Is Football Bankrupt?' *Money Week*, 22 January 2010 (available online: <http://www.moneyweek.com/news-and-charts/economics/is-football-bankrupt-47010.aspx>, last accessed 2 May 2010).

every two years.[34] Post *Bosman*, teams are changing them on a yearly basis in addition to the use of a home and an away jersey. The supporters are 'paying for the salary increases, which make it arguably a competition law violation'.[35]

It is interesting to note that the ECJ did not give judgment on the compatibility of the transfer and quota system with the competition provisions. However, in his opinion, Advocate General Lenz did consider those matters and suggested that both practices violated Article 85 of the EC Treaty (now Article 101 of the TFEU). An opinion of an Advocate General is not binding on the Court of Justice.

Bosman and Non-EU Players

After *Bosman* there were a number of cases involving non-EU players and the payment of transfer fees for out-of-contract players. This issue arose in *Balog v ASBL Charleroi Sporting Club*, where Balog, a Hungarian national, played for Belgian club Charleroi.[36] In a similar situation to Bosman, Balog's contract was about to expire and he refused a new contract and was placed on the transfer list. The transfer fee was excessive and Balog found it impossible to find a club that would pay that amount for an out-of-contract player. A transfer fee was required as he was not an EU national; Hungary did not join the EU until 2004. Balog argued that he should be treated the same as an EU national and be allowed to transfer without the need for a fee. The matter was settled by FIFA and the Belgian court decreed that it would be pointless to send the case to the ECJ as it had been resolved.[37]

The rights of non-EU players were recognised in two further cases, *Kolpak*[38] and *Igor Simutenkov v Spanish Football Federation*.[39] Kolpak, a Slovak national and goalkeeper for a second division handball team, was resident in Germany and held a valid residence permit. Kolpak was

---

[34] Camatsos, 'European Sports, the Transfer System and Competition Law', at 175.
[35] *Ibid*.
[36] Tribunal de Première Instance de Charleroi by judgment of the court of July 1998 in the case of *Tibor Balog v ASBL Royal Charleroi Sporting Club (RCSC)*.
[37] Agreement reached between FIFA and Tibor Balog on 28 March 2001 (available online: <http://www.fifa.com/aboutfifa/federation/releases/newsid=87210.html>, last accessed 2 May 2010).
[38] C-438/00, *Deutscher Handballbund e.V. v Maros Kolpak* (2003/C146/07). Slovakia became a member state of the EU on 1 May 2004.
[39] ECJ press release No 03/35, 11 January 2005 – Opinion of Advocate General Stix-Hackl in case C-265/03. C-265/03, *Simutenkov v Spanish Football Federation* ECR 2005 I-02579.

issued with a player's licence, which included the letter A. This identified Kolpak as a non-EU player who did not enjoy the privilege of equal treatment. Under the league rules, a team could only field two players with an 'A'-marked licence. Kolpak requested that he be re-issued with a licence that did not contain the letter A, as he had rights similar to an EU national due to an Association Agreement between the EU and Slovakia.[40] The ECJ held in Kolpak's favour that the restriction was a form of discrimination under European law.[41]

In *Simutenkov v Spanish Football Federation*, Simutenkov, a Russian national who played for Spanish club Deportivo Tenerife, endeavoured to rely on Article 23 of the Association Agreement between Russia and the EU. Similar to Kolpak, Simutenkov wished to have his licence converted to an EU player's licence. His application was rejected. The case was sent to the ECJ for a preliminary reference. The ECJ held in favour of Simutenkov, holding that Article 23 of the Association Agreement allows a professional sportsperson of Russian nationality, who is lawfully employed by a club established in a member state, to play for a domestic club without any restriction. A club or federation may only impose restrictions in situations where the players are not party to an association agreement.

On 1 May 2004, ten new member states joined the EU – Cyprus, the Czech Republic, Estonia, Hungary, Latvia, Lithuania, Malta, Poland, Slovakia and Slovenia. On 1 January 2007, Romania and Bulgaria joined the EU. With this enlargement, the effects of *Kolpak* and *Simutenkov* were somewhat diminished as many of the associated countries are now member states of the EU.

Transfers Since *Bosman*

The *Bosman* decision applies only to players who are out of contract. For players still in contract, there are two transfer windows during the season and during these windows the player may be transferred.[42] The

---

[40] Article 38(1) of the Europe Agreement establishing an association between the European communities and their member states, of the one part, and the Slovak Republic, of the other part, approved on behalf of the communities by Decision 94/909/ECSC, EEC, EURATOM of the Council and the Commission of 19 December 1994 (OJ 1994 L 359, at 1).

[41] The *Kolpak* decision has had implications for a number of sports, in particular cricket in the United Kingdom. See P. Wood, 'The Kolpak Effect' (available online: <http://www.cricketweb.net/blog/features/10.php>, last accessed 2 May 2010).

[42] In September 2009, FIFA banned Chelsea from making any more new signings for the next two transfer windows after it was found that Chelsea had induced Gael Kakuta

transfer windows are the result of negotiations between FIFA and the Commission. It is up to each national association to decide when the transfer windows take place. The first transfer window is for 12 weeks and the second is for 4 weeks. In England, the first window is from 1 June to 31 August and the second is from 1 January to 2 February. There have been calls to have the transfer windows reviewed by FIFA, but FIFA has no immediate plans to do. In the January 2010 window, the Barclays Premier League spent only £30 million on transfers in comparison to £170 million spent in the same period in 2009.[43] The 2010 figures are the lowest figures since the transfer window system was introduced in 2003.

The FIFA Regulations on the Status and Transfer of Players were updated in October 2009.[44] The main regulations provide for:

1. Training compensation for players under 23 to replace transfer fees[45]

---

to breach his contract with Racing Club de Lens (RC Lens) two years previously. Chelsea and Kakuta were ordered to pay a joint compensation fine of £680,000. Chelsea was also ordered to pay £114,000 to Lens for training fees. Kakuta was banned from playing in official international matches for four months. However, Chelsea appealed the ban to the Court of Arbitration for Sport (CAS), resulting in the CAS ratifying an agreement between Chelsea and Lens in February 2010.

[43] 'FIFA to Leave Transfer Windows in Place', 10 February 2010, (available online: <http://www.rte.ie/sport/soccer/2010/0210/transferwindow.html>, last accessed 2 April 2010).

[44] The rules were introduced in 2001 and revised in 2005 and 2008. The most recent rules are available at <http://www.fifa.com/aboutfifa/federation/administration/playersagents/regulationstatustransfertsplayers.html> (last accessed 16 August 2010).

[45] In a recent case, the payment of compensation fees for young players in France was challenged. On 16 March 2010, the CJEU handed down its decision in C-325/08 *Olympique Lyonnais SASP v Oliver Bernard and Newcastle United*. The Professional Charter of the French Football Federation contains rules relating to the employment of footballers in France. The charter contains specific provisions relating to young players. A *joueur espoir* is a footballer between the ages of 16 and 22 on a fixed-term contract. The charter obliges such a footballer to sign with the club that first trained him, if the club so requires. Bernard had a three-season *joueur espoir* contract with Lyonnais and, on expiration of the contract, he refused to sign with Lyonnais and instead joined Newcastle United. Lyonnais sued Bernard for €53,357.16, one year's salary had Bernard signed with Lyonnais. The French court sent the matter to the CJEU under the preliminary reference procedure. The question referred to the CJEU was whether the requirement that the young player had to sign with the club that trained him on expiration of his *joueur espoir* contract constituted a breach of the free movement of workers provisions. The CJEU was satisfied that Bernard's contract was gainful employment and thus constituted an economic activity for the purposes of EU law. Equally, the charter had the status of a collective bargaining agreement aimed at regulating gainful employment, which also fell within the ambit of EU law. The CJEU held that the

2. Protection of contracts for the first two to three years by a sporting sanction of a four-month suspension for a player who unilaterally breaches their contract within this period; compensation paid to the club reflects the wages and period left on the player's contract in accordance with national law
3. Movement for players only allowed in two transfer 'windows' per season
4. Redress to an independent and objective disciplinary and arbitration system to deal with contractual disputes and compensation

In 2008, FIFA suggested the introduction of the 6+5 rule. Under this rule, at the beginning of each game, each club must field at least six players eligible to play for the national team of the country of the club. However, there is no restriction on the number of non-EU players a club can sign on or on the number of non-EU substitutes brought on during a match. At the end of a match it could be 3+8.

The Commission rejected the rule as it was deemed to be a direct form of discrimination and contrary to the free movement of persons provided for in the EC Treaty. FIFA, in response, commissioned a report by an independent body, the Institute for European Affairs (INEA). The INEA found that the rule did not breach European law. FIFA hope to introduce the rule by the start of the 2012–2013 season. However, it is likely that the Commission will uphold its rejection. The INEA found that the proposed rule is indirectly discriminatory. Indirect discrimination is permitted if it can be objectively justified. FIFA argue that the rule will protect young indigenous players who are often left on the bench and replaced by cheaper and fully trained players from other countries.[46]

---

obligation on the player to sign with the club that trained him had the effect of discouraging a player from going to another club as he could be sued. The CJEU held this to be a restriction on the free movement of workers. However, the CJEU recognised the social importance of sport and thus the objective of encouraging the recruitment and training of young players must be acceptable as legitimate. It held that a scheme which guarantees compensation to a club which has trained a young player, where that young player decides to sign with another club within the EU, is not a breach of the free movement of workers provisions so long as the scheme is suitable to ensure the attainment of that objective and does not go beyond what is necessary to attain it. However, in the case of Lyonnais, the French scheme went beyond that which was necessary to encourage the recruitment and training of young players and to fund those activities.

[46] FIFA's 6+5 rule does not conflict with EU law, claims a report dated 26 February 2009 (available online <http://www.guardian.co.uk/football/2009/feb/26/fifa-6-5-eu-law-independent-report-bosman-ruling-sepp-blatter>, last accessed 12 March 2010). However, the Commission held otherwise.

The Commission has accepted UEFA's homegrown players rule. UEFA's rules on homegrown players require clubs participating in the Champions League and the UEFA Cup to have a minimum number of homegrown players, i.e. players who, regardless of their nationality, have been trained by their club or by another club in the same national association for at least three years between the ages of 15 and 21. UEFA introduced the rule in three phases:

1. Season 2006–2007: minimum of 4 homegrown players in 25-man squad
2. Season 2007–2008: minimum of 6 homegrown players in 25-man squad
3. Season 2008–2009: minimum of 8 homegrown players in 25-man squad

There are no nationality restrictions and a club is not obliged to field homegrown players. The rule provides that there must be 8 homegrown players in a 25-man squad.[47] The Commission will review the situation in 2012.

SPORTING BODIES:
COMPETITION LAW AND THE FREEDOM TO PROVIDE A SERVICE

The question recently arose as to whether sporting bodies were subject to competition provisions. Articles 85 of the EC Treaty (now Article 10 of the TFEU) and 86 (now Article 102 of the TFEU) were deemed not to be applicable in *Bosman*, although the Advocate General opined that the provisions did apply. However, in the case of *Meca-Medina and Majcen v Commission*, the ECJ held that the IOC was engaged in an economic activity and thus European competition law applied.[48]

Meca-Medina and Majcen were professional long-distance swimmers who tested positive for nandrolone. The IOC suspended the two swimmers for four years; this was reduced to two years by the Court of Arbitration for Sport. The swimmers made a complaint to the Commission, arguing that the IOC's doping rules were a violation of European competition law and in breach of the freedom to provide a service. The Commission rejected the complaint by way of a decision on 1 August 2002.

---

[47] See <http://www.uefa.com/uefa/footballfirst/protectingthegame/youngplayers/news/newsid=943393.html> (last accessed 16 August 2010).
[48] C-519/04 P, *Meca-Medina and Majcen v Commission* [2006] ECR I-06991.

The Commission's decision was appealed to the Court of First Instance (CFI).[49] The CFI upheld the Commission's decision, holding that the IOC's doping rules did not come within the rubric of either competition law or services.[50] The CFI reiterated the earlier dicta from the ECJ and held that sport, insofar as it constitutes an economic activity, is subject to the provisions of European law, for example, rules restricting the number of foreign players or the requirement of a transfer fee for out-of-contract players. However, Union law did not extend to purely sporting rules and matters which have nothing to do with economic activity, for example, the composition of national teams or the number of players on the field.

The swimmers appealed the CFI decision to the ECJ on the grounds that the CFI had erred in law. The ECJ agreed and held that the CFI had erred in dismissing the application on the grounds that the anti-doping rules in question were subject to neither the freedom to provide a service nor competition law. The ECJ overturned the decision of the CFI. However, it held that the Commission decision was not to be annulled as the penalty imposed was not excessive; it was proportionate.[51]

In *Piau*, a French soccer players' agent lodged a complaint with the Commission in 1998.[52] He argued that the FIFA Agent Regulations were 'excessive, opaque and discriminatory', contrary to the competition provisions of Articles 81 (now Article 101 of the TFEU), 82 (now Article 102 of the TFEU) and 49 (now Article 56 of the TFEU) of the EC Treaty on the freedom to provide a service.[53] In response, the Commission issued FIFA with a statement of objections. The Commission was of the opinion that the 1994 regulations constituted a decision by an association of undertakings within the meaning of Article 81(1).[54] It

---

[49] Now referred to as the General Court.
[50] T-313/02, *Meca-Medina and Majcen v Commission* [2001] ECR II-3291.
[51] *Ibid.*, see paras 54 and 55 of the judgment.
[52] T-1 93/02, *Laurent Piau v Commission* [2005] ECR II-209, [2005] 5 CMLR 2; appeal dismissed by the ECJ, C-171/05P, [2006] ECR 1-37.
[53] A sportsperson who is an independent contractor, i.e. not part of a team but a solo competitor (e.g. tennis or golf), falls under the provision of services. A service provider may go to another member state to take part in a competition and will then return to their usual place of residence. A worker, on the other hand, is someone who moves to another member state to work there. A worker is defined as someone who provides a service in return for remuneration under the direction of another, see C-66/85 *Lawrie Blum v Land Baden-Württemberg* [1986] ECR 2121, which sets out the criteria for a worker.
[54] The Commission *White Paper on Sport*, 2007 defines an association of undertakings in relation to sport as follows: 'The sports association is an "association of undertakings" if its members carry out an economic activity. In this respect, the question will become

also questioned the compatibility with European law of the licence requirement, the exclusion of legal persons, prohibition on the use of an unlicensed agent, the requirement of a bank guarantee and the sanctions. Under the 1994 rules, an interview was required.[55] FIFA subsequently amended the rules but Piau challenged them in the CFI. FIFA contended that the regulations were necessary in order to raise moral standards and levels of professional qualification, and could be given an exemption under Article 81(3) of the EC Treaty. The CFI agreed with FIFA and upheld the regulations. Piau appealed the decision of the CFI to the ECJ. However, the ECJ upheld the lower court's decision.[56]

In *Deliège v Ligue de Judo*, the ECJ, consistent with its earlier judgments, held that selection criteria did not come within the ambit of European law.[57] Deliège practised judo at an advanced amateur level and had obtained excellent results in her 52 kg category since 1987. She had been declared a national champion on a number of occasions. Deliège argued that the Belgian judo federation had improperly impeded her career by not allowing her to compete in a number of competitions, including the 1992 and 1996 Olympics. She argued that she was carrying out an economic activity for the purposes of European law. Eligibility for the Olympics is decided by pre-determined national quotas set by the national federation. The question for the ECJ was 'whether or not it is contrary to the Treaty of Rome, in particular Articles 59, 85 and 86, to require professional or semi-professional athletes or persons aspiring to professional or semi-professional activity to be authorised by their federation in order to be able to compete in an international competition which does not involve national teams competing against each other'.

---

relevant to what extent the sport in which the members (usually clubs/teams or athletes) are active can be considered an economic activity and to what extent the members exercise economic activity. In the absence of "economic activity" competition provisions do not apply.'

[55] Agents are discussed in Chapter 6. Agents no longer have an interview. Instead they sit a multiple choice examination.

[56] On 17 June 2010 the European Parliament adopted a resolution requesting the introduction of a European licensing system for football agents in order to prevent illegal practices. The Parliament estimates that 30 per cent of all transfers are done by unlicensed agents. It is not just the effect that such activity has on football but, according to Belgian MEP Ivo Belet, the activities of unlicensed agents 'opens the gateway to human trafficking, money laundering, fraud and corruption', see 'Parliament Wants Sports Agents to Get EU Licence', 17 June 2010, (available online: <http://www.euractiv.com/en/sports/parliament-wants-sports-agents-get-eu-license-news-495352>, last accessed 21 June 2010).

[57] C-51/96 and C-191/97, *Deliège v Ligue de Judo* ECR I-2549.

The ECJ held that such rules did not fall within the ambit of the freedom to provide a service 'as long as it derives from a need inherent in the organisation of such a competition', although the individual concerned may be affected financially. The ECJ gave considerable latitude to the governing body in fixing selection criteria in sporting events.[58] So long as the rules are reasonable, justifiable and proportionate, such restrictions should not attract the application of EU law.

BROADCASTING RIGHTS

Competition Policy and Broadcasting

Broadcasting contracts in sport must comply with Articles 101[59] and 102[60] of the TFEU. The Commission has applied competition rules on a case-by-case basis and has found broadcasting rights to fall within the ambit of its competition policy. In assessing whether an agreement comes within the ambit of Article 101, the Commission must establish the relevant market. This is examined by looking at the following: the type of television;[61] the type of sport;[62] live and recorded sport;[63] and the geographical market.[64]

---

[58] Weatherill, 'Fair Play Please!', at 3. See also the case of C-176/96, *Lehtonen et al. v FRSB*, [2000] ECR 1-2549. Lehtonen, a professional basketball player from Finland, wished to move to a club in Belgium. Lehtonen was prevented from participating in the remaining games of the season as he registered after a transfer deadline set by the Belgian Basketball Federation. Lehtonen claimed that the restriction was contrary to the free movement of workers. The ECJ accepted that such a rule could be justified to prevent a player leaving one league at the end of the season to join another league where the season was still in progress. Similar to *Deliège*, the ECJ accepted that a governing body could justify certain restrictive rules.

[59] Article 101 of the TFEU prohibits any agreements which purport to restrict the supply of products, agreements which restrict market access, price fixing agreements and any collusion to manipulate the market.

[60] Article 102 of the TFEU provides that any abuse by one or more undertakings of a dominant position within the common market or in a substantial part of it shall be prohibited as incompatible with the common market insofar as it may affect trade between member states.

[61] Is it free to air or pay-per-view?

[62] M. Beloff *et al.*, *Sports Law* (Oxford: Hart Publishing, 1999), at para 6.52, states, 'Football is the only sport which has been able to generate the demand for pay-TV in a sufficiently large proportion of the population, [and,] along with the screening of the first run of Hollywood films, has been responsible for the success of pay-TV.'

[63] Beloff *et al.*, *Sports Law*, at para 6.54, notes that price is an indicator of a separate market for live sport.

[64] Beloff *et al.*, *Sports Law*, at para 6.55, notes that TV is split along national lines and if an agreement only affects one member state then Articles 101 and 102 cannot be applied.

Collective Selling of Broadcasting Rights

Often television rights are sold collectively by the league and not by the individual clubs. The Commission has taken the view that the collective selling of broadcasting rights in football in various member states may violate Article 101 of the TFEU, as it may allow clubs to collectively reduce their input and fix a collective price.[65] The Commission has also looked at the selling of exclusive rights, from the point of view of the consumer, and has expressed concerns that the selling of such rights for a long period of time to a single broadcaster or a group of broadcasters may increase prices and reduce choice for the consumer.[66] Collective selling may also constitute an abuse of a dominant position under Article 102, as it may result in the league or association abusing its market power.[67]

From the point of view of the broadcaster, exclusivity of broadcasting rights is desirable as it increases the value of such rights.[68] By its nature, exclusivity may be viewed as anti-competitive and in breach of Article 101.[69] The Commission has endeavoured to reconcile these conflicting issues and has granted exemptions under Article 101. The Commission, in the case of the *German Film Purchases*,[70] granted an exemption under then Article 85(3) of the EC Treaty (now 101(3) TFEU), as it allowed other broadcasters to access the films for short periods during the term of the 15-year agreement.

The Commission has long been a proponent of the regulation of broadcasting rights at national level.[71] This has caused problems for Ireland and England as Irish and English law does not recognise a property right in a sports event itself or in the news emanating from the event. Problems arise when there is an objection made in relation to the collective selling of a governing body's broadcasting rights.[72] This

---

[65] N. McCarthy, 'The European Commission as Referee: Sport and the Law' [2002] 20 *Irish Law Times* 217–218.

[66] McCarthy, 'The European Commission as Referee'.

[67] Beloff *et al.*, *Sports Law*, at para 6.56.

[68] D. Griffith-Jones, *Law and Business of Sport* (London, Edinburgh, Dublin: Butterworths, 1997), at 87.

[69] *Ibid.*

[70] Decision of the Commission in Film Purchases by German Television Stations, Case OJ L 248. The European Court of Justice indicated that it is not against exclusivity *per se* in C-262/81 *Coditel v Cine Vog Films SA* [1982] ECR 3381. See Parrish, *Sports Law and Policy in the European Union*, at 125.

[71] Cox, Schuster and Costello, *Sport and the Law*, at 443.

[72] *Ibid.*

situation could invoke either Article 101 or Article 102.[73] Sections 4 and 5 of the Irish Competition Act, 2002 are based largely on Articles 101 and 102 respectively.[74] For example, the question arises whether the decision concerns the decision of a single dominant undertaking, such as a federation, and thus invokes Article 102 (or section 5), whether it amounts to a concerted practice or whether it is an agreement involving many separate undertakings, namely, the clubs, which would invoke the application of Article 101 (or section 4).[75] In the first example, the federation would be the single undertaking and this would be the situation if the governing body were deemed to own the rights to the event.[76] In the latter situation, the separate undertakings would be the clubs if the clubs own the individual rights to their own home games.[77]

Single Entity Theory

While it would appear that Irish law does not recognise broadcasting rights *per se* in a sporting event, for an event manager or a governing body to secure exclusive broadcast rights over a sporting event, a contractual agreement must be negotiated.[78] This agreement provides that only the official broadcaster can gain access to the venue for the purpose of broadcasting the footage of the event in question.[79] Following from this, the rationale would be that the venue owner (which would be the club hosting the game in question) should be the person entitled to exploit the exclusivity rights.[80] Arguably, the league would be considered a single entity rather than a group of sub-entities.[81] Using the single entity theory, 'what is being sold to the broadcasting company is the right to broadcast the real-life soap opera that is the league campaign or cup campaign and of which each game is a component part and not a stand-alone attraction'.[82]

---

[73] *Ibid.*
[74] Section 4(2) allows the Competition Authority to licence agreements, decisions and concerted practices which contribute to the improvement in production or supply of goods or provision of services or which promote technical or economic progress. This is similar to the exemption in Article 101(3).
[75] Cox, Schuster and Costello, *Sport and the Law*, at 443.
[76] *Ibid.*
[77] *Ibid.*
[78] *Ibid.*, at 364.
[79] *Ibid.*
[80] *Ibid.*
[81] *Ibid.*
[82] *Ibid.*, at 449.

One may take the view that it is the league organising body that owns the rights in the event as it is this body that created and organised the event.[83] It is interesting to note that the single entity theory has not enjoyed favour with the Commission.[84] If the single entity theory is accepted, it results in the application of Article 102, which requires one or more undertakings, whereas Article 101 requires two or more undertakings. The situation moves from being an anti-competitive agreement under Article 101 to one involving an abuse of a dominant position under Article 102.

SUMMARY

European law applies to sport so long as sport constitutes an economic activity. If an activity is of purely sporting interest and has nothing to do with economic activity, then EU law has no application. European law has been invoked in cases involving the free movement of workers, the provision of services and competition law. Broadcasting rights have also been subject to the scrutiny of the EU.

European law has a role to play in the regulation of sport. In order to exercise the free movement of workers or the freedom to provide a service, the individual must move to another member state.[85] The Court of Justice's failure to address the competition provisions in *Bosman* resulted in much criticism.[86] While the decision allowed players to move freely throughout the EU, it has resulted in the increase of players' salaries and consequently some clubs are facing financial ruin. Perhaps a future case will give the Court of Justice an opportunity to provide a more concrete discussion of the application of Articles 101 and 102 to sport. In addition, the Directorate General for Competition has become more involved of late in sporting cases.[87]

Although criticised for its creation of the sporting exception, the ECJ (now the Court of Justice) has been instrumental in creating a body of European sports law. The decision in *Bosman* marked a turning point in the EU's involvement in sport. After this decision, the Commission

---

[83] *Ibid.*, at 149.
[84] *Ibid.*
[85] If a matter is a purely internal matter, European law does not apply. See joined cases of C-35/82 and C-36/82, *Morson and Jhanjan v State of the Netherlands* [1982] ECR 3723.
[86] See Camatsos, 'European Sports, the Transfer System and Competition Law'.
[87] See <http://ec.europa.eu/competition/sectors/sports/overview_en.html> and <http://ec.europa.eu/competition/sectors/sports/policy.html> (last accessed 2 May 2010).

came under pressure to include a Declaration on Sport in the Treaty of Amsterdam. While viewed as aspirational, it was a much welcomed development. With Articles 6 and 165 of the TFEU providing the EU with a soft competence in regard to sport, it will be interesting to see how EU sports policy will develop in the near future.

CHAPTER 8

Alternative Dispute Resolution

INTRODUCTION

The law has showed more of a willingness to intervene in the determinations of the governing bodies. As discussed in Chapter 1, sport is considered to be a private activity and, as such, is regulated by private rule. However, the public law has intervened in cases where there is an allegation of a breach of natural justice. The involvement of the public law can be attributed to the increased commercialisation of sport; the stakes are higher for sports bodies and persons. There are merits to seeking redress in the courts of the land. As Little and Morris note, judicial intervention embodies a 'copper bottomed guarantee of ultimate justice for individual sportsmen embroiled in stormy long running (invariably disciplinary) disputes with their governing bodies'.[1] Lord Woolf MR in *Modahl v British Athletic Federation* made a similar point and argued 'generally a court will not interfere with the findings of fact by an independent tribunal, because an independent tribunal is somebody who has the experience of matter. But it does have a right to interfere where a point of law is involved, or where there is alleged to be a breach of natural justice.'[2]

BENEFITS OF RECOURSE TO THE COURTS

Under the Irish Constitution, there is a separation of powers. The legislature drafts legislation, the executive implements legislation and the

---

[1] P. Morris and G. Little, 'Challenging Sports Bodies' Determinations' (1998) 17 *Civil Justice Quarterly* 128–148, at 129.
[2] An unreported interlocutory judgment of the Court of Appeal, dated 28 July 1997, at 32.

judiciary interprets and applies the law. Each institution has a delineated role and must adhere to its limits as provided by the Constitution. In a system of separation of powers, no institution holds all the power. By dividing the power between the three institutions, there is an element of checks and balances.

However, there is no such separation of powers in national sports governing bodies. While the governing body may be judged to be in the best position to regulate its own sport, a number of cases have been referred to the courts.[3] These cases have established a set of principles which the governing bodies must adhere to. The main principles which have been established are:

• Governing bodies must respect the concept of natural justice (including the right to fair procedures and due process)
• Governing bodies must conduct themselves in conformity with well recognised principles of fairness.
• Governing bodies must act in good faith and the athlete must be able to trust the information provided by the national federation[4]
• Governing bodies must not reach a decision that is biased − justice must not only be done but be seen to be done. See *Modahl v British Athletic Federation (No. 2)*[5]

---

[3] As Mrs Justice Ebsworth held in *Jones v Welsh Rugby Football Union* (WRFU), *The Times*, 6 March 1997: 'There are likely to be many people who take the view that the processes of the law have no place in sport and the bodies which run sport should be able to conduct their own affairs as they see fit and that by and large they have done so successfully and fairly over the years. It is a tempting and attractive view in many ways, particular to those (and I almost said those of us) who grew up on windy and half deserted touchlines. However, sport today is big business. Many people earn their living from it one way or another. It would, I fear, be naïve to pretend that the modern world of sport can be conducted as it used to be not very many years ago.'
[4] CAS 1996/149 *Cullwick/FINA*.
[5] [2001] EWCA Civ 1447. British athlete Diane Modahl had tested positive for the banned substance testosterone. The disciplinary committee of the British Athletic Federation (BAF) found that Modahl had committed a doping infraction and banned her for four years. Modahl appealed the decision to the independent appeal panel and the panel found that new scientific evidence showed that there was a possibility that the sample had been contaminated by bacteria, which could affect the accuracy of the tests. Modahl sought compensation on the grounds that she was unable to earn a livelihood from the time of the ban to the acquittal and that members of the panel had been biased against her, which constituted a breach of contract on the part of the BAF. There was no written contract but the court held that there was an implied contract and a term of that contract was that the BAF should operate a fair disciplinary process. On the issue of bias, the court rejected the claim holding that any bias which allegedly existed at the time of the panel hearing would have been rendered irrelevant by the hearing of the independent appeal panel.

- Governing bodies must not act unreasonably, capriciously or arbitrarily; see *Nagle v Feilden*[6]
- Governing bodies must adhere to their own rules and regulations and not misinterpret the rules
- Governing bodies must not decide a disciplinary case without hearing the accused[7]
- Governing bodies, in applying the doctrine of fair procedures, must consider an appeal *de novo* (from the beginning) and not by way of review of a decision of another body[8]

Under the Irish Constitution every individual has the right to fair procedures. Implicit in the concept of natural justice is the right to fair procedures and due process of law. Every individual possesses inalienable rights which are derived from their mere existence. In *Quirke v Bord Lúthchleas na hÉireann* (BLE), Quirke, a discus thrower, was informed by a BLE official that he had been selected for drug testing.[9] Quirke was due to participate in the discus-throwing event and asked the official if he could return to the doping control station after this event. However, on his return he was unable to provide a sample. The plaintiff was given a glass of water and was asked to stay in the room until he provided a urine sample. After half an hour Quirke asked if he could collect his valuables and contact his coach and he would then return to the doping control centre. He was accompanied by an official to the track and was escorted to the door of the doping control station. However, Quirke failed to return to the station. A few days later the athlete telephoned a BLE official to explain his failure to return to provide a urine sample. He was advised to write a letter explaining his actions. A few weeks after receipt of the letter, the BLE wrote to Quirke informing him that a doping infraction had occurred by virtue of his failure to provide a urine sample. Quirke was suspended from all BLE competitions for a period of 18 months.

---

[6] [1966] 2 QB 633. See Chapter 6 and restraint of trade for details of the case.

[7] See *Quirke v Bord Lúthchleas na hÉireann* (1988) IR 83; (1989) ILRM 129.

[8] See P. McCutcheon, 'Judicial Scrutiny of Sports Administration' (1995) 13 *Irish Law Times* 171–175. McCutcheon provides a detailed discussion on the case of *Clancy v Irish Rugby Football Union* [1995] 1 ILRM 193 and rule changes enacted by the IRFU. The changes were applied retrospectively, meaning that Clancy was prevented from moving to a new club in the next season. He appealed the rule change but the appeal tribunal simply reviewed the decision of the disciplinary panel. The court held that Clancy had the right to have his case heard in its entirety and anew.

[9] (1988) IR 83; (1989) ILRM 129.

Quirke challenged the decision in the High Court on the grounds that his suspension violated his right to fair procedures. Barr J held that there were two important factors in the case, namely, the suspension and the concept of natural justice. Barr J was sympathetic to Quirke's claim for the following reasons: this was the first time such procedures were being used and participants had not been previously informed. Quirke had not been presented with the notice form as prescribed by the IAAF. Barr J contended that a suspension could take two different forms. An association can impose a 'holding operation', which is merely an allegation and an investigation is pending, or an association can impose a suspension that is 'not holding'. In this situation a person has been found to have breached the rules and has been penalised. Barr J held that suspension fell within the ambit of the latter form. As Quirke had been banned for 18 months, he would be unable to compete in the Olympics. Barr J argued that the 'moral implications' of the suspension would remain long after the ban. Barr J then turned to the second issue of natural justice and held that 'no man shall be condemned unheard' and those who have a duty to act judicially must observe this principle. Barr J also held that Quirke should have been permitted to have his own defence heard before being punished, and, perhaps most importantly, all persons and bodies had a duty to act 'judicially'.[10] The suspension was overturned and Quirke was permitted to return to competition.

DISADVANTAGES OF RECOURSE TO THE COURTS

There are a number of disadvantages in seeking redress in the courts. A court case can be very expensive and time consuming. This point was made by Scott Baker LJ in *Flaherty v National Greyhound Racing Club Limited*: '...it seems to me inherently unsatisfactory that a hearing before a sporting tribunal lasting between 1 and 2 hours should be followed by a High Court hearing lasting 10 days and an appeal taking up a further day and a half.'[11]

Often sportspersons can use the courts to obtain an interlocutory injunction. An interlocutory injunction is granted during a trial to restore the status quo. It is a temporary measure that is granted pending the final hearing. The court must be satisfied that there is a fair and *bona fide* (in good faith) question to be tried and the balance of

---

[10] *Ibid.*
[11] [2005] EWCA Civ 111, at para 19.

convenience favours the granting of the injunction. In one case, West-meath GAA player Rory O'Connell applied to the High Court for an interlocutory injunction in order to resume playing for his county, even though he had been suspended following an alleged stamping incident involving an opponent, Paschal Kelleghan.[12] The interlocutory injunc-tion was granted, which allowed O'Connell to be reinstated on the Westmeath team. The judge emphasised the point that this was an interlocutory hearing and he was not adjudicating on how O'Connell would succeed at the final hearing. However, the case was never heard at full hearing as O'Connell was reinstated and eligible to play for Westmeath in the Leinster Football Final, thus eliminating the need for a full hearing. Similarly, the High Court granted an interlocutory injunction in a case involving David Bardon, a Longford player. Bardon had been banned for six months by the Games Administration Committee (GAC) of the GAA. The injunction allowed Bardon to be reinstated on the team.[13]

The decision of the court to grant the injunction attracted sharp crit-icism from members of the GAA. Liam Mulvihill, the director general of the GAA at the time of the case, contended that O'Connell had no right to take the action before the High Court as it created a right of appeal that is not permitted under the GAA rules. He added that play-ers are voluntary members of the GAA and they agree to be bound by the rules of the organisation.[14]

In some cases the issue of a contractual relationship between the player and the organisation has been a deciding factor for the court. In *Law v National Greyhound Racing Club Ltd*, the Court of Appeal held that the rules of the sporting organisation provided that those who partici-pated were deemed to have submitted to the rules and jurisdiction of that sport.[15] Similar sentiment was echoed in *Korda v ITF* where a tennis player was held to be in a contractual relationship with the governing body in relation to its disciplinary jurisdiction.[16] Lord Denning in *Lee v The Showman's Guild of Britain*[17] submitted that the jurisdiction of 'domestic tribunals' was based in contract and such tribunals must

---

[12] *O'Connell v GAA* (2004) Record 2004 105 34 P (High Court).
[13] See L. Donnellan, 'The GAA Disciplinary Procedures and Player Reinstatement?' (2004) 11(6) *Sports Law: Administration and Practice* 14–16.
[14] *Ibid.*
[15] [1983] 3 All ER 300.
[16] [1999] All ER (D) 337. See I. Blackshaw, 'Running Free' (2002) 157 *New Law Journal* 477–481.
[17] [1952] 2 QB 329.

comply with the rules of fairness, but such an obligation does not have to arise from contract.[18]

United States figure skater Tanya Harding availed of an injunction so that she could compete in the 1994 Winter Olympics in Norway. Harding was accused of being involved in the assault of fellow skater Nancy Kerrigan. The incident took place shortly before the 1994 Games. The United States Figure Skating Association (USFA) was of the opinion that Harding, due to her suspected involvement in the assault, had breached the Olympic code of fair play. The United States Olympic Committee decided that a disciplinary hearing would take place in Norway. Harding sought an injunction in an American court to prevent the hearing taking place.[19] The court granted the injunction and Harding was allowed compete in the Games. Her hearing was deferred until after the Games. The USFA subsequently stripped her of her title from the 1994 Games and banned her for life.

ALTERNATIVE DISPUTE RESOLUTION IN IRISH SPORT: THE DISPUTE RESOLUTION AUTHORITY

While the intervention of the courts has been a welcome development in some respects, there are drawbacks as the above cases demonstrate. Litigation in the courts is expensive, it may take months for the case to come before the court and the parties may face adverse publicity. Sports governing bodies have become more amenable to the use of alternative dispute resolution. Instead of seeking redress in the courts, an increasing number of sports have embraced arbitration,[20] negotiation[21] and mediation.[22] The use of specialised tribunals has assumed greater importance.[23]

---

[18] Blackshaw, 'Running Free'.

[19] *Harding v United States Olympic Committee* No. CCV-942151 (Clackamas Country Cir. Or., 13 February 1994).

[20] Arbitration involves a third party who is given the power impose a decision upon two or more parties who are seeking agreement in relation to an issue that affects the parties involved. For a discussion of the use of arbitration in sport, see L. Donnellan, 'Player Eligibility and Club Sanctions: The Position in Ireland' (2007) 14(2) *Sports Law Administration and Practice* 12–16.

[21] Negotiation involves two or more parties seeking to reach an agreement in regard to an issue affecting them both. The parties involved have direct control over what is discussed.

[22] Mediation is a type of negotiation between two or more parties whereby a mediator facilitates and coordinates the discussion. The mediator may introduce issues for discussion.

[23] Arbitration is not appropriate in all situations; it is usually appropriate where there

At the GAA Annual Congress in 2005, the GAA adopted an arbitration rule and a disputes resolution code. A Disputes Resolution Authority (DRA) was established to implement the code. The DRA is independent of the GAA and bound only by provisions of the code. The DRA has a panel of arbitrators, consisting of solicitors, barristers, arbitrators and persons 'who, by virtue of their experience and expertise in the affairs of the Association, are properly qualified to resolve disputes relating to the Rules of the Association'.[24] These rules provide that there can be no fewer than 30 panel members and these members are assigned to arbitration tribunals. The panels comprise of three members. In order to bring a claim, the claimant fills out the necessary forms and lodges €1,000 with the DRA. In the event of the claimant being successful, he or she will be reimbursed. The respondents are required to reply and a hearing then follows. The parties may avail of mediation and negotiation at any time during the dispute resolution proceedings. The main types of cases the DRA hears are cases involving fair procedures, player eligibility (transfers and the 'parish rule'),[25] and failure to abide by its own rules, interpretation or misapplication of the rules or an irrational decision or sanction.[26]

The arbitrators are all independent and impartial and decisions are usually given within one to two weeks.[27] As of yet, no decision of the DRA has been appealed to the courts.[28] This would suggest that the system is working.[29] Recourse to the DRA is limited to GAA sports. However, it could be adapted for any sport in Ireland.[30]

---

is a dispute between an individual sportsperson and a sports governing body. See N. Cox, A. Schuster and C. Costello, *Sport and the Law* (Dublin: First Law, 2004), 20.

[24] Rule 1.1. The code is available online: <http://www.sportsdra.ie/dracode.htm> (last accessed 23 June 2010).

[25] Under the parish rule, players are confined to playing for clubs from the player's native parish. The parish is defined as the parish in which the player's parents were living at the time of his birth. For more details see the GAA, *Official Guide Part 1*, 2009, (available online: <http://www.gaa.ie/content/documents/publications/official_guides/Official_Guide_2009_Part1_100109203732.pdf> (last accessed 7 July 2010).

[26] This information was gathered from a presentation, 'The Use of Alternative Dispute Resolution in Sport', given by Dr Jack Anderson, senior lecturer at Queens' University Belfast, in a talk organised by the International Commercial and Economic Law (ICEL) Group at the School of Law, University of Limerick on 17 February 2010. Dr Anderson is an arbitrator in the DRA. See also J. Anderson, *Modern Sports Law* (Oxford: Hart Publishing, 2010), Chapter 3.

[27] Anderson, 'The Use of Alternative Dispute Resolution in Sport'.

[28] *Ibid.*

[29] *Ibid.*

[30] A Sports Dispute Tribunal was established in New Zealand in 2003. It comprises

THE COURT OF ARBITRATION FOR SPORT

The Court of Arbitration for Sport (CAS) was created by the International Olympic Committee (IOC) in 1983.[31] The CAS is an independent body that resolves sports-related disputes through arbitration or mediation. It is not a court in the strict sense of the word, but rather an arbitration body that hear disputes that are directly or indirectly related to sport. It hears cases brought by natural persons (individuals) and legal persons (governing bodies and associations). It is up to the parties to choose the relevant law to be applied in their case; Swiss law applies if they do not. The CAS has approximately 300 arbitrators from 87 countries. All arbitrators are persons with specialist knowledge of arbitration and sport, and are appointed by the International Council for Arbitration for Sport (ICAS). Arbitrators are appointed for a renewable term of four years and must sign a letter of independence on appointment. Ireland has one arbitrator, Ercus Stewart, SC, who is also a committee member of the Irish Sports Council. The CAS has a permanent president who is also president of the ICAS.

The CAS is based in Lausanne, Switzerland and has two permanent outposts (decentralised offices) in Sydney (Oceania) and New York (North America).[32] Hearings in the CAS are held in private and, depending on the nature of the case, decisions may be confidential. The CAS hears an average of 300 cases per year.

History of the CAS

In the early 1980s there was an increase in sports-related disputes going before the courts. The then President of the IOC, H.E. Juan Antonio Samaranch, put forward the idea of creating a specialised authority that would hear sports cases. The process would be inexpensive, speedy and offer both athletes and sporting bodies an alternative form of redress. The IOC ratified the statutes of the CAS in 1983 and it came into force in June 1984. The CAS is governed by its statute and a set of procedural regulations.[33] Initially, the IOC bore the costs of the CAS except in cases that involved commercial disputes;

experienced legal professionals and sportspeople. It hears doping cases, and cases involving challenges to decisions of the New Zealand Olympic Committee and national governing bodies.

[31] See <http://www.tas-cas.org/>.

[32] The North American office was previously located in Denver, Colorado. The office moved to New York in 1999.

[33] Both the statute and regulations were slightly amended in 1990.

in these cases both parties would contribute to the costs. At this time, the CAS was very closely tied to the IOC. The CAS statute could be modified only by the IOC session, at the proposal of the IOC executive board. Doubt was cast on the independent nature of the CAS in light of its close workings with the IOC. Matters came to a head in the case of *Gundel v FEI/CAS* in 1992.[34] Gundel, a horse rider, was banned and fined by the FEI (Fédération Equestre Internationale) after a doping infraction. Gundel challenged the decision of the FEI to the CAS.[35] The CAS reduced Gundel's suspension from three months to one month. However, Gundel was not satisfied with the outcome and appealed the decision of the CAS to the Swiss Federal Tribunal.[36] The tribunal held that the CAS:

> ... therefore represents an alternative to state justice, while, of course, respecting certain inalienable fundamental rights. This neutral and independent institution is therefore in a position to pronounce final and enforceable awards which have the force of a judgment.

However, the Swiss Tribunal referred to the close connection between the CAS and IOC, in terms of funding, appointment powers and the power of the IOC to amend the CAS statute. The tribunal stated that there was a need for the CAS to become more independent of the IOC. In 1993, the IOC convened the International Conference on Law and Sport in Lausanne and established the International Council for Arbitration in Sport (ICAS). The ordinary arbitration division and appeal arbitration division were also created at this time.

The Swiss Federal Tribunal was given the opportunity to comment on the restructured CAS in 2003 in a case involving two Russian cross-country skiers. The Federal Tribunal recognised the independent nature of the CAS.[37]

---

[34] Published in the *Recueil Officiel des Arrêts du Tribunal Fédéral* [Official Digest of Federal Tribunal Judgments] 119 II 271, the Federal Tribunal (FT).

[35] CAS 1992/63 G /FEI.

[36] It is important to note that judicial recourse to the Swiss Federal Tribunal is allowed on a very limited number of grounds, such as lack of jurisdiction, violation of elementary procedural rules (e.g. violation of the right to a fair hearing) or incompatibility with public policy.

[37] In 2000, Andrea Raducan, a Romanian gymnast who had been stripped of her gold medal and banned after testing positive for pseudoephedrine, challenged the decision of the CAS before the Swiss Federal Tribunal. However, the tribunal dismissed the appeal and did not discuss the independence of the newly restructured CAS. The Swiss Federal Tribunal will only hear appeals from decisions of the CAS in the narrowest of situations.

The Code of Sports-Related Arbitration

A new code was introduced in 1994.[38] It was revised in 2003 and, more recently, it was updated. The new code has been in force since 1 January 2010. The code provides for the procedures in ordinary and appeal arbitration cases. It also provides for advisory opinions and mediation.[39]

Role of the ICAS

The primary function of the ICAS is to ensure the independence of the CAS. It is responsible for running the CAS in terms of both finance and administration. The ICAS comprises 20 members appointed by the international sports federations, the national olympic committees and the IOC. In order to amend the code, all members of the ICAS must be present and a 2–3 majority is required. In other situations, a simple majority is sufficient so long as half the members are present.

Types of Cases Heard by the CAS

The CAS sits in three divisions:

Ordinary Arbitration Division: hears disputes of first instance. Judgments are confidential unless the parties agree otherwise. This division hears cases involving contractual disputes, sponsorship deals, the sale of television rights and other commercial disputes.

Appeals Arbitration Division: hears cases where the applicant is appealing a case made by their governing body and the particular sport provides for recourse to the CAS. The decisions are not confidential unless the parties otherwise agree. This division hears disciplinary cases, including doping cases,[40] cruelty to horses, violence on the field

---

[38] The changes are found in a document known as the *Paris Agreement*, as the various federations, IOC and NOC endorsed the changes in Paris on 22 June 1994.

[39] The CAS gives advisory opinions on matters which are not the subject of an existing dispute. Opinions are not binding.

[40] See 17.12.2009 – Final Award – CAS 2009/A/1926 & CAS 2009/A/1930 *ITF/WADA v Richard Gasquet*. French tennis player Gasquet tested positive for cocaine. His defence was that he had kissed a girl in a nightclub and had ingested cocaine from the kiss. The ITF banned him for 12 months. By the time he appealed the decision to the CAS, he had served a two-and-a-half-month ban. The CAS did not formally annul the decision of the ITF. However, it ruled that Gasquet's suspension should not count as a doping offence on his record. The panel was of the opinion that the traces of cocaine were so minute that it could not have been from a recreational user.

of play and abuse of a referee.[41] An applicant must first exhaust all the internal remedies of the sport before seeking redress from the CAS. The appeal must be lodged within 21 days of the communication of the decision from the governing body.

Ad Hoc Division: hears cases at particular events such as the Olympic Games. Decisions are given within 24 hours.[42] The Ad Hoc Division was first used at the Olympic Games in Atlanta in 1996.[43] Since Atlanta, the Ad Hoc Division has been used at the Summer and Winter Olympic Games, the Commonwealth Games since 1998, the UEFA European Championships since 2000 and the ad hoc division set up for the first time at the FIFA World Cup in 2006. The Irish women's bobsleigh team were involved in an Ad Hoc Division decision at the Winter Games in Vancouver in February 2010. The Australian women's team challenged a decision of the Committee Fédération Internationale de Bobsleigh et de Tobboganing (FIBT) which decided that Australia would not be included in the line-up of 20 teams. Australia argued that the team should be entered under the wild card provision which provides for one team from Oceania and one other from Asia. A compromise was reached between the Irish and Australian Olympic Committees, which provided that 21 teams would participate.[44]

Who May Bring a Case Before the CAS?

In order to bring a case before the CAS, there must be a clause allowing for this either in the contract between the individual and the sporting body or it must be provided for by the statute and regulations of the national governing body or international federation. This clause will provide that, in the event of a dispute, the parties agree for the

[41] For example, the Irish Women's Hockey team appealed a discussion of the International Hockey Federation's Disciplinary Commission. The Disciplinary Commission decided that the Irish women's team would have to re-qualify for the 2002 Hockey World Cup after an improperly conducted penalty shoot-out between Ireland and Lithuania in the qualifying tournament in September 2001. The CAS held in favour of the team and struck down the ruling of the international federation. See CAS 2001/A/354, *Irish Hockey Association (IHA)/Lithuanian Hockey Federation (LHF) and International Hockey Federation (FIH)*, and CAS 2001/A/355, *Lithuanian Hockey Federation (LHF)/International Hockey Federation (FIH)*, Award of 15 April, 2002.
[42] It hears disputes between the opening and closing ceremonies of the particular event.
[43] Rule 59 of the Olympic Charter provides: '... any dispute arising on the occasion of or in connection with the Olympic Games, shall be submitted exclusively to the Court of Arbitration for Sport, in accordance with the Code of Sports Related Arbitration.'
[44] CAS OG 2010/01 *AOC/FIBT*.

matter to be submitted to the CAS. Participants in the Olympics are required to sign a standard form athletic agreement which provides that all disputes during the period of the Games will be submitted to the CAS. Cox *et al.* argue that it would be against public policy and arguably unconstitutional for such a clause to oust the jurisdiction of the courts absolutely in such matters.[45] However, once a matter has been subject to the jurisdiction of the CAS, national courts are very reluctant to overturn a decision.[46]

How Is a Case Taken to the CAS?

If the case involves an issue at first instance, a written request for arbitration is filed in the court office of the CAS. If it is an appeal case, a statement of appeal is filed. If the claimant is seeking ordinary arbitration, a brief statement describing the relevant legal issue must be provided and the claimant must set out in detail what is being sought. The claimant must include a copy of the relevant arbitration clause or arbitration agreement. The court office will then ascertain if the CAS has jurisdiction to hear the matter. If the CAS is found to have jurisdiction, the office forwards the application to the opposing body, setting out the relevant time limits and the procedures for choosing the arbitrators. The respondent will be required to furnish an answer to the questions raised by the claimant. A defence will usually be included in the response. The respondent may question the jurisdiction of the CAS and may also file a counterclaim.

After the necessary formalities have been followed, the parties are summoned to a hearing for the taking of evidence and oral pleadings. The parties can be represented at the hearing by a person of choice, who is not necessarily a lawyer. The panel consists of three arbitrators, one chosen by each side; the two arbitrators select a president from the

---

[45] Cox, Schuster and Costello, *Sport and the Law*, at 21.
[46] In 2000, Angela Raguz was dropped by the Australian Olympic judo team after Rebecca Sullivan successfully challenged her omission from the team in the CAS; see CAS 2000/A/282 *Sullivan/Raguz* and CAS 2000/A/284 *Sullivan*. Raguz had initially been chosen but, after Sullivan challenged this before the CAS, Raguz was dropped from the Australian Olympic team. Raguz appealed the CAS decision to the Supreme Court of New South Wales (NSW). The proceedings were removed to the New South Wales Court of Appeal. The Court of Appeal held that the Supreme Court did not have jurisdiction to hear the case and leave to appeal was denied; see *Raguz v Sullivan* (2000) NSWCA 240 (unreported). See D. Sturzaker and K. Godhard, 'The Olympic Legal Legacy' [2001] 11 2(1) *Melbourne Journal of International Law* 241–248. See also J. Anderson, 'Arbitration in Sport: The Australian and New Zealand Experience' (2004) 11(5) *Sports Law Administration and Practice* 11–14.

CAS.[47] Arbitrators must be completely independent and not have been previously involved in the case. The procedures are conducted in English or French. In certain circumstances, another language may used. In the ordinary arbitration procedure, the parties are free to choose the applicable law, but if there is no agreement Swiss law is applied. In appeal arbitration, the applicable law is that of the jurisdiction where the governing body is domiciled. The arbitrators apply the relevant rules and procedures of the particular sport. The ordinary procedure lasts between six and twelve months. In terms of the appeals procedure, a decision must be made within three months of the file being given to the panel. In certain urgent cases, the CAS can grant interim measures or can suspend the execution of an appeal against a decision. Awards are made in the form of a majority verdict or, where this is not possible, a verdict from the president of the panel. The decision is in writing and will state the reasons behind the award. The award is final and binding as soon as it is communicated to the court office of the CAS. Appeals are possible, on very limited grounds, to the Swiss Federal Tribunal.[48]

Advantages of the CAS

It is relatively simple to bring an action to the CAS. The CAS website (http://www.tas-cas.org) provides details in relation to cost and the application procedure. The parties lodge 500 Swiss francs with the court office in order to have the application for arbitration or appeal to be registered. There are also administrative costs which vary depending on the case.[49] The arbitrators have both legal expertise and an interest in and understanding of sport.

Problems Associated with the CAS

Although the CAS was restructured, the IOC still has a close affiliation with the CAS. Not all sports recognise the jurisdiction of the CAS, for example, professional boxing, motor sports and other non-Olympic sports. If an individual's governing body or federation does not recognise the CAS, the athlete will not be permitted to bring a case before the CAS. FIFA did not recognise the jurisdiction of the CAS until 2002.

---

[47] In exceptional cases, either where both parties agree or where the CAS deems it appropriate, a single arbitrator may be appointed.
[48] CAS awards are enforced in accordance with the New York Convention on the recognition and enforcement of arbitral awards, which more than 125 countries have signed.
[49] For more details, see <http://www.tas-cas.org/arbitration-costs> (last accessed 23 June 2010).

CONCLUSION

The CAS, although a relatively new creation, has been instrumental in creating an international corpus of sports law. Beloff, as an arbitrator in the CAS, offers an insightful discussion on the role of the CAS. He makes an important comment in relation to its jurisdiction.[50] There are certain matters that will never go before the CAS, for example, the decisions of referees. However, the issue is not as straightforward as one may think. It is often difficult to distinguish between rules and the rule of law. Beloff notes that refereeing decisions may not of themselves gives rise to the intervention of the CAS; however, 'appeals from them could raise questions of fair procedures and other recognised grounds of interference which might engage the attention of the CAS or other international arbitral bodies.'[51]

The use of alternative dispute resolution procedures in sport is a welcome development. There are situations when recourse to the courts will still be necessary. However, the use of alternative dispute resolution procedures is a more flexible, efficient and cost-effective method of redress. As organisations such as the DRA and CAS comprise legal experts with an inveterate interest in and knowledge of sport, a more specialised system will emerge which will be of benefit to the sport and competitors alike.[52]

---

[50] M. Beloff *et al.*, *Sports Law* (Oxford: Hart Publishing, 2000), at 263, para 8.108.
[51] *Ibid.*
[52] See also I. Blackshaw, 'The Court of Arbitration for Sport: An International Forum for Settling Disputes Effectively "Within the Family of Sport"' (2003) 12(2) *Entertainment Law* 61–83; I. Blackshaw, 'CAS: Analysis of Revised Rules of Procedure' (2010) 8(1) *World Sports Law Report* 10–11.

CHAPTER 9

Animals in Sport

INTRODUCTION

It is important to note from the outset that Irish law relating to animals and to sport mirrors that of the United Kingdom until the early part of the twentieth century. The 1911 Protection of Animals Act applied to both Ireland and the United Kingdom. In Ireland, the Protection of Animals Act, 1965 was introduced to amend certain parts of the 1911 Act. In 2007, the Irish Government pledged its commitment to the introduction of contemporary animal health and welfare legislation. The result was the drafting of a proposal by the Minster for Agriculture, Food and Fisheries to amend and repeal some of the earlier legislation. Submissions were requested from interested parties in relation to the proposed Animal Health and Welfare Bill. It has been almost two years since the deadline for submissions; the text of the Bill has yet to be published. It is expected to be available by the end of 2010. The Programme of Government 2007–2012 was reviewed in October 2009 and more animal welfare measures were proposed, including the Wildlife (Amendment) Act, 2010.

In order to understand animal involvement in modern-day sport, it is necessary to examine the historical evolution of the role of animals in sport (and indeed sport in general) from the early modern period to the early part of the nineteenth century. The evolution of sport cannot be examined in a vacuum but must be placed within the context of class, politics and religion. Many sports were prohibited at one time or another, whether it was because of the gambling or excessive drinking that accompanied them or the King's need to build up an army of proficient archers. In the United Kingdom sport was often used as a political tool by the King or by those in public office, a notable example being the restrictions on hunting. The *Book of Sports* contributed to the tensions between church and state during the reigns of James I and his son Charles I, tensions that culminated in civil war.[1]

Sport was an activity that all members of society engaged in, from the King to small children. While some sports were almost exclusively played by different social classes, a number of animal sports brought the wealthy and poor together. Cockfighting was commonly associated with the lower orders but was a sport enjoyed by the upper classes too. Many of the famous cockpits in Westminster, London were located near the courts and the Parliament. This Parliament introduced the first anti-cruelty statute in 1822, which applied to both Ireland and the United Kingdom.

Animal involvement in sport can be traced back centuries. One of the earliest documented cases involved the hunting of boars by the Celts upon their arrival in 1000 BC in Britain as part of a military sport.[2] Primitive man hunted as a form of self-defence against wild creatures. After he became accustomed to eating meat, he hunted for food in a group.[3]

---

[1] The Puritans banned their congregation from participating and watching Sunday sports due to the drinking and gambling that accompanied such sports. The King instructed a local bishop to draw up a declaration that was to be read out to the congregation in Lancashire and the surrounding areas. While Sunday services were taking place, all social amusements were to be suspended until the services had finished. The King was pleased with the compromise and ordered the declaration to be read from all pulpits in England, Wales and Scotland. This revised declaration became known as the *Book of Sports*. Some Puritan clergymen refused to read out the declaration, losing their positions as a consequence. Relations became increasingly fraught between the more conservative members of society and their secular counterparts and, as a result, support for the *Book of Sports* waned. James I was forced to retreat and no longer demanded that preachers read the declaration from the pulpit. The *Book of Sports* soon faded into obscurity; however, it was to be revived by James's son Charles I. Charles I held Puritans in even lower regard than his father and ordered the re-issue of the *Book of Sports*. Clergymen were mandated to read the book from their pulpits. Puritan clergymen who refused to do so were forced into exile, while others were censured and suspended, and thus deprived of their ability to earn a livelihood. Over time, Puritans assumed greater control in Parliament. Strained relations culminated in the outbreak of civil war in 1642. With England in the midst of a civil war, the Puritans took the opportunity to redress the laxity of rules and morals introduced by the Stuart kings. In May 1643, Parliament issued an ordinance prohibiting the following pursuits: 'wresting, shooting, bowling, ringing of bells for pleasure or pastime, masque, wake, otherwise called feasts, church ale, dancing, games, sport or pastime whatsoever'. All copies of the *Book of Sports* were destroyed. Charles I was sent the Tower of London and was beheaded in 1649. See J. Parker Lawson, *The Life and Times of William Laud DD, Lord Archbishop of Canterbury, Volume II* (London: C.J.G. & F. Rivington, 1829), at 46–47.
[2] Boars had special significance for the Celts; see D. Birley, *Sport and the Making of Britain* (Manchester: Manchester University Press, 1993), at iiv. The boar has long been associated with Celtic iconography.
[3] Birley, *Sport and the Making of Britain*, at 129.

The slain animal became communal property to be shared among the group and humans realised that they could make nature work for them by digging pits, building traps and camouflaging themselves.[4]

In the early modern period, hunting was limited to the ruling classes and certain areas of land.[5] This restriction continued after the Norman invasion of England with only rabbits and wolves being the subject of a 'hunting for all' mandate. In the early modern period hunting became a sport of gentlemen and hunting privileges were reserved for royalty and landed gentry. Hunting privileges not only excluded the poorer class but provided for imprisonment, transportation and even death to those who ignored its edict.

The Black Act of 1723 made it an offence punishable by death to hunt or poach in royal forests and on private lands.[6] This statutory measure was not introduced to protect the deer but as a way for the Crown (who had its interests and those of the landed gentry in mind) to intervene in the lives of the power class. Game laws gave the gentry a monopoly over hunting, laws which were enforced by themselves through the legislature and judiciary.[7]

As new sensibilities emerged in the eighteenth century, the popularity of animal sports, particularly baiting, began to wane. Cockfighting, one of the earliest spectator sports, is illegal in most Western countries. While a popular sport among all classes and ages during the height of its popularity in the sixteenth and seventeenth centuries, by the early eighteenth century it had faded into relative obscurity. Sensibilities changed and a civilization process emerged during the sixteenth century. People began to keep pets; animals featured in family portraits and in literature. Societal attitudes towards the treatment of animals began to change. Religion was influential as it encouraged benevolence and charity towards animals for the sake of humankind. The belief

---

[4] *Ibid*. Over time, other animals were employed in the hunt. The Normans used bloodhounds to follow the scent of an animal trail.

[5] *Ibid*.

[6] The Black Act was introduced during the reign of King George I and passed by the Whig Government. An offence was only committed if the offender appeared in disguise or with a blackened face. It was not an offence to simply appear with a weapon. Section 1 of the Act made it a capital offence to appear in disguise or with a blackened face on high roads, open heaths, commons, downs, forests, parks, paddocks and enclosed grounds. The Black Act was intended to be a three-year temporary measure. However, it was renewed in 1725 (for five years), 1733 (for a further three years), 1737 (new clauses were added), 1744 and 1751, and was made permanent in 1758. See E.P. Thompson, *Whigs and Hunters* (London: Allen Lane, 1975).

[7] P.B. Munsche, *Gentlemen and Poachers 1671–1831* (Cambridge: Cambridge University Press, 1981), at 1.

centred on the hypothesis that cruelty to animals would have an effect on the human agents who inflicted harm. A more moderate approach began to emerge. It was accepted that animals could be domesticated and used for food; however, they were not to be subjected to unnecessary harm or cruelty.[8]

Fox hunting has presented an anomaly as it continues to remain legal in Ireland[9] and socially acceptable, although it has roused vehement opposition. It has experienced a longevity not shared with other animal sports. Perhaps its longevity can be attributed to the fact that many modern sports have evolved from hunting and there exists a partiality to the sport that has superseded sensibilities and the civilization process.[10]

Hunting was regulated by the Black Act, 1723 in order to protect the privileges of the gentry. Other animal sports were not subject to a similar mandate. Animal baiting was a popular sport among all sectors of society dating back to the twelfth century. Baiting was finally prohibited in 1835. The class concerns of hunting were not an issue in baiting. Baiting was enjoyed by the royal family and lower orders alike. However, in mid-Victorian times, attitudes changed among the higher orders and baiting became increasingly associated with ruffians of the lower classes. Selective sensibilities emerged among the more affluent members of society: while hunting remained a socially acceptable activity, baiting had become an affront.

ANIMAL SPORTS: FROM THE TWELFTH CENTURY

Bear-Baiting

Cockfighting and the baiting of bears and bulls were popular activities for many centuries in England.[11] While cockfighting was more

---

[8] K. Thomas, *Man and the Natural World: Changing Attitudes in England, 1500–1800* (London: Allen Lane, 1983), at 153.

[9] In the United Kingdom, hunting with dogs has been illegal since 2004. This will be discussed in detail later in this chapter.

[10] Thomas, *Man and the Natural World*. As humans needed food to survive, they needed to hunt. In order to hunt, they needed tools, which were developed over time: the spear, the harpoon, the boomerang, the bow, the arrow, nets and the sling. Like fox hunting, pheasant shooting has enjoyed continued support.

[11] R.L. Greaves, *Society and Religion in Elizabethan England* (Minneapolis, MN: University of Minnesota Press, 1981), at 444. It is interesting to note that during medieval times animals were often prosecuted for crimes. Usually pigs were the principal culprits (often committing infanticide) but bulls were also condemned to death. In 1314, a bull escaped from a farm and made its way to the road where it attacked a man,

commonly associated with the lower orders of society, bear-baiting was the preferred pastime of the royal family. The first documented evidence of bear-baiting dates back to the twelfth century, when bear-baiting was introduced to England from Italy. Although increasingly popular, bear-baiting was not as common as cockfighting. King Edward III (1327–1377) denounced bear-baiting as among the most 'dishonest, trivial and use-less' of activities.[12] However, subsequent monarchs were to prove more amenable to the sport. During the reign of King Henry VIII (1509–1547), bear-baiting became increasingly associated with the royal family and the nobility. The Paris Garden was built at Bankside, Southwark in London. It contained two bear gardens, circular in shape and likened to an inferior imitation of a Roman amphitheatre.[13] Scaffolds were erected and patrons could watch from the scaffold, although an extra penny (in addition to the penny paid at the entrance) was required and a third penny if they wished to observe near the pit.[14]

Queen Elizabeth (1533–1603) had owned bears since the age of six and would use the bears for entertaining foreign ambassadors at her residence at Whitehall.[15] So popular was the sport of bear-baiting that in July of 1591 the Privy Council issued an order forbidding plays to be performed on Thursdays as this was traditionally a day for bear-baiting.

Cock-Throwing, Cockfighting and Seasonal Festivals

In the sixteenth century blood sports became increasingly associated with major seasonal festivals.[16] Cock-throwing became a popular pas-time on Shrove Tuesday.[17] Occasionally, cock-throwing would be

which resulted in the man's death some hours later. The bull was seized and impris-oned by officers of Charles, Count of Valois, a region in France. The bull was tried and convicted and subsequently hung. Similarly, a bull residing near Beauvais was con-demned to death on 16 May 1499. The bull had killed a boy of 14 or 15 who had worked as a farm hand. See E.P. Evans, *The Criminal Prosecution and Capital Punishment of Animals* (New York: EP Dutton & Co., 1906), at 160–162.

[12] 'Bear-Baiting' in R. Chambers (ed.) *The Book of Days: A Miscellany of Popular Antiquities Anecdote, Bibliography and History Curiosities of Literature and Oddities of Human Life and Character, Volume II* (London and Edinburgh: W. & R. Chambers, 1864), at 57. The bear would be tied or tethered to a stake while dogs (usually mastiffs) were specifically trained to bite and attack. Bears were expensive commodities and would often be used in subsequent baits.

[13] W. Hone, *The Table Book, Volume I* (London: Hunt & Clark, 1827), at 490.

[14] Hone, *The Table Book, Volume I*.

[15] Greaves, *Society and Religion in Elizabethan England*, at 445.

[16] Birley, *Sport and the Making of Britain*, at 16.

[17] Birley, *Sport and the Making of Britain*, at 17. Also known as cock-threshing, shying at cocks, cock running, cock-squailing and, in Devon, it was referred to as cock-kibbit.

performed at wakes and fairs.[18] This form of amusement has been cited as a precursor for the development of modern-day fairground entertainment.[19] Cock-throwing was very popular among school boys who brought the cocks to school on Shrove Tuesday, a custom which is said to have stemmed from its popularity with the aristocracy and race-goers.[20] Its rules were simple yet crude. The bird was tied to a stake with strings.[21] Passersby, standing twenty yards away, would pay to throw stones or a broomstick at the cock.[22] The cock would endeavour to avoid the thrown object. The owner of the bird would often charge two pence for three throws.[23] If the thrower hit the bird and reached the animal before it got up on its feet, the cock was his.[24] Then he could set himself up as a promoter. A well-trained cock could earn good money for its master.[25] For those less skilled cocks, their legs were often broken and death shortly ensued.

The popularity of cock-throwing waned in the mid-eighteenth century as magistrates began to fine participants for public order offences. This served to undermine the sport in the minds of the more affluent members of society.[26] The sport became synonymous with unruliness, as the death of a thirteen-year-old boy in Leeds in 1783 demonstrates.[27] As the cock was tethered and could not defend himself, the sport was accused of being 'unmanly'.[28]

Like with cock-throwing, all sectors of society engaged in cockfighting and by the eighteenth century many large towns in England had cockpits or inns.[29] Cockfighting was also often associated with Shrove

---

See T. Collins, 'Cock-throwing' in *Encyclopaedia of Traditional British Rural Sports* (eds. T. Collins, J. Martin and W. Vamplew) (Oxford: Routledge Sports Reference Series, 2005), at 75.

[18] R.W. Malcolmson, *Popular Recreations in English Society, 1700–1850* (Cambridge: Cambridge University Press, 1973), at 48.

[19] *Ibid.*

[20] Birley, *Sport and the Making of Britain*, at 134.

[21] *Ibid.*

[22] Malcolmson, *Popular Recreations in English Society, 1700–1850*, at 48.

[23] *Ibid.*

[24] *Ibid.*

[25] *Ibid.*

[26] Collins, 'Cock-throwing', at 75.

[27] *Ibid.*

[28] *Ibid.*

[29] R. Holt, *Sport and the British: A Modern History* (Oxford: Clarendon Press, 1989), at 17. Cockfighting dates back to 517 BC when the first recorded cockfight took place in China. It was introduced to Britain by the Romans in the first century. See J. Harris, 'The Rules of Cockfighting' in *The Cockfight: A Casebook* (ed. Alan Dundes) (Madison, WI:

Tuesday. On that day school boys would bring a cock to school. They would pay the teacher one penny, the 'cock penny'. The teacher would take home the dead or unwanted cocks for food and the money collected from the children would augment his teacher's salary.[30]

During the reign of Edward III, cockfighting was declared unlawful as the King felt that the time could be better spent engaging in archery. Cockfighting was also prohibited during the reigns of Oliver Cromwell (1654–1658) and Charles II (1660–1685). Cockfights attracted 'riff raff' and it was feared that a rebellion could be instigated by disquiet at the pit.[31] King Henry VI expressed a similar sentiment. However, during the reign of King Henry VIII cockfighting experienced a revival culminating in the building of the cockpit at Westminster.[32] Soon more cockpits were built around the country. James I enjoyed cockfighting as much as horse racing and it is believed that he was responsible for the cockpit at Newmarket, as he often frequented the area.[33]

Cock-throwing was declared illegal in some towns, while cockfighting continued to be popular. By the 1800s the city of Newcastle alone had seven cockpits.[34] Cockfights were often advertised in the newspapers. While the advertisements appealed to the gentlemen, the common person was not excluded from the sport.[35] Cockfighting was one activity that transcended class lines, with gentlemen and miners becoming enthusiastic cockers.[36] The cock of the gentleman could be pitted against the cock of the common man. The cocks would be matched by weight, their beaks would be filed down and their wings clipped. Most fights pitted one cock against one other, although the Welsh main involved 32 cocks and only 1 could survive.[37]

University of Wisconsin Press, 1994), 9–16. See H. Cunningham, *Leisure in the Industrial Revolution c.1780–c.1880* (London: Croom Helm, 1980). See also B. Harrison, *Drink and the Victorians: The Temperance Question in England, 1815–1872* (Keele: Keele University Press, 1994).
[30] E. Lile, 'Cockfighting' in the *Encyclopaedia of Traditional British Rural Sports* (eds. T. Collins, J. Martin and W. Vamplew) (Oxford: Routledge Sports Reference Series, 2005), 69–74, at 69.
[31] C.H. McCaghy and A.G. Neal, 'The Fraternity of Cockfighters: Ethical Embellishments of an Illegal Sport' (1974) 8(3) *Journal of Popular Culture* 557–569, at 559.
[32] Lile, 'Cockfighting', at 69.
[33] *Ibid.*
[34] Holt, *Sport and the British*, at 17.
[35] Malcolmson, *Popular Recreations in English Society*, at 49.
[36] *Ibid.*
[37] *Ibid.*, at 50. A main is defined as a series of odd-numbered fights between two parties. The party that has the most wins during a day or a two-day period is deemed to be the winner. Cocks were matched according to their weights. The Welsh main would

After the ban on cockfighting and other amusements on the Sabbath day, the sport's popularity was somewhat affected. However, it resurfaced in the eighteenth century and early nineteenth century. During this period the sport was considered a socially acceptable mainstream activity.[38] As discussed below, by the early nineteenth century, the cruelty of the sport became an issue. More morally respectable pastimes were emerging; the continued practice of blood sports did not sit easily within this new vista.

BLOOD SPORTS IN THE EIGHTEENTH CENTURY

The popularity of bear-baiting and indeed other blood sports had waned by the eighteenth century. Sensibilities had changed, and not only was religion a factor (since it encouraged benevolence and charity towards non-humans), but the continued practice of blood sports undermined the emerging social morality.[39] The landed gentry proved to be most immutable when it came to the treatment of animals. Bear-baiting in public was declared unlawful. However, it continued in private.

Bull-Baiting, Bull Running and Badger-Baiting

Bears were in short supply (and also costly), so bulls were being increasingly used. By the eighteenth century, a number of animal sports were no longer practised. However, bull-baiting remained a prominent activity.[40] Bull-baiting often accompanied wakes, festivals, local elections and holidays. It usually took place in a publican's yard, a field or a market.[41] It was also believed that the quality of the meat would be improved if the bull was baited prior to it being slaughtered.[42] Indeed, baiting to tenderise the meat was required by some bye-laws.[43] One such law in 1710 provided for financial penalties for butchers who killed or sold

---

begin with eight pairs of chickens, although some began with sixteen pairs. This was a single elimination tournament where the cock would continue to fight in a series of battles until he lost. Then the winner would proceed to the next round. See Harris, 'The Rules of Cockfighting', at 11.

[38] Lile, 'Cockfighting', at 69.

[39] J. Walvin, *Leisure and Society, 1830–1950* (London and New York: Longmans, 1978), at 9.

[40] Malcolmson, *Popular Recreations in English Society*, at 45.

[41] *Ibid.*, at 46.

[42] Holt, *Sport and the British: A Modern History*, at 18.

[43] Malcolmson, *Popular Recreations in English Society*, at 45.

meat from an unbaited bull.[44] Baiting sports also tested the skill and courage of the dogs.[45]

Bulls were not only subjected to baiting but would often be allowed roam the streets where they would be goaded with sticks, and people would hang from their horns and swing off their tails.[46] This was known as bull running and was popular in Tutbury, Staffordshire, Stamford, Lincolnshire and a couple of other towns.[47] A more competent bullard (participant) would often be placed in a barrel and would entice the bull to toss the barrel. The barrel would protect the bullard from being directly exposed to the bull.[48] At the Tutbury and Stamford festivals, bulls were often thrown over the parapet into the water (called brigging) by bullards.[49] If the bull could not be 'brigged', he would be allowed live, otherwise the bull would be chased and baited by dogs waiting at an adjacent meadow and then slaughtered.[50] The meat would then be sold cheaply to the poor or served in public houses.[51] Bull running was also popular in London and in 1816 the vicar of Bethnal Green complained of the noise caused by the rambunctious crowd on the Sabbath day.

Bull-baiting, badger-baiting and bull running continued into the nineteenth century. According to Holt, the continued use of animal combatants into the early part of the nineteenth century 'underlies the point that attitudes are perhaps more important than the physical environment in determining what is and what is not permissible in play'.[52]

ANIMAL SPORTS IN THE NINETEENTH CENTURY: REFORM

As discussed in Chapter 1, by the 1850s sports and pastimes noted for their brutality, disorganisation and rowdiness – among them street games, blood sports and local festivals – had waned in popularity.[53]

---

[44] W. Hylton Dyer Longstaffe, *The History and Antiquities of the Parish of Darlington, in the Bishoprick* (Darlington, London and Newcastle-upon-Tyne: The Darlington And Stockton Times, J.H. Parker and G.B. Richardson, 1854), at 295.

[45] Malcolmson, *Popular Recreations in English Society*, at 47.

[46] Holt, *Sport and the British*, at 18 and Malcolmson, *Popular Recreations in English Society*, at 47.

[47] Malcolmson, *Popular Recreations in English Society*, at 46.

[48] *Ibid.*

[49] Holt, *Sport and the British*, at 18.

[50] *Ibid.*

[51] Malcolmson, *Popular Recreations in English Society*, at 47.

[52] Holt, *Popular Recreations in English Society*, at 18.

[53] R. Vorspan, "'Rational Recreation" and the Law: The Transformation of Popular

These sports gave way to more 'morally respectable' pastimes, namely seaside vacations and spectator sports.[54]

By the early part of the nineteenth century, the legislature decided to introduce an animal anti-cruelty statute, much to chagrin of the poorer classes. The 1822 Ill Treatment of Cattle Act introduced reforms into the lives of working animals. Baiting was not prohibited until 1835, when the Cruelty to Animals Act was introduced. This Act brought an end to most animal sports, the notable exception being fox hunting. The introduction of anti-cruelty legislation caused much consternation. Not only was the government involving itself in lives of the working class, but it was introducing legislation to protect animals at a time when many humans were suffering hardship. As the poorer classes traditionally, although not exclusively, engaged in the sports of cockfighting, cock-throwing, dog fighting, prizefighting and bear- and bull-baiting, attempts to legislate against such activities were viewed as an indirect invasion of the lives of the lower classes.[55] As gambling accompanied these activities, there was a public order interest in their prohibition.

The Ill Treatment of Cattle Act, 1822 (also known as Martin's Act) was the culmination of tiresome campaigning on the part of a few men who argued that liberation was not just a human concern but one that should also be extended to animals. Against the backdrop of the abolition of slavery and the slave trade, the revolutions in America and France, reform of the criminal justice system,[56] improvements to conditions in mental hospitals and the quest for Catholic emancipation in Ireland, the animal movement gained momentum. Animal welfare supporters, including the anti-slavery supporter and subsequent animal welfare advocate William Wilberforce, realised that human and animal rights issues had in common the fight against oppression and the protection of the vulnerable.[57]

Urban Leisure in Victorian England' (2000) 45 *McGill Law Journal* 894–973, at 894.

[54] *Ibid.*

[55] While, traditionally, the sports of the poorer classes, these sports were occasionally enjoyed by the more affluent members of society, both men and women. Although cockfighting was commonly associated with the working classes, a number of famous cockpits were located near the Inns of Court, and another next to Westminster, the seat of the English Parliament.

[56] The Peel Acts consolidated 316 Acts of Parliament into four statutes which covered almost 80 per cent of all offences. These reforms included the abolition of the death penalty for forgery in 1837, and horse and sheep stealing and coining became non-capital offences in 1832 under the Coinage Offences Act, 1832, 2 & 3 Will. 4, c. 34 (repealed). This Act abolished the death penalty in all cases of counterfeiting and allowed for the provision of legal representation to the poor.

[57] K. Shevelow, *For the Love of Animals: The Rise of the Animal Protection Movement* (New

Shortly after the 1822 Act, the Society for the Prevention of Cruelty to Animals was established. Following subsequent approval by Queen Victoria, it was renamed the Royal Society for the Prevention of Cruelty to Animals (RSPCA). The Cruelty to Animals Act, 1835 extended the 1822 Act. This Act outlawed bull-, bear- and badger-baiting, and cockfighting. The 1835 Act was repealed and replaced by the Cruelty to Animals Act, 1849. The 1849 Act reiterated the offences of beating, ill-treating, over-driving, abusing and torturing animals with a maximum penalty of £5 and compensation of up to £10. This Act was again amended by the Cruelty to Animals Act, 1876. Some 110 years later the 1876 Act was replaced by Animals (Scientific Procedures) Act, 1986. This later Act is not concerned with animal cruelty but was introduced to protect researchers from prosecution. More recently, the Animal Welfare Act, 2006 was enacted in Britain. This Act pertains to animal welfare in general.

In Ireland, modern anti-cruelty legislation dates back to the Protection of Animals Act, 1911. The proposed Animal Health and Welfare Bill is the most recent piece of animal welfare legislation; however, this Bill has yet to become law.

MODERN REGULATION OF ANIMALS IN SPORT

The use of animals in sport can be placed in three categories:[58]

- The use of the animals in the pursuit of excellence (horse-related sports: show jumping, horse racing and polo)
- The use of animals in fighting (animals fighting each other, for example, dog fighting, cockfighting, baiting)
- Legal regulation of blood sports: 'where the animal is pitted against human in test of athletic excellence by use of a gun, other instrument or animal agency'.[59] These sports are referred to as blood sports and include angling (one of most popular and highly regulated sports in the United Kingdom and Ireland), hunting (deer, mink and stag) and hare coursing.[60]

ANIMALS USED IN THE PURSUIT OF EXCELLENCE

The governing body of equestrian sports in Ireland is Horse Sport Ireland (HSI). There are 18 affiliate bodies:

York: Henry Holt & Co., 2008), at 13.

[58] S. Gardiner, *et al.*, *Sports Law* (3rd ed., London: Cavendish, 2006), at 119.

[59] *Ibid.*, at 121.

[60] *Ibid.* Bullfighting would come within this third category. Bullfighting is popular in Spain but would not be considered a sport in Ireland or the United Kingdom.

1. Association of Irish Riding Clubs
2. Carriage Driving Section of HSI
3. Dressage Ireland
4. Eventing Ireland
5. Irish Long Distance Riding Association (ILDRA)
6. Irish Pony Society
7. Irish Pony Club
8. Irish Universities Riding Club Association (IURCA)
9. Para-Equestrian Ireland
10. TREC Ireland (Tourism Related Equestrian Competitions Ireland)
11. Department of Defence
12. Irish Polo Cross
13. Medical Equestrian Association (MEA)
14. Royal Dublin Society (RDS)
15. The Federation of Irish Polo Clubs
16. Riding for the Disabled Association Ireland (RDAI)
17. Association of Irish Riding Establishments (AIRE)
18. Show Jumping Ireland (SJI)

Horse racing in Ireland is regulated by Horse Racing Ireland (HRI). The Horse and Greyhound Racing Industry Act, 2001 established HRI, which replaced the Irish Horseracing Authority.[61] The Horseracing Authority was established under the Irish Horse Racing Industry Act, 1994. There are 17 pieces of legislation that regulate the horse racing industry in Ireland. There are three Acts that govern the industry: Horse and Greyhound Racing (Betting Charges and Levies) Act, 1999; Horse and Greyhound Racing Act, 2001; and the Horse Racing Ireland (Membership) Act, 2001.[62]

While horse racing enjoys widespread support in Ireland and in the United Kingdom, Australia, the United States and Dubai, animal welfare proponents have criticised the industry. For example, in some flat races, a thoroughbred race horse can run up to 30 miles an hour with a person on their back. Young horses begin training while their skeletal system is still growing. In maiden races, a two-year-old horse races for the first time in a race against other two-year-old horses. Horses that break their legs in a fall are usually euthanised immediately at the

---

[61] Prior to the 1994 Act, the Racing Board, founded in 1945 under the Racing Board and Racecourse Act, was the regulating body in Ireland.
[62] The 1994 Act repealed two earlier acts, the Racing Board and Racecourses Act, 1945 and the Racing Board and Racecourses (Amendment) Act, 1975.

track.[63] In the United States there have been calls for reform. However, 'whether any such reform can remove the perils inherent in a sport in which 1,200 pound animals run full throttle in traffic on spindly legs' is another matter.[64]

The Australian state of Victoria has banned steeplechase and hurdle racing.[65] A report found that 20 (12 in 2008 and 8 in 2009) horses had died in the previous two years.[66] Animal welfare groups greatly welcomed the announcement, which was made in late 2009. The ban will not come into effect until after the end of the 2010 season in order to 'soften the impact' for the trainers, owners and jockeys involved.[67] Racing Victoria Limited (RVL), which announced the ban, will introduce a programme of high-weight races (where the jockey is heavier than the accepted weight; this is being introduced to help with the transition from hurdle racing to non-hurdle racing) for the 2011 season.[68] Not surprisingly, the decision has not been greeted with much enthusiasm by those involved in the sport. South Australia is the last remaining state to permit jump racing. It is expected that many of those who oppose the ban will begin competing in South Australia. The three-day Grand Annual Steeplechase carnival in Warmambool, which took place in May 2010, was the last after 138 years. However, Racing Victoria Limited will give AUS$1 million to help promote the 2011 carnival, which will become a flat-race event.[69]

Doping in Horse Sport: Recent Developments

Doping in horse sports is also an issue.[70] There are two important considerations when it comes to doping and horses. If a horse is being

---

[63] According to W.C. Rhoden, from January 2009 to 19 March 2009, seven horses died at one track called the Aqueduct. W.C. Rhoden, 'Horse Racing Begins Reform, but Legal Drugs Are Still an Issue', *New York Times*, 19 March 2009.

[64] Rhoden, 'Horse Racing Begins Reform'.

[65] P. Mercer, 'Australian State of Victoria Bans Jump Racing', *BBC News Sydney*, 27 November 2009 (available online: <http://news.bbc.co.uk/2/hi/8382072.stm>, last accessed 10 April 2010).

[66] Judge David Jones made a number of safety recommendations in a report in December 2008. The report resulted in the implementation of safety provisions; however, the fatalities continued to increase. See 'Jumps Racing to End after 2010', *National News*, 27 November 2009 (available online: <http://www.news.com.au>, last accessed 10 April 2010).

[67] Mercer, 'Australian State of Victoria Bans Jump Racing'.

[68] 'Australian State Bans Hurdle Racing' (available online: <http://inform.com/world/australian-state-bans-hurdle-racing-756228a>, last accessed 7 July 2010).

[69] *Ibid.*

[70] Although banned in 1903, it took a further seven years for the doping of horses to be

doped in order to enhance performance, there is an element of cheating, which is against the principles of clean and fair competition. There is also an animal welfare issue if a substance is given to a horse either to enhance performance or to mask an injury. In the latter situation, the horse should not compete until the injury has fully healed.

The Fédération Equestre Internationale (FEI) is the world governing body of equestrian sports. Horse Sport Ireland is affiliated to and bound by the rules of the FEI. On 5 April 2010 new FEI Equine Anti-Doping and Controlled Medication Regulations took effect.[71] The new rules are in response to requests to the president of the FEI, HRH Princess Haya of Jordan, and from participants who felt that the previous rules lacked clarity. In addition, at the Beijing Olympics in 2008, six horses failed drug tests. In response, the FEI convened a Commission on Equine Anti-Doping and Medication under the chairmanship of Professor Arne Ljungqvist, vice-president of WADA, to review the FEI's anti-doping regulations.

The commission received submissions and feedback from the various national federations. It published a report which formed the basis for the Anti-Doping and Controlled Medication Regulations. The regulations were to come into force on 1 January 2010. While some provisions were implemented by that date, others were delayed until 5 February 2010.[72] The new rules provide that the principle of strict liability does not apply to support personnel. This was in response to criticisms and feedback received by the FEI during its consultation process. However, the rules have been widened when it comes to the liability of others involved in equestrian sport. Previously only the rider could be held responsible. Under the new rules, coaches, grooms and veterinary surgeons may also be held responsible.

There are two sets of rules governing substances. There are rules pertaining to banned substances and rules relating to allowed medications. If a medication used is not allowed, it falls under the banned substance

---

prohibited. By 1910 it was possible to test for the presence of alkaloids in the saliva of horses. See M. Verroken, 'Drug Use and Abuse in Sport' in *Drugs In Sport* (ed. D. Mottram) (2nd ed., London: E & FN Spon, 1996), 18–55, at 19.

[71] The previous were the FEI Equine Anti-Doping and Medication Control Rules, effective from 1 June 2006, updated with modifications approved by the General Assembly, effective 1 June 2007 and with modifications approved by the Bureau, effective 10 April 2008.

[72] See <http://www.feicleansport.org/rules.html> (last accessed 26 March 2010). The revised rules can be found at <http://www.feicleansport.org/Rules.pdf> (last accessed 26 March 2010).

list. According to Article 10(2), anyone who is found to have used or has attempted to use, or is found to be in possession of a banned substance or method, will face a two-year suspension.[73]

The burden of proof that a doping infraction has occurred is placed on the FEI.[74] In line with recent developments in the WADA code, the standard of proof in all cases is greater than a mere balance of probability, but less than proof beyond a reasonable doubt.

Hansen v Fédération Equestre Internationale (FEI)

The Court of Arbitration for Sport (CAS) recently delivered an arbitral award in the case of *Hansen v Fédération Equestre Internationale*.[75] Hansen was part of a Norwegian team that won the bronze medal in the team jumping event at the Beijing Olympics. Hansen was disqualified from the team and his own individual event and received an additional suspension after his horse, Camiro, tested positive for the prohibited substance Capsaicin. The team event results were recalculated to exclude Hansen and he was forced to forfeit all prize money and medal points won at the Games.[76] Hansen was disqualified for 4.5 months (113 days) and fined 3,000 Swiss francs.[77] Hansen brought the FEI before the CAS to request the annulment of the FEI tribunal decision on a number of grounds. The applicant argued that at the FEI tribunal hearing he was denied 'a fair and transparent hearing'. However, this was not an issue for the CAS on the grounds that the case was being heard *de novo* (anew) and thus 'any procedural defects which occurred in the internal proceedings of a federation are cured by arbitration proceedings before CAS'. Hansen further argued that Capsaicin was not expressly stated as a prohibited substance. The FEI admitted that it was not expressly stated in the material at the time; however, the error would be corrected in the near future. Medical

---

[73] Anyone who is found to have engaged in trafficking or attempted trafficking in any banned substance or banned method will face a four-year ban, according to Article 10(6).

[74] Article 3.1. This article further provides: 'Where these Equine Anti Doping Rules place the burden of proof upon the Persons Responsible and/or member of their Support Personnel to rebut a presumption or establish specified facts or circumstances, the standard of proof shall be by a balance of probability, except where a different standard of proof is specifically identified.'

[75] CAS 2009/A/1768.

[76] FEI tribunal decision, dated 22 December 2008 (Positive Medication Case No. 2008/23).

[77] The suspension commenced on the date of the application of the provisional suspension of 21 August 2008.

evidence provided that Capsaicin fell within the definition of a prohibited substance.

The CAS reiterated the principle of strict liability and its importance in maintaining the element of fairness in competition.[78] The issue for the CAS was whether Capsaicin had been in the body of Camiro before being detected in the horse's urine or whether it had found its way into the urine sample during or after the process of collection of the sample.[79] There was no evidence to suggest that the sample had been tampered with.[80] Both sample A and sample B were found to have Capsaicin. The CAS upheld the decision of the FEI tribunal.

ANIMAL FIGHTING SPORTS

Illegal Fighting Sports

Dog fighting,[81] quailing and cockfighting are illegal in most countries. Cockfighting survives as a national sport in Latin America, Pakistan and the Middle East.[82] Cockfighting is illegal in all states in the United

---

[78] The CAS referred to the earlier decisions of CAS 1994/129 *USA Shooting/UIT*, paras 14–16 and CAS 1995/41 *C/FINA*, at para 137.

[79] Hansen argued that Camiro could have ingested the substance by biting wood in a stable impregnated with it, or breathing in airborne particles or eating feed contaminated with it (all without knowledge of the rider). The tribunal dismissed this argument as the horses of five other riders were found to have ingested Capsaicin and three confirmed they had used Equi-Block, which contains Capsaicin. It was highly improbable that the other two horses ingested it through contamination.

[80] There was conflicting evidence whether the tester had worn gloves when taking the urine sample. A blood test was also taken and tested. The blood test showed traces of Capsaicin.

[81] Dog fighting, although illegal in many countries, continues to be a popular underground sport. Michael Vick, an NFL quarterback for the Atlanta Falcons, was found to have 66 fighting dogs, a dog-fighting pit and blood-stained carpets on his premises. Vick was sentenced to 23 months in prison. In Northern Ireland, the BBC programme *Spotlight* exposed 15 illegal dog-fighting gangs. Gerard Cavlan, a Tyrone GAA player and All-Ireland medalist, was found to be a senior figure in dog fighting in Northern Ireland. The GAA allowed Cavlan to continue playing for Tyrone after the Ulster Society for the Prevention of Cruelty to Animals raided a kennel and seized more than a dozen dogs that were bred for fighting. Cavlan was identified as co-owner of the raided facility and he pleaded guilty in April 2007 to possession of a dangerous dog and was fined £650. The Dungannon Magistrates Court was led to believe that the player had merely collected the dogs from kennels for a man in Dublin and was not involved in any other illegal activities. See 'Spotlight Special Unmasks Local Sporting Hero as Hardened Dog Fighter' (available online: <http://www.bbc.co.uk/pressoffice/press-releases/stories/2007/08_august/30/dog.shtml>, last accessed 4 May 2010).

[82] Lile, 'Cockfighting', at 69.

States, most recently banned in Louisiana in 2007 with the ban taking effect in August 2008.

Lawful Fighting Sports

Greyhound racing and hare coursing are lawful in Ireland. The Irish Greyhound Board (or Bord na gCon) regulates the greyhound racing industry in the Republic of Ireland. The board is a semi-state body that was established under the Greyhound Act, 1958. Under the Act, the board has wide-ranging powers, including the licensing of tracks and the issuing of permits to officials, bookmakers and trainers. The board ensures that the rules pertaining to the industry are enforced. There are 17 licensed tracks in Ireland, 9 of which are owned by the board. The remainder are run by private enterprises.

The primary piece of legislation is the Greyhound Industry Act, 1958 (the principal act). This was amended by the Greyhound Industry (Amendment) Act, 1993. The 1993 Act amended Article 9 on membership of the board and Article 36 of the principal act. Article 36, as amended, provides that the Minister may make regulations for the following: the muzzling of greyhounds, the prohibition of a greyhound at an event that is not muzzled or not muzzled in accordance with the regulations, the supervision by a veterinary surgeon of hares prior to and after the event, the marking of a hare before the hare's release into the wild after an authorised event, and the prohibition of the use of a hare that has been used in a previous authorised event. The 1993 Act introduced the compulsory muzzling of greyhounds. In light of these amendments, hare coursing and greyhound racing have become safer, in line with animal welfare legislation.

There are 105 pieces of legislation pertaining to the greyhound industry in Ireland. The vast majority are statutory instruments. For example, there are statutory instruments on admission charges, race card charges, greyhound trainers, artificial insemination of greyhounds, betting charges and levies, totalisation (jackpots) and various commencement order regulations. There are four Acts: the Greyhound Industry Act, 1958, the 1993 Greyhound Industry (Amendment) Act, the Horses and Greyhound (Betting, Charges and Levies) Act, 1999 and the Horse and Greyhound Racing Act, 2001.

BLOOD SPORTS

Fox hunting with dogs is legal in Ireland. There have been calls for its abolition, but as yet the Government has not banned fox hunting. There are 38 recognised fox-hunting packs registered with the hunt governing body, the Masters of Foxhounds Association. In order to hunt foxes a licence is not required as the fox is not a protected animal. Various groups, including the Irish Council against Blood Sports and the Green Party, had called for the abolition of the Ward Union Hunt (the deer hunting club) and the introduction of restrictions on hunts and hunt kennels. On 10 July 2010, the Wildlife (Amendment) Bill, 2010 was signed into law. The Wildlife (Amendment) Act, 2010 prohibits the hunting of deer with two or more dogs.

The Wildlife (Amendment) Act, 2010 amends the principal act, the Wildlife Act, 1976. It will not be an offence where the person has been granted permission under section 42 of the Wildlife Act, 1976 to use dogs to drive deer off land where they are causing serious damage to tree plantations or crops. Section 7 amends section 74 of the 1976 Act. Section 7 increases the maximum fines for breaches of the Act: on summary conviction the maximum fine is increased to €1,000 from £500 for a first offence, to €2,000 from £1,000 for a second offence and to €5,000 from £1,500 for a third or subsequent offence and/or 12 months in prison. The maximum fine for conviction on indictment is increased to €100,000 from £50,000 and/or two years in prison. The maximum prison terms remain unchanged.[83] As yet, there has been no legislative ban on hare coursing or fox hunting in Ireland.

Background to the Hunting Act, 2004

Britain banned hunting with dogs in 2005.[84] The Hunting Act, 2004 was passed under the Parliament Act, 1949 after repeated rejections in the House of Commons.[85] It took a number of years for the Bill to be enacted. The Bill would progress to a certain stage but the Government would invariably decide to back down.

In June 2001, Labour won the general election and again promised that the issue of hunting would be resolved. Pressure was placed on the

---

[83] See section 68 of the Wildlife (Amendment) Act, 2000.
[84] Prior to the Hunting Act, 2004 there had been several British laws on animal welfare, such as the Protection of Animals Act, 1911, the Protection of Badgers Act, 1992 and the Wild Mammals (Protection) Act, 1996. However, the 1996 Act contained specific exemptions for hunting activities, thereby preventing prosecutions of hunts for activities that might otherwise have been considered cruel.
[85] Two attempts in the form of private members' bills were made to ban fox hunting in 1949. In 1969 and 1977 the House of Commons passed legislation to ban hare coursing but neither became law. Three more private members' bills were introduced in the 1990s; again, these bills never became law.

Government by the House of Commons to take a vote on the banning of hunting. The Government introduced the Hunting Bill, 2002; however, this Bill proposed a licensing system and not the banning of hunting. This was not what the Commons had intended. The Bill was amended to include a complete ban on hunting. It was cleared by the Commons but rejected by the House of Lords. The bill ran out of parliamentary time and subsequently collapsed.

The Government, facing increasing pressure from backbenchers, introduced a similar bill to the Commons in September 2004. The bill to ban hunting was accepted by 66 per cent of the Commons, but again it was rejected by the Lords. The Bill continued to go back and forth between the Commons and the Lords when finally the Commons speaker Michael Martin invoked the Parliament Acts, 1911 and 1949 and pushed the Bill into law.[86] The Act became law without the approval of the House of Lords, which favoured an act that regulated hunting as opposed to banning hunting with dogs.

The Act received royal assent on 18 November 2004. The Act took effect on 18 February 2005. In February 2005, the Countryside Alliance (a coalition formed in 1995 to campaign against any prohibition of fox hunting and the general way of life in the country) challenged the validity of the Parliament Act, 1949 on the grounds it was not a lawful statute. In the case of *R. (on the Application of Jackson) v the AG*, the validity of the 2004 Act was questioned.[87] As the Act had come into being without the approval of the House of Lords as required under the Parliament Acts, 1911 and 1949, the applicant sought a declaration that the 2004 Act was not an Act of Parliament. Lord Justice Maurice Kay and Mr Justice Collins held that the 1949 Act was a lawful statute validly made under the 1911 Act, and therefore the Hunting Act, 2004 was also lawful. The court dismissed the application, but granted leave to appeal. The case was subsequently appealed, with the court upholding the validity of the 2004 Act.[88]

Those who support fox hunting refer to the need to control the number of foxes as they are considered pests to the farmer. Fox hunting is seen as being part of the natural order. Those who are against fox hunting reject the view that foxes are a major problem in the country and argue that hunting is not the best method of dealing with the problem.

---

[86] E. Griffin, *Blood Sport Hunting in Britain Since 1066* (New Haven, CT and London: Yale University Press, 2007), at 220.
[87] [2005] EWCA Civ 126.
[88] [2006] 1 AC 262.

They argue that there are more humane ways of culling foxes. From an animal rights perspective, the argument is that animals have the right not to be hunted. Irrespective of the arguments, the 2004 Act prohibits the hunting of wild mammals with dogs except in exceptional circumstances. The Act permits trailing hunting, exercising of hounds, and rabbit and rat hunting. However, there are loopholes. Foxes can still be killed so long as it is accidental and unintentional. For example, a hunt could set out to kill rabbits, which is legal (it is unlawful to kill hares, as provided for by Part 1, section 5 of the 2004 Act);[89] however, the dogs could pick up the scent of a fox, pursue the fox and kill it. In this way the fox's death is unintentional and accidental. In this situation, it is lawful and the hunt will not be exposed to any liability. Drag hunting remains legal. Drag hunting involves the planting off an artificial scent. As for many the thrill of hunting is in the chase, the continued practice of drag hunting should satisfy the chase element.[90]

There are also problems with flushing.[91] In Scotland, the flushing of foxes by a pack of dogs is preserved by the Protection of Wild Animals (Scotland) Act, 2002. In England and Wales, flushing with two dogs is permitted if it is undertaken to prevent or reduce the damage a wild mammal may cause to livestock (Schedule 1, para 1, (2)(a)(i)), crops (Schedule 1, para 1, (2)(a)(iv)) and other property (Schedule 1, para 1, (2)(a)(vii)). It is also possible that a number of separate groups with two dogs could set out at the same time and in the same area. In this situation, the groups can circumvent the rules on flushing.

The power of the police is also somewhat limited. Under Part 2, section 8 of the Act, the police can only enter private lands if there is a reasonable suspicion of illegality. This section adds a human rights dimension. The Countryside Alliance has challenged the Act under the European Convention on Human Rights (ECHR). The challenge has centred on Article 1 of Protocol 1, which concerns the right to peaceful enjoyment of property, and Article 8, which concerns the right of an individual to respect for his or her family life, his home and correspondence. The Burns Report had predicted that actions might be brought under the Human Rights Act, 1998.[92] The report noted the importance of the principle of proportionality in the balancing of rights

---

[89] Hare coursing is legal subject to certain restrictions. See the Hares Act, 1848 and the Protection of Animals Act, 1911.
[90] Griffin, *Blood Sport Hunting in Britain Since 1066*, at 229–230.
[91] Schedule 1 of the Act.
[92] The British Government set up an inquiry into hunting under Lord Burns. The report,

under the ECHR, namely, the general interest of society versus the protection of an individual's rights. The Countryside Alliance brought an action to the English High Court under the ECHR and under European law. The alliance argued that the ban on hunting with dogs was contrary to the free movement of goods under Article 28 of the EC Treaty (now Article 41 of the TFEU), the free movement of persons under Article 39 of the EC Treaty (now Article 45 of the TFEU) and the free movement of services under Article 49 (now Article 56 of the TFEU). In the case of *R. (Countryside Alliance and Others) v Attorney-General and Another* and *R. (Derwin and Others) v Same*, the House of Lords rejected the contention that the 2004 Act was incompatible with the Human Rights Act, 1998 and the treaty establishing the European Union.[93]

Conservative Prime Minister David Cameron stated in the run-up to the general election of 6 May 2010 that, if elected, he would offer a free vote in the House of Commons to repeal the 2004 Act. Cameron, a hunting advocate, maintains that the Act was 'a mistake' as 'it is difficult to enforce'.[94]

COMMENTARY AND ANALYSIS

Is there a social interest in prohibiting blood sports? Those who support fox hunting argue that foxes are pests and are going to be killed by farmers in any event. However, those who view hunting as barbaric point to the effect hunting has on society. Anti-hunting groups question the morality of hunting and its effect on those who engage in it and those who watch hunting. It is interesting to note that in Victorian times foxes were under control, yet breeding programmes were introduced so that foxes would be in plentiful supply for hunting. It leads to the question of whether or not the use of animals in sport should be prohibited outright or reformed from within. Often analogies are made between boxing and animal sports. As with boxing, if animal sports that are currently legal were to be made illegal, there is a danger that the sport could go underground. At least if the sports are legal there can be some safeguards for the animals involved.

---

known as the *Burns Report, Report of the Committee of Inquiry into Hunting with Dogs in England and Wales*, was published in June 2000.
[93] [2007] UKHL 52. For a discussion on the cases, see 'Hunting Law Not Incompatible with Human Rights or EU Law', Law Reports, *The Times*, 27 November 2007.
[94] S. Adams, 'David Cameron: Hunting Ban "a Mistake"', *Daily Telegraph*, 1 April 2010,

SUMMARY

Animal involvement in sport can be traced back centuries. Cockfighting is one of the earliest spectator sports.While reports differ on the exact date, some historians have traced it back to 2500 BC. Hunting has been cited as the precursor of many modern sports. The skills early man acquired in hunting enabled him to create other sports using nets, spears and boomerangs. Originally hunting provided man with food and clothing necessary for survival. It soon developed into a pastime that brought communities together and forged relationships between individuals. Cockfighting, cockthrowing, bull-baiting and bear-baiting were at their most popular up until the early nineteenth century. During the nineteenth century, new sensibilities emerged. Formalised holidays and recreational activities became the norm, sports including football were regulated and the Football Association was established in 1863. This change in perception caused some people to question the use of animals in sport. For others, the gambling and alcohol that accompanied animal sports were an affront to this middle-class evangelism that was enveloping England. Bare-knuckle fighting was banned and the more civilised sport of boxing was regulated under the Queensbury Rules.

In the nineteenth century, the legislature intervened and the very first modern animal anti-cruelty statute was enacted in 1822.[95] Subsequent legislation banned bear-, bull- and badger-baiting.

In Ireland, and indeed most countries, horse racing, greyhound racing and hare coursing are lawful sports. However, the Horse and Greyhound Racing Act, 2001 provides that the Minister can make regulations that protect the hare and allow for muzzling of greyhounds. Fox hunting with dogs remains legal in Ireland. The 2004 Hunting Act in Britain banned hunting with dogs. There are numerous loopholes that have denigrated the effectiveness of the Act and there have been calls to repeal it by pro-hunting groups and politicians. It remains to be seen whether Ireland will follow suit and introduce a similar ban.

(available online: <http://www.telegraph.co.uk/news/newstopics/politics/7545774/David-Cameron-hunt-ban-a-mistake.html>, last accessed 19 April 2010).

[95] The 1822 Act is often referred to as the world's first animal anti-cruelty statute; however, this Act was preceded by three earlier acts: a Code in Maine from 1821 which forbade intentional cruelty to horses, sheep or cattle and another animals; the Act Against Plowing by the Tayle and Pulling the Wooll of Living Sheep, 1635 (an Irish Act), and 'Off the Bruite Creature' (Liberties 92 and 93 of the *Body of Liberties of 1641* in Massachusetts).

References

Anderson, J., *Modern Sports Law* (Oxford: Hart Publishing, 2010).

Anderson, J., 'The Use of Alternative Dispute Resolution in Sport', seminar to students and staff, University of Limerick, 17 February 2010.

Anderson, J., 'Law and a New Order', *Tribune*, 16 November 2008.

Anderson, J., *The Legality of Boxing: A Punch Drunk Love* (Oxon: Birkbeck Law Press, 2007).

Anderson, J., 'Policing the Sports Field: The Role of the Criminal Law' (2006) 2 *International Sports Law Review* 25–31.

Anderson, J., '"These Boots Are Made for Advertising" – Ambush Marketing, Sport and the Law' (2005) 12(8) *Commercial Law Practitioner* 207–213.

Anderson, J., 'Arbitration in Sport: The Australian and New Zealand Experience' (2004) 11(5) *Sports Law Administration and Practice* 11–14.

Anderson, J, 'Ignorance of the Law Is No Defence', *Irish Times*, 18 December 2004.

Anderson, J., 'The Practice of Sports Law', seminar to the Professional Practice Course, Law Society of Ireland, Dublin, 11 November 2003.

Anderson, J., 'Pugilistic Prosecutions: Prize Fighting and the Courts in Nineteenth Century Britain' (2001) 21(2) *The Sports Historian* 37–57.

Anderson, J., 'International Sports Law Perspective: Citius, Altius, Fortius? A Study of Criminal Violence in Sport' (2000–2001) 11 *Marquette Sports Law Review* 87–106.

Anderson, J., 'Mens Sana In Corpore Sano? Violence in Sport and the Criminal Law' (1998) 6 *Irish Student Law Review* 64–78.

Barnes, J., *Sports and the Law in Canada* (3rd ed., Butterworths: Toronto & Vancouver, 1996).

Beloff, M., *Sports Law* (Oxford, Portland Oregon: Hart Publishing, 1999).

References

Bhattacharjee, S. and Rao, G., 'Tackling Ambush Marketing: The Need for Regulation and Analysing the Present Legislative and Contractual Efforts' (2006) 9(1) *Sport in Society* 128–149.

Bird, E.J. and Wagner, G.G., 'Sport as a Common Property Resource' (1997) 41(6) *Journal of Conflict Resolution* 750–766.

Birley, D., *Sport and the Making of Britain* (Manchester: Manchester University Press, 1993).

Blackshaw, I., 'CAS: Analysis of Revised Rules of Procedure' (2010) 8(1) *World Sports Law Report* 10–11.

Blackshaw, I., 'The Court of Arbitration for Sport: An International Forum for Settling Disputes Effectively "Within the Family of Sport"' (2003)12 (2) *Entertainment Law* 61–83.

Blackshaw, I., 'Running Free' (2002) 157 *New Law Journal* 477–481.

Blackshaw, I., 'Regulating Sport Globally' (2000) 150 *New Law Journal* 617–619.

Blainpain, R. and Instone, R., *The Bosman Case: End of the Transfer System* (London: Sweet & Maxwell, 1996).

Brasch, R., *How did Sports Begin?* (London: Longman, 1972).

Brayne, H., Sargeant, L. and Brayne, C., 'Could Boxing Be Banned? A Legal and Epidemiological Perspective' (1998) 316(7147) *British Medical Journal* 1813–1815.

Breaking News.ie, 'GAA Clarify "Mark" Experimental Rule', 12 January 2010.

Burns, L., Edwards, V., Marsh, J., Soulsby, L. and Winter, M., *Report of Committee of Inquiry into Hunting with Dogs in England and Wales* (London: Stationery Office, 2000).

Buti, T. and Fridman, S., 'Drug Testing in Sport: Legal Challenges and Issues' (1999) 20(2) *University of Queensland Law Journal* 154–185.

Caddell, R., 'The Referee's Liability for Catastrophic Injuries – A UK Perspective' (2005) 15(2) *Marquette Sports Law Review* 415–424.

Caiger, A. and Gardiner, S., *Professional Sport in the European Union: Regulation and De-Regulation* (Cambridge: Cambridge University Press, 2000).

Camatsos, S., 'European Sports, the Transfer System and Competition Law: Will They ever Find a Competitive Balance' (2005) 12 *Sports Law Journal* 155–179.

Campbell, A. and Sloane, P.J., *Discussion Paper No. 97-02: The Implications of the Bosman Case for Professional Football* (Aberdeen: University of Aberdeen/Dept of Economics, 1997).

Canadian Law Reform Commission, *Working Paper on Assault* (1984).

Cashmore, E., *Sports Psychology: The Key Concepts* (Oxon, Routledge, 2002).

Chambers, R. (ed.) *The Book of Days: A Miscellany of Popular Antiquities Anecdote, Bibliography and History Curiosities of Literature and Oddities of Human Life and Character, Volume II* (London and Edinburgh: W & R Chambers, 1864).

Charlish, P., 'Sports Ordinary Negligence in the Final Furlong' [2005] 4 *Journal of Personal Injury* 314–325.

Clark, R. and Clarke, B., *Contract Cases and Materials* (3rd ed.) (Gill & MacMillan, 2004).

Cole, C.L., 'One Chromosome Too Many' in *The Olympics at the Millennium: Power Politics and the Games* (eds. K. Schaffer and S. Smith) (Rutgers University Press, New Brunswick, New Jersey, 2000), 128–146.

Collins, T., 'Cockthrowing' in the *Encyclopaedia of Traditional British Rural Sports* (eds. T. Collins, J. Martin and W. Vamplew) (Oxford: Routledge Sports Reference Series, 2005), 75.

Connolly, C., 'The Sponsorship Contract as a Mechanism of Safeguarding and Influencing the Level of Return on Investment in Sport Sponsorship' (2005) 12(8) *Commercial Law Practitioner* 199–206.

Cox, N. and Schuster, A. and Costello, K., *Sport and the Law* (Dublin: First Law, 2004).

Cozzillio, M.J. and Levinstein, M.S, *Sports Law Cases and Materials* (Carolina Academic Press, 1997).

Cunningham, H., *Leisure in the Industrial Revolution c.1780–c.1880* (London: Croom Helm, 1980).

Davis, C., 'The Draft System in Professional Team Sports and the Restraint of Trade Doctrine: Is the AFL Draft Distinguishable from the NSWRL Draft?' (2006) 1(1) *Australian and New Zealand Sports Law Journal* 80–102.

Davis, T. 'What Is Sports Law?' (2001) 11 *Marquette Sports Law Review* 211–244.

Dobson, S. and Goddard, J.A., *The Economics of Football* (Cambridge: Cambridge University Press, 2001).

Donnellan, L., 'TV Rights in Irish Football' in *TV Rights in Europe* (eds. R. Siekmann and Professor I. Blackshaw) (The Hague: TMC Asser Press, 2009), 373–387.

Donnellan, L., 'Gender Testing at the Beijing Olympics' (2008) 16(1) *Journal of Sport and the Law* 20–28.

Donnellan, L., 'Player Eligibility: Player Eligibility and Club Sanctions – The Position in Ireland' (2007) 14(2) *Sports Law Administration and Practice* 12–16.

Donnellan, L., 'The Regulation of Football Agents in Ireland' in *Player's Agents Worldwide: Legal Aspects* (eds. R. Siekmann, R. Parrish, R. Branco Martins and J. Soek) (The Hague: TMC Asser Press, 2007), 295–308.

Donnellan, L., 'The GAA Disciplinary Procedures and Player Reinstatement?' (2004) 11(6) *Sports Law Administration and Practice* 14–16.

Donnellan, L., 'Strict Liability in Drug Cases?' (2002) 10(6) *Sports Law Administration and Practice* 13–16.

Donnellan, L., 'The Right to Privacy and Drug Testing: An Irish Perspective' (2002) 10(5) *Sports Law Administration and Practice* 11–16.

Dubin, C.L., *Commission of Inquiry into the Use of Drugs and Banned Substances intended to Increase Athletic Performance* (Ottawa: Canadian Government Publishing Centre, 1990).

Duncan, J., *Sport in American Culture from Ali to X Games* (ABC-CLIO, California, 2004).

Dunning E.,'Social Bonding and Violence in Sport' in *Quest for Excitement Sport and Leisure in the Civilising Process* (eds. N. Elias and E. Dunning) (Oxford: Blackwell, 1986), 224–244.

Editorial, 'The Sad Story of Santhi Soundarajan', *The Times of India*, 9 January 2007.

Elias, N. and Dunning, E., *Quest for Excitement Sport and Leisure in the Civilising Process* (Oxford, UK; Cambridge, MA: Blackwell Publishers, 1986).

Ellis, H., *Modern Irish Commercial and Consumer Law* (Jordons: Bristol, 2004).

Ettman, J.M., 'Vernonia Case Comment: High School Students Lose Their Rights When They Don Their Uniforms' (1996–1997) 13 *New York Law School Journal of Human Rights* 625–662.

European Commission, *European Model of Sport* (Brussels: European Commission, 2000).

European Commission, *White Paper on Sport* (Brussels, 11.7.2007 COM (2007) 391 final).

Evans, E.P., *The Criminal Prosecution and Capital Punishment of Animals* (New York: EP Dutton & Co., 1906).

Fainaru-Wada, M. and Williams, L., 'Giambi Admitted Taking Steroids', *San Francisco Chronicle*, 2 December 2004.

Fewell, M., *Sports Law: A Practical Guide* (Sydney: LBC Information Services, 1995).

Finlay M. and Plecket H., *The Olympic Games: The First Thousand Years* (London: Chatto and Windus, 1976).

Finney Boylan, J., 'The XY Games', *New York Times*, 3 August, 2008.

Flakne, G.W. and Caplan, A.H., 'Sports Violence and the Prosecution' (1977) 13 *Trial* 33–35.

Forde, M., *Commercial Law* (3rd ed., Haywards Heath: Tottel Publishing, 2005).

Friel, R.J., *The Law of Contract* (Dublin: Round Hall, 1995).

Fry, C.B., *Life Worth Living: Some Phases of an Englishman* (London: Ian Allen, 1957).

Fulbrook, J., *Outdoor Activities, Negligence and the Law* (Surrey: Ashgate, 2005).

Gardiner, S. and Felix, A., 'Juridification of the Football Field: Strategies for Giving the Law the Elbow' (1994–1995) 5 *Marquette Sports Law Journal* 189–220.

Gardiner, S., O'Leary, J., Welch, R. and Boyes, S., *Sports Law* (3rd ed., London: Cavendish, 2006).

Gardiner, S., O'Leary, J., Welch, R. and Boyes, S, *Sports Law* (2nd ed., London: Cavendish, 2001).

Genel, M., 'Gender Verification No More?' (2000) 5(3) *Medscape Women's Health* (available online: <http://www.medscape.com/viewarticle/408918>, last accessed 5 July 2010).

Goldman, B., *Death in the Locker Room* (South Bend: Icarus Press, 1984).

Griffith-Jones, D., *Law and Business of Sport* (London, Edinburgh, Dublin: Butterworths, 1997).

Grayson, E., *Sport and the Law* (3rd ed., London, Edinburgh, Dublin: Butterworths, 2000).

Grayson, E., 'Sport and the Law: A Return to Corinthian Values' (1998) 6(1) *Sport and the Law Journal* 5–12.

Grayson, E., *Sport and the Law* (2nd ed., London: Butterworths, 1994).

Greaves, R.L., *Society and Religion in Elizabethan England* (Minnesota: University of Minnesota Press, 1981).

Greenfield, S. and Osborn, G. (eds.) *Law and Sport in Contemporary Society* (London: Frank Cass, 2000).

Griffin, E., *Blood Sport Hunting in Britain Since 1066* (New Haven and London: Yale University Press, 2007).

Gunn, M. and Ormerod, D., 'Despite the Law: Prize-Fighting and Professional Boxing' in *Law and Sport in Contemporary Society* (eds. S. Greenfield and G. Osborn) (London: Frank Cass, 2000).

Harris, J., 'The Rules of Cockfighting' in *The Cockfight: A Casebook* (ed. Alan Dundes) (Wisconsin: University of Wisconsin, 1994), 9–16.

Harrison, B., *Drink and the Victorians: The Temperance Question in England, 1815–1872* (Keele: Keele University Press, 1994).

Healey, D., *Sport and the Law* (4th ed., Sydney: University of New South Wales Press, 2009).

Hechter, W., 'The Criminal Law and Violence in Sports (1976–1977) 19 *Criminal Law Quarterly* 425–453.

Holt, R., *Sport and the British: A Modern History* (Oxford: Clarendon Press, 1989).

Hone, W., *The Table Book, Volume I* (London: Hunt & Clark, 1827).

Horne, J., Tomlinson, A. and Whannel, G., *Understanding Sport: An Introduction to the Sociological and Cultural Analysis of Sport* (London: Spon Press, 1999).

Houlihan, B. and White, A., *The Politics of Sports Development: Development of Sport or Development through Sport?* (London: Routledge: 2002).

Husa, A. and Thiele, S., 'In the name of the Game: Hockey Violence and the Criminal Justice System' (2001–2002) 45 *Criminal Law Quarterly* 509–529.

Hylton Dyer Longstaffe, W., *The History and Antiquities of the Parish of Darlington, in the Bishoprick* (Darlington and London, 1854).

Ireland, J., 'He shoots, She Scores', *In These Times*, 27 July 2007, (available online: <http://www.inthesetimes.com/article/3232/he_shoots_she_scores/>, last accessed 29 June 2010).

Irish Examiner, 'O'Mahoney Has Provisional Drug Suspension Lifted', 22 November 2008.

Irish Times, 'GAA Man in Assault Donates €10,000', 11 January 2005.

Jackson, D., 'The Constitution Expelled: What Remains of Students' Fourth Amendment Rights?' (1996) 28 *Arizona State Law Journal* 673–698.

James, M., *Sports Law* (London: Palgrave MacMillan, 2010).

James, M., 'Liability for Professional Athletes' Injuries: A Comparative Analysis of Where the Risk Lies' [2006] 1 *Web Journal of Current Legal Issues* (available online: <http://webjcli.ncl.ac.uk/2006/issue1/james1.html>, last accessed 18 March 2010).

James, M., 'The Trouble with Roy Keane' (2002) 1(3) *Entertainment Law* 72–92.

James, M. and Deeley, I., '*The Standard of Care in Negligence Cases Caldwell v Maguire and Fitzgerald [2001] EWCA 1054*' (2002) 1(1) Entertainment Law 104–108.

Jenkins, S., *Sports Science Handbook: The Essential Guide to Kinesiology, Sports and Exercise Science* (Multi-Science Publishing, Essex, 2000).

Kerr, J.H., 'Examining the Bertuzzi-Moore NHL Ice Hockey Incident: Crossing the Line between Sanctioned and Unsanctioned Violence in Sport' (2006) 11 *Aggression and Violent Behaviour* 313–322.

Kerr, J.H., *Motivation and Emotion in Sport: Reversal Theory* (Hove: Psychology Press, 1997).

Law Commission, *Criminal Law: Consent in the Criminal Law* (LCCP 139) (London: HMSO, 1995).

Law Commission, *Consent and Offences against the Person* (LCCP 134) (London: HMSO, 1994).

Law Reform Commission, *Report on Non-Fatal Offences against the Person* (LRC-45–1994) (Dublin: LRC, 1994).

Law Society, *A Guide to Professional Conduct of Solicitors in Ireland* (2nd ed., Dublin: Law Society of Ireland, 2002).

Lenehan, P., *Anabolic Steroids and Other Performance-Enhancing Drugs* (London: Taylor and Francis, 2003).

Lile, E., 'Cockfighting' in the *Encyclopaedia of Traditional British Rural Sports* (eds. T. Collins, J. Martin and W. Vamplew) (Oxford: Routledge Sports Reference Series, 2005), 69–74.

Ljungqvist, A., 'Gender Verification' in *Women in Sport: Volume VIII of The Encyclopaedia of Sports Medicine* (eds. Barbara L. Drinkwater and IOC Medical Committee in collaboration with the International Federation of Sports Medicine) (Blackwell Science Ltd, London, 2000), 188.

Ludd, S.O. 'Athletics, Drug Testing and the Right to Privacy: A Question of Balance' (1991) 34 *Howard Law Journal* 599–632.

McArdle, D., 'Swallows and Amazons, or the Sporting Exception to the Gender Recognition Act' (2008) 17(1) *Social and Legal Studies* 39–47.

McArdle, D., *From Boot Money to Bosman* (London: Cavendish, 2000).

McAuley, F. and McCutcheon, P., *Criminal Liability* (Dublin: Round Hall Sweet & Maxwell, 2000).

McCaghy, C.H. and Neal, A.G., 'The Fraternity of Cockfighters: Ethical Embellishments of an Illegal Sport' (1974) 8(3) *Journal of Popular Culture* 557–569.

McCarthy, N., 'The European Commission as Referee-Sport and the Law' [2002] 20 *Irish Law Times* 217–218.

McCutcheon, P. 'Negative Enforcement of Contracts in Sports Industries' (1997) 17 *Legal Studies* 65–100, at 78.

McCutcheon, P., 'Judicial Scrutiny of Sports Administration' (1995) 13 *Irish Law Times* 171–175.

McCutcheon, P., 'Sports Violence and Consent and the Criminal Law' (1994) 45(3) *Northern Ireland Legal Quarterly* 267–284.

McFee, G., *Sport, Rules and Values Philosophical Investigations into the Nature of Sport* (London: Routledge, 2004).

McGonagle, M., *Media Law* (2nd ed., Dublin: Thomson Roundhall, 2003).

Mackay, D., 'Whitaker Becomes Latest Banned Briton to Overturn BOA Doping Bye-law', *Inside the Games*, 17 March 2010.

McMurtry, W.R., *Investigation and Inquiry into Violence in Amateur Hockey* (Toronto: Ministry of Community and Social Services, 1974).

McNally, F., 'McCartan Found Guilty of Assaulting Westmeath Player', *Irish Times*, 2 November 2004.

McNally, F., 'FAI Defends €7m Sky Deal for Soccer Ties', *Irish Times*, 6 July 2002.

Malcolmson, R.W., *Popular Recreations in English Society*, 1700–1850 (Cambridge: Cambridge University Press, 1973).

Mercer, P., 'Australian State of Victoria Bans Jump Racing', *BBC News Sydney*, 27 November 2009.

Moore, C., *Sports Law and Litigation* (2nd ed., Welwyn Garden City: CLT Professional Publishing, 2000).

Morris, P. and Little, G., 'Challenging Sports Bodies' Determinations' (1998) 17 *Civil Justice Quarterly* 128–148.

Munsche, P.B., *Gentlemen and Poachers 1671–1831* (Cambridge: Cambridge University Press, 1981).

Murphy, P., Williams, J. and Dunning, E., *Football on Trial Spectator Violence and Development in the Football World* (London and New York: Routledge, 1990).

Musto, D.F., 'Opium, Cocaine and Marijuana in American History' (1991) 265(1) *Scientific American* 40–47.

Nafziger, J., *International Sports Law* (2nd ed., Ardsley, NY: Transnational Publishers, 2004).

Nafziger, J. 'Dispute Resolution in the Arena of International Sports Competition' (2002) 50 *American Journal of Comparative Law* 161–179.

Nafziger, J. 'International Sports Law as a Process for Resolving Disputes' (1996) 45 *International and Comparative Law Quarterly* 130–149.

National News, 'Jumps Racing to End after 2010', 27 November 2009 (available online: <http://www.news.com.au>, last accessed 10 April 2010).

Neville, J.W., 'Baseball and the Antitrust Laws' (1947) 16 *Fordham Law Review* 208–230.

Opie, H., 'Condon v Basi' (1986) 15 *Melbourne University Law Review* 756–62.

O'Riordan, I., 'Cooney Insists that GAA Have Not Gone Soft on Discipline', *Sunday Independent*, 31 January 2010.

Parker Lawson, J., *The Life and Times of William Laud DD, Lord Archbishop of Canterbury* (Volume II) (London: C. J. G. & F. Rivington, 1829).

Parpworth, N., 'Boxing and Prize Fighting: The Indistinguishable Distinguished?' (1994) 2 *Sport and the Law Journal* 5–8.

Parrish, R., *Sports Law and Policy in the European Union* (Manchester: Manchester University Press, 2003).

Parrish, R. and Miettinen, S., *The Sport Exception in European Union Law* (The Hague: TMC Asser Press, 2008).

Pendlebury, A., 'Perceptions of Playing Culture in Sport: The Problem of Diverse Opinion in the Light of Barnes' (2006) 4(2) *Entertainment and Sports Law Journal* (available online: <http://go.warwick.ac.uk/eslj/issues/volume4/number2/pendlebury>, last accessed 6 July 2010).

Porter, D., 'Amateur Football in England, 1948–1963: The Pegasus Phenomenon' (2000) 14(2) *Contemporary British History* 1–30.

Quill, E., *Torts in Ireland* (2nd ed., Dublin: Gill & Macmillan, 2004).

Reeb, M., *Digest of CAS Awards II 1998–2000* (The Hague: Kluver Law International, 2002).

Rees, P., 'Salary Cap for England's Premiership Clubs to be Increased to £4 million', *Guardian*, 5 January 2008.

Reeser, J.C., 'Gender Identity and Sport: Is the Playing Field Level?' (2005) 39 *British Journal of Sports Medicine* 695–699.

Reilly, J., 'Courts Soft on Violent Tackles on Sports Field', *Independent*, 1 April 2007.

Rhoden, W.C., 'Horse Racing Begins Reform, but Legal Drugs Are Still an Issue', the *New York Times*, 19 March 2009

Rose, N. 'Agent of Change?' (2005) 102(31) *Law Society Gazette* 18–20.

RTE News, 'Government Withdraws Transgender Appeal', 21 June 2010, (available online: <http://www.rte.ie/news/2010/0621/foyl.html>, last accessed 21 June 2010).

Saner, E., 'The Gender Trap', *The Guardian*, 30 July 2008.

Shevelow, K., *For the Love of Animals: The Rise of Animal Protection Movement* (New York: Henry Holt & Co., 2008).

Shropshire, K., 'Introduction: Sports Law?' (1998) 35 *American Business Law Journal* 181–184.

Simpson, J.L, Ljungqvist, J.A. and Ferguson-Smith, M.A et al, 'Gender Verification in the Olympics' (2000) 284(12) *The Journal of the American Medical Association* 1568–1569.

Slater, M., 'Legal Threat to Anti-Doping Code', *BBC Sport*, 22 January 2009.

Smith, A. and Porter, D., *Amateurs and Professionals in Post-War British Sport* (London: Frank Cass, 2000).

Sports Council, 'Recognition of Activities and Governing Bodies' Sports Council Paper SC (93) 68.

Standen, J., 'The Manly Sports: The Problematic Use of Criminal Law to Regulate Sports Violence' (2009) 99(3) *Journal of Criminal Law and Criminology* 619–642.

Sturzaker, D. and Godhard, K., 'The Olympic Legal Legacy' [2001] 11 2(1) *Melbourne Journal of International Law* 241.

Strutt, J., *Sports and Pastimes of the People of England* (London: Thomas Tegg & Son, 1838).

Sweeney, E., 'GAA Can't Avoid the Ugly Truth', *Irish Times*, 31 January 2010.

The Times, 'Hunting Law not Incompatible with Human Rights or EU Law', Law Reports, 27 November 2007.

Thomas, K., 'A Lab Is Set to Test the Gender of Some Female Athletes', *New York Times*, 30 July 2008.

Thomas, K., *Man and the Natural World: Changing Attitudes in England, 1500–1800* (London: Allen Lane, 1983).

Thompson, E.P., *Whigs and Hunters* (London: Allen Lane, 1975).

Thorpe, D., Buti, A., Davies, C., Fridman, S., *Sports Law* (Victoria, Australia: Oxford University Press, 2009).

Trapp, R., 'Professional foul? You'll be hearing from my solicitor. Can a player be held liable for the injury of an opponent? Or is it all part of the game?' *Independent*, 19 July 1995.

Verroken, M., 'Drug Use and Abuse in Sport' in *Drugs In Sport* (ed. Mottram, D.) (2nd ed., London: E & FN Spon, 1996), 18–55.

Vines, G., 'Last Olympics for the Sex Test? The world's biggest sports body has just banned sex tests, branding them unfair and unnecessary. But the old guard at this year's Olympics still insists the practice must go on', *New Scientist*, Issue 1828, 4 July 1992, 39–42.

Vorspan, R., '"Rational Recreation" and the Law: The Transformation of Popular Urban Leisure in Victorian England' (2000) 45 *McGill Law Journal* 891–973.

Voy, R., *Drugs, Sport and Politics* (Champaign, Illinois: Leisure Press, 1991).

Weatherill, S., 'Fair Play Please! Recent Developments in the Application of EC Law to Sport' (2003) 40 *Common Market Law Review* 51–93.

Weiler, I., 'The Predecessors of the Olympic Movement, and Pierre de Coubertin' (2004) 12(3) *European Review*, 427–443.

Weistart, J.C. and Lowell, C.H., *The Law of Sports* (Indianapolis: Bobbs-Merrill Co., 1979).

Welch, R., 'A Snort and a Puff: Recreational Drugs and Discipline in Professional Sport' in *Drugs and Doping in Sport* (ed. J. O'Leary) (London: Cavendish 2001), 75–90.

Whelan, D., 'Sport Here Must Take Arbitration Route', *Irish Times*, 6 November 2004.

White, D., 'Sports Violence as Criminal Assault: Development of the Doctrine by Canadian Courts' (1986) 6 *Duke Law Journal* 1030–1054.

White, F., *Commercial Law* (Dublin: Thomson Roundhall, 2002).

Wilkinson, T., 'Boyer Fined £600 for On-Pitch Brawl', *Independent*, 5 July 2006.

Williams, J., 'Sport and the Elite in Early Modern England' (2008) 28(3) *Sport in History* 389–413.

Wilson, S., 'Is Football Bankrupt?' *Money Week*, 22 January 2010.

Wise, A., 'Strict Liability Drug Rules of Sports Governing Bodies' (1996) 146 *New LJ* 1161–1164.

Woolf, B., *Behind Closed Doors* (New York: Atheneum, 1976).

Yaniv, O., 'Caster Semenya, Forced to Take a Gender Test, Is a Woman...and a Man', *New York Daily News*, 10 September 2009.

Yasser, R.L., *Torts and Sports Legal Liability in Professional and Amateur Athletics* (Westport, Connecticut; London: England: Quorum Books, 1985).

Yates, J. and Gillespie, W., 'The Problem of Sports Violence and the Criminal Prosecution Problem' (2002–2003) 12 *Cornell Journal of Law & Public Policy* 145–168.

Zorpette, G., 'The Chemical Games' (2000) 3 *American Scientific Presents, Quarterly* 16–17.

REPORTS OF THE EUROPEAN PARLIAMENT

European Parliament Committee on Culture and Education, *Report on the Future of Professional Football in Europe*, A6-0636/2007, 2006/2130 (INI) (Belet Report).

European Parliament, *Professional Sport in the Internal Market*, commissioned by the Committee on the Internal Market and Consumer Protection of the European Parliament on the initiative of Toine Manders, project no.: IP/A/IMCO/ST/2005-004.

European Parliament, *Report on the Commission Report to the European Council with a View to Safeguarding Current Sports Structures and Maintaining the Social Function of Sport within the Community Framework – The Helsinki Report on Sport*, A5-0208/2000 (Mennea Report).

European Parliament, *Report on the Role of the European Union in the Field of Sport*, A4-0197/97 (Pack Report).

European Parliament, *Report of the Committee on Culture, Youth, Education and the Media on the European Community and Sport*, CA3-0326/94, Part A (27/4/94); Part B (29/4/94) (Larive Report).

European Parliament, *Report on behalf of the Committee on Legal Affairs and Citizens' Rights on the Freedom of Movement of Professional Footballers in the Community*, 1 March 1989, A2-415/88 (Van Raay Report).

Index